A WORLD TOUR BY

BICYCLE BOOK 1

Until the Road Ends

Cycling the Americas

Jacob Ashton

Preface

Here it is! Book One of my world tour by bicycle, adapted from my journal covering about 19,837 miles (31,925 km) in 21 countries. I've written it in both primary measurement systems (Imperial and Metric) where applicable; it makes things a little less clean-cut but easier to understand internationally. Everything really happened just like I wrote it here; honestly, it did. As is often the case with non-fiction, some names may have been changed.

Special thanks to:

Me, I did it all myself. No, not really. Thanks to my parents for being accepting of my current choice to live a nomadic lifestyle, despite the fact that it's an unusual choice, and for everything else they've done for me too. Love you both! A huge thank you to the people of this world; most of y'all are pretty cool and a select percentage of you are the superstars that make traveling by bicycle so incredible and worthwhile, despite the occasional challenge. Thanks to you, the reader, as well. It means a lot to me that you'd spend your, probably hard-earned, money on my book; it's probably not perfect but I put a ton of effort into it. In all likelihood, I'll use the money to keep cycling. Last but not least, thanks to all the friends and family that helped me edit and proofread this book into something that kind of makes sense, especially Chris and Sean.

CONTENTS

PART ONE

*Eagle, Idaho, USA to
Cartagena, Colombia*

CHAPTER 1

Day 1, February 1, 2016

Eagle, Idaho, USA

They say you pack your fears with you when you travel. If that's true, I was terrified. All my equipment had been meticulously researched to be the best blend of durability, comfort, and function. Weight wasn't a huge consideration; my bike probably weighed 120 pounds (55 kg) loaded as it was with cold weather gear for the sub zero Fahrenheit (-17 C) temperatures that I expected to encounter within the first few days of my world tour. It didn't matter anyway; I was going to travel the world by bicycle for the adventure and it sounded fun too.

This was it, the culmination of years of saving and planning; this was the day I'd begin to fulfill my dream of traveling the world by bicycle. My heavily loaded recumbent bicycle sat in the garage of my parents' house in Eagle, Idaho, USA. I'd chosen a recumbent bike to counter some back issues I have as the laid-back position (similar to a recliner) would be far more comfortable than a traditional bike. My ambitious plan involved starting from home, in mid-winter, and riding south as far as I could by road. If everything went according to plan, I'd be in decent weather after a week on the road and the timing would be perfect to cross the equator in June or so. With luck, I'd be all the way to the southernmost end of South America, a city called Ushuaia, in the middle of the Austral (southern hemisphere) summer near the end of December.

I awoke in the wee hours of the morning; I jerked awake, convinced I'd overslept my alarm. Without success, I tried to go back to sleep, but just laid there in the dark until almost six in the morning. I climbed up the stairs into the kitchen where my mom was cooking breakfast: cinnamon rolls and scrambled eggs. Normally, I'd devour half a dozen eggs without thinking about it but, I could only eat a few bites because of how nervous I was. My lack of experience in traveling didn't help me relax; my longest bicycle tour before this was only three days. A long weekend away from work was the best I could manage previously. My only experience traveling internationally was a family trip to Canada and some overseas travel for work, but I'd never left the country alone. I made an effort to find someone to cycle the world with me; many people were interested although no one actually committed.

After another once-over on my bike to make sure I had everything, I said my goodbyes to my parents and siblings, not knowing when I'd see them again. I planned to be gone for a few years, at least, and I didn't intend to return home before I finished. I waved and said goodbye one more time as I wobbled down the street and turned the corner, southbound; it was the farthest I'd ever ridden my bike this heavily loaded.

No, I didn't have an emotional breakdown once I was out of sight; I was excited to leave and as soon as I started down the road and turned the corner, all the nervous energy disappeared.

I made it less than a mile before I pulled over on a bike path to rearrange some gear and take a picture of the sunrise over the mountains. Since the temperatures were below freezing, I put on my waterproof jacket for warmth. I made it a few more miles before stopping yet again, then, as I was trying to get my sunglasses, my kickstand broke from the weight of my bike!

Perhaps it was an omen of things to come, one last attempt by the universe telling me to turn around and go home before it was too late, but I continued. Soon, the road turned uphill. I shifted into an easier gear; this was a moment I'd trained for.

I strained at the pedals and muscled my heavy bike up and over my first climb, then coasted down the other side. It was only a freeway overpass, but I had to start somewhere. A tailwind aided my progress south and the extra cinnamon rolls my mom had packed for me made a great second breakfast somewhere along the highway. Mountains covered in snow and desert scrub glided by; near dusk, I turned onto a dirt road to take a shortcut to Idaho State Highway 51. I found an unused patch of ground, well away from any houses or the road, and set up my tent for the night. At my goal budget of roughly $20 US per day, I wouldn't be able to afford hotels very often, especially in expensive countries like the US. In the process of assembling my tent, I realized I'd lost a water bottle and walked back to the road to look for it without success. When I turned around, I couldn't see my bike or tent, even with my flashlight. I had to find and follow my tire tracks to locate it in a tense process that felt much longer than the few minutes it actually took. Reunited with everything I had, I went to sleep.

My alarm went off at 6:00 am the next morning. Because of the short days of winter, I wanted to maximize the available daylight by waking up early. It quickly became obvious that my bags were not organized. I got dressed for the freezing weather and packed everything. Then I realized I'd packed my gloves; I had to dig through all my panniers (the bicycle equivalent of saddle bags) to find them before packing them up again and noticing that I needed something else. Pack, unpack, and repack. Almost two hours had passed before I was ready to ride, and I'd already wasted half an hour of precious daylight. Since all of my food and water had frozen overnight, I gnawed on a leftover (and also frozen) cinnamon roll for breakfast. I tucked the smaller of my frozen water reservoirs into my jacket in the hope that my body heat would thaw it out. The road climbed and I watched some planes from the nearby military base fly across the sky, keeping my mind off of my slow progress.

Some people in a pickup truck stopped and offered me

some water which I gladly accepted; I'd been unable to thaw more than a few sips of my frozen water all morning. I drank the bottles they gave me right away, before they froze and became even more useless weight.

Once I was onto a high desert plateau, the roads were covered with ice and a frigid headwind was blowing. I congratulated myself on switching to studded tires (to grip the ice) only a few days before I left home. The novelty of being on a grand, round-the-world adventure began to wear away quickly in the cold, windy, and ice-covered landscape so, I listened to music to help the time pass. Sadly, there weren't any shops to buy food. I had plenty of food with me but, it was all frozen solid; I hadn't anticipated that happening. By the end of the day, I'd cycled 54 miles (87 km) in eight hours of pedaling time and it was dark when I found a gap between some fences where I could put my tent.

It was cold enough that my lighters had frozen and it took me nearly an hour to warm them up enough to get my stove lit. Since I had no liquid water, I took advantage of my surroundings and melted some snow to make instant noodles. It was the best bowl of instant noodles I'd ever had. I set up my tent in the dark. I was so cold, so tired, and so uncomfortable that I almost hoped I had frostbite on my toes so I'd have a good excuse to call my parents to come bail me out so I could try again when it was warmer. I took off my boots and examined my feet; they were fine. No excuse to quit meant I'd keep going.

A cold night followed, even with my zero degree Fahrenheit (-17 C) sleeping bag, I didn't quite stay warm. Since I'd sweated through my sleeping bag after getting too hot during my first night, the down had compressed and thus failed to provide proper insulation. Happily, packing my gear went a little faster on the morning of my third day. I was only a few miles away from a gas station. Anxiously, I waited for it to open. They had donuts inside which were calling my name. Also, I'd wasted most of the fuel for my stove trying to get it started last night. I filled up my fuel bottle with gasoline and the shop-keeper told me it was -5 F (-20 C) outside.

The donuts in my stomach boosted my morale and I felt like I could conquer the world. Ice from my breath condensed into the beginnings of an ice beard as I crossed into Nevada. Past the state line, a rather grizzled looking couple, with probably half a set of teeth between them, got out of their truck and offered me a ride and a beer. A beer sounded great; I accepted it, though saved it for later, and turned down the lift. I was cycling the world after all, not riding a bicycle around the world except for that time I rode in a truck because it was cold. One of my goals was to cycle every inch overland, under my own power, and, if just traveling around the world on a bicycle wasn't hard enough already, this seemed like a noble challenge to add.

I climbed ever higher along a river up to 6,200 feet (1,880 meters) in elevation. I tried to dry out my sleeping bag in the sun so that I would not have to endure another cold night with compressed down. The sun was warm but, the air temperature was low enough that I wasn't sure if the sun did anything for my sleeping bag. Another day ended and I pitched my tent in another field near another road. My stove wasn't working properly; I got the water heated to barely a simmer before it spluttered and died. Tragically, it wouldn't restart. I dined on crunchy pasta with the beer I'd been given early that day and felt like it had been a successful day; even with the adverse conditions, I'd cycled 79 miles (127 km).

I made it to Elko the next day; the first city I'd seen since leaving home. I went directly to a McDonald's and treated myself to a greasy cheeseburger and fries while I made a call home. My morale was high.

Some internet research showed that I'd bought the wrong fuel for my stove when I refilled it, so I found some kerosene at a supermarket in town. I bought several packs of cookies and instant noodles too; I'd already given up on trying to eat healthy. That day was the tipping point after which everything began to go smoother. With the correct fuel, my stove started easily. I learned to always carry my lighters close to my body in cold weather to keep them operable and I learned to buy food that wouldn't freeze solid overnight.

On day eight, it finally warmed up enough that I could ride in shorts; my pale legs contrasted starkly with the burnt and tanning reflection of my face that I saw in my rearview mirror. On day nine, I ended the day only half a day's cycle away from Las Vegas.

After only a week of cycling and camping in cold snowy weather, my plan to ride south into warmer weather had worked! A few hours into my tenth day, on the road it was warm enough to ride in short sleeves again. I followed rolling hills through the desert. Then, over the crest of one hill, I saw the city of Las Vegas. I almost choked up with emotion at the realization I could actually get somewhere just by riding a bicycle.

I rode down Las Vegas Boulevard and onto The Strip, marveling at the opulence of the hotels and casinos around me. I pedaled up to the replica of the Eiffel Tower and tried to get someone to take a picture of me and my bike in front of it. People completely ignored me or brushed me off rudely, to them I was just another homeless person begging for change. To be fair, I was covered in ten days' worth of sweat and road grime and I hadn't bathed since I left home. After giving up on finding someone to take my picture, I explored more of the city. As evening approached, I rode into the suburbs on the east side of Las Vegas toward my Warmshowers.org hosts' house.

Warmshowers.org is a global hospitality network of people, usually cyclists, who sign up to offer a free place to stay for people who are traveling by bicycle. I'd never used the site before, or been in a position to host people myself, but what better time to start? I had had to message a few people before I got a reply, but eventually I found someone. In complete contrast to the people who ignored me just a few hours earlier, I was warmly welcomed into my hosts' home and shown a room that I'd have to myself. My hosts were a retirement aged couple who'd done several tours around the US and who were now opening their home to cyclists in need of a place to stay.

After the obligatory hot shower and an excellent meal prepared by my hosts, I felt like a new man. I was ready to take on the world again, or at least I would be after I took a rest day there.

CHAPTER 2

Day 12, February 12, 2016

Las Vegas, Nevada, USA

I spent my rest day exploring the city. I wasn't confident enough about figuring out the city's bus system so, I rode my bike to the sights I hadn't seen yesterday, then I went back to my host's house and made a call home to my parents to let them know I was doing well. The next morning, I was ready to go again and, after giving my thanks to my hosts, I began riding out of the city, a process that took most of three hours. Daytime temperatures climbed into the mid-70s F (~24 C) and, after spending much of the last week outside in freezing weather, it felt hot! I sweated up the climbs and began to adjust to riding on the busy highway. It was the only road I could find going toward my next destination.

The next morning, after descending to the Colorado River and crossing a bridge, I was in Arizona; the third state of my tour. I got off the main road and onto the world famous Route 66. As the road climbed away from the Colorado River, the temperature rose to 90 F (32 C) and I was sweating buckets. I pedaled through Oatman, Arizona, a tourist town fixed up to look like something out of the Wild West. Donkeys roamed freely.

While I was taking pictures, someone approached me and said there was a free place to camp about a mile up the road. Surprisingly, the distance they gave me was accurate; they must have been a cyclist too. The only problem was that the area was overrun with a motorcycle gang, some of whom were shooting at targets in a gravel pit. They saw me surveying the site, invited me in, and showed me a place where I could camp. On first impression, they seemed friendly enough and I cautiously accepted their invitation. After I pitched my tent, they invited me over for a beer. Never one to turn down free alcohol, I joined them for a drink. One of them offered me some moonshine too and, true to form, I had a generous serving of that as well. I started talking with them and they all seemed like relatively normal people who just liked to ride motorcycles together. We talked and drank well into the night; they all got a kick out of my story about how I'd cycled there from Idaho and planned to continue all the way through South America. It was an unforgettable experience and I hoped to have more like it.

It was my third day on Route 66; the last couple of days had been filled with red deserts and clear blue skies and this day was promising to be more of the same. I checked my tires' pressures in the morning; they felt alright although it'd been a week since I pumped them up. A few miles later, my rear tire went flat, "Murphy's Law", I muttered to myself and set about changing it. The rounded inside of a tire stud on my ice tires had worn through the tube and caused the leak. I switched out to a normal tire, one of four spares I was carrying. Suddenly, my bike was quieter and half of the constant clicking noise from the tire studs, which sounded like I was perpetually riding on gravel, disappeared.

While I was refilling my water in the public park of a small town, some people walked over and gave me a few pieces of fruit. They'd hiked the Pacific Crest Trail and had experienced people's generosity themselves. They told me they were paying it forward now that they were able. I liked that idea and resolved to do the same someday. A few miles out of town, my cycle-computer showed me I'd ridden 1,000 miles (1,600 km) since I started my tour just over two weeks ago. It seemed like a long way when I thought about it, though it had passed incredibly quickly. I wondered if I'd ever reach 100,000 miles (160,000 km) cycled on tour; that seemed like a nice round number and I added that as one of my goals.

A few days later I was cycling the last miles toward Grand Canyon National Park when I saw something slowly approaching me on the opposite side of the road. When it came into view I recognized it as another cycle tourist, the first I'd seen on my entire tour! He introduced himself as "John from New York"; he'd been cycling around the perimeter of the US and had pedaled about 4,000 miles (6,450 km) which seemed pretty impressive to me. It had taken him 4 1/2 months. He had just left a free campground where he had stayed for 4 days; he said he had enjoyed the experience. To each his own, I wouldn't have enjoyed sitting around that long. We chatted for a while before continuing our separate ways. I rode into Grand Canyon National Park and stopped at the first viewpoint; it really was grand though perhaps 'Incredible Canyon' or 'Awesome Canyon' would be a better name, but neither has the same ring to it. Several people came by to talk to me over the course of the afternoon: some retirement age couples from Canada in motor homes, a trio of men from Minnesota traveling in a van, a couple from Australia traveling by car, and lots of people from Asia traveling in massive tour buses and begging for photos with me. All of them on their own separate journeys; all of them united in awe of nature.

I rode alone along the rim of the Grand Canyon, stopping frequently at viewpoints for pictures or to just enjoy the scenery and the moment. The day passed quickly and, before long, it was getting dark. Carefully selecting a campsite close to an overlook, I set my alarm for early the next morning. It went off about 90 minutes before dawn and I packed quickly; with all the practice I'd had, I could get going in less than 45 minutes if I tried. Excitedly, I rode to an overlook in the dark and waited for sunrise. The black and white colors of the canyon came into view as the first light of dawn came over the horizon. Changing into red and orange tones of exposed rock,

the
sunr
befo
ext
ove

de
a t
no
pr
w
a
h
a
a

s
sk

Jacob Ashton

(9 meters) from the road, I waited for darkne
invisible to passing cars before setting up m
I was on I-40 after a few miles the next
into Winslow, Arizona in about an ho
town and anticlimactic in such a f
my comprehension why it would
song by the Eagles. Perhaps it
called 'Take It Easy' for thos
ing on a corner doesn't
Contradicting the son
went to the superm
fore riding out of
Back on the
ride. I passe
and turne
went o
that
Ve

Here was a crossroads, thr...
staff on highway, or into the desert of the Navajo reservation
on questionable dirt roads. Highways got boring quickly and I
turned into the desert, after loading up on water at a gas station. The wind abated slightly and the dirt roads across the
reservation were almost entirely free of cars. I had to push
through some sandy sections, but I didn't mind it much.

I camped in the desert, somewhere in the reservation, that
night and the road conditions were much worse the next day.
Approximately 10 miles (16 km) of riding took two hours, on
mostly flat terrain. I had to get off and push my bike through
several sections of deep sand and bounced slowly over washboard so rough that it was as slow as walking. The 45 miles
(72 km), on flat to rolling roads, took all day. Finally, I made
it a small town called 'Leupp' and then filled up on water at a
church. After that, I was on paved roads and the distance went
by much faster; ending the day in a gravelly area not 10 yards

ss to render me
y tent.
morning and I cycled
ur. It was a quiet sort of
shion that it was beyond
be mentioned in a particular
just rhymed well. The song is
unfamiliar with the band. Stand-
take long so I tried it just because.
g, there were no fine sights to see, so I
arket and found wifi at a McDonald's be-
own.
Interstate once more, I continued my days'
through the town of Holbrook at midafternoon
d onto US-180. A few miles out of town, the road
ver the Little Colorado River and there was a turnout
had access to the river; I hadn't bathed properly since Las
gas, so something that resembled bathing was well over-
due. A short path through the trees opened up to a sandy beach
with easy access to the river and a rock wall, worn smooth by
the ages, made a backdrop to the swimming hole. I made my
way into the water and almost instantly sunk over a foot into
the mud and silt on the river bed. The water was freezing and
my bath was much shorter than it should have been. Thanks
to the mud and silt, I was covered in splotches of grey colored
dirt after I dried off. Even so, I was likely cleaner than before
considering that I'd ridden through a sandstorm a couple of
days earlier as I was leaving the Grand Canyon. I wiped as much
of the silt off as I could while I waited for my clothes to dry in
the sun.

A couple of evenings later, I considered paying for a campground; a real shower sounded nice since bathing in the Little
Colorado River hadn't done much. I rode by Lyman Lake State
Park and checked out the campground there; it looked like a
nice place, grassy sites and of course right by a lake. It was
also crowded, loud, and they wanted $20 a night. I'd rather

sleep on dirt for free, so I rode a few more miles then setup my tent off the road behind some bushes. It was well below freezing when I crawled out of my tent in the morning and frost covered the ground. I hadn't noticed the night before, because of the wind, but I'd camped near a waste water treatment plant and, when I opened the door to my tent, the pungent aroma of sewage hit me full in the face. Nauseously, I did my best not to vomit as I got everything ready to ride and then pedaled a few miles before eating breakfast.

I had a big pass to climb and I was getting overexcited at the thought. At 8,550 feet (2,590 meters) above sea level, the Alpine Divide would be the highest pass I'd climbed yet. A large roller took me into a river valley lined on all sides with pine trees and snowy mountains in the distance. Slowly, I worked my way up the mountain on the inconsistent climb, a few hundred feet up and a little bit less far down. Reaching the summit was anticlimactic; it almost came as a surprise that it was over so soon. I followed the road down into the village of Alpine, Arizona and had a slice of rhubarb pie with ice cream at a cafe to celebrate my new highest-elevation-of-the-trip and an early celebration of entering the fourth state on my journey. Having had minimal human interaction for over a week, I was happy when the owner of the cafe came by and struck up a conversation. They asked where I was from, what I was doing there, and they were impressed when I told them I'd just cycled over the Alpine Divide pass. More concerning to them was where I said I was going next, Mexico. They regaled me with tales of people being kidnapped by the cartel and having pieces of their body mailed to their family until a huge ransom was paid. This wasn't an uncommon theme, almost everybody I spoke with told me how dangerous Mexico was but I was not deterred. After leaving the cafe, I crossed into New Mexico a few miles later, the fourth state on my journey.

I slept in a bit the next morning, an extra 30 minutes, and woke up at 6:00 am. I'd planned for an easy day, ride the remaining 15 miles (24 km) into Silver City, and then stop for the day at a campground there. I took my time getting ready and made some of the instant coffee that I'd been carrying the entire time. I sat drinking a cup of the entire thermos-full I'd just made, when a realization came to me as the sun was coming over the hills; this was how most people cycle tour. Most of them average much less than the 65 miles (105 km) per day I'd been averaging over the past few weeks. I continued packing my gear, utterly baffled by that idea; what would I do with all the extra time if I wasn't riding?

I started pushing my bike towards the road at 7:45, then, I saw my front tire was low on air. Nothing serious, I'd had to pump it up every morning for the past couple of days; it seemed to lose a couple of pounds of pressure per hour and I was feeling too lazy to change it. My thermos happened to be in the same pannier as most of my tools and, after pumping it up, I had another cup of coffee while I gathered my thoughts concerning my epiphany of the morning.

A couple of hours later, I was climbing at a leisurely pace that suited my idea of an easy day, Riding uphill toward Silver City, the summit of which happened to be the Continental Divide, the line marking the separation of the eastern and western watersheds of the US. I rode into Silver City and got all my errands done: buy tire patches at the bike shop, stock up on food at the supermarket, and send my ice tires home at the UPS office. With everything done, I went to the campground; $15 for the night seemed a bit steep but, they had wifi and I really wanted a hot shower. It was also the first time I'd paid for a place to sleep in the entire trip. Since I'd spent most of my budget for the week, I decided I'd avoid spending money until I got to Mexico.

I crossed from New Mexico into Texas a few days later, my fifth and final state on my first leg of the US, and I rode into El Paso soon after. I had a few things to do before I left the US; I bought kerosene for my stove and enough peanut butter and cookies for me to last for a few days in case I had any problems finding food in Mexico. Making my way through the hills of

El Paso, I stopped just before the border to make a call home since I wouldn't have cell service outside the US. My tasks done, I rode over to the border and into my second country. The process was surprisingly simple; I had nothing to declare, the border guard took a quick look at my passport, asked a few questions, said "Welcome to Mexico", and just like that, I was in. I expected him to stamp my passport coming into the country but he just waved me off. With one border crossing down I had probably 100+ to go; cycling through at least 100 countries was another goal I added to my list.

The border city of Ciudad Juarez was similar to what I expected it to be: there were significant amounts of garbage lining the streets, buildings in disrepair, electrical lines were above ground in a messy jumble, and the number of stares I was receiving increased dramatically. Juarez used to be the murder capital of the world, but they've since cleaned up their act, and now it's something of a tourist destination for day trips from Texas.

Some of the side roads through the city seemed to have been recently paved, but the construction crew appeared to have forgotten to grade the road smooth before laying the asphalt. I bounced along the road and found that highway 45D would take me south for the next few hundred miles.

The glue-less patches that I'd been using to fix flat tires decided to melt off in the 85+ F (30 C) heat and I found myself on a sidewalk that inexplicably lined the highway, fixing the same couple of punctures I'd already repaired all over again. This time, I used vulcanizing patches, the people at the bike shop in Silver City told me they would work better.

I'd been studying a bit of Spanish on my way south so I knew: how to count to 10, ask directions to a few important amenities, say please and thank you, and ask how much something cost. Since I didn't know any numbers larger than ten, I learned how to ask someone to write it down too.

Asking for directions from someone in Spanish, I found my way to the nearest ATM and ended up pushing my bike up one of the steepest paved roads I had ever seen. The directions were correct and I soon had some pesos in hand, though not before taking a low speed spill in front of a crowded bus stop while I tried to get over a sloping curb. I usually don't get embarrassed easily, but having close to 50 people staring at me as I picked my bike up off the ground did the trick.

When I was getting close to being out of the city, I went to a burrito shop to try some real Mexican food. I managed to get two burritos for a few dollars which seemed like a pretty good deal. When I was done eating, I was sweating as much from the spicy food as I was from the sun!

A few miles away from the city, I came upon a federal police checkpoint. I stopped just out of sight to hide the rest of my American dollars and mentally prepared myself to be harassed by the police. The 'Policia Federales' or 'federal police' had a reputation for being as powerful as they were corrupt; I expected to be questioned and searched or at least asked for a bribe, but the police just waved me through. I waved back and gave a thumbs up as if to ask if I was clear to go; they returned it and I rode into the Chihuahua Desert. The desert was quite empty and the complete lack of fences made camping easy but, I pushed my bike a lot father off the road than normal before setting up camp. Peacefully, I cooked some pasta and listened to coyotes howling while I ate. Mexico didn't seem too dangerous, yet.

CHAPTER 3

Day 30, March 1, 2016

Chihuahua Desert, Mexico

My first days in Mexico were mostly highway riding; the Chihuahua desert was pretty empty and there didn't seem to be any options for smaller roads. People seemed friendly, so far; they stared, took my picture with their phones, and even shouted encouragement as I rode through most every town, but I didn't mind it much.

Approaching the city of Chihuahua, late one day, I followed a non-highway road option that wound through the hills; it seemed like there would be better options for camping. The road climbed about 500 feet (150 meters) before the descent into Chihuahua. I hadn't found anywhere to camp yet, though there was a church at the crest. I tried to ask permission to camp there from some people I saw outside the building. As I was riding toward the church, two dogs ran toward me from behind one of the buildings; they barked throughout my approach but didn't attack.

Through a combination of my incredibly limited Spanish, pointing at my still packed tent, and some hand signs, I got permission to stay the night there. They offered to let me sleep in one of the sheds on the property but, I preferred to sleep outside as I did not like the idea of staying somewhere I could be locked in. Just as it was getting dark and I was ready to go to bed, one of the men I had spoken with invited me inside for dinner. Gladly, I accepted, never expecting that they would be so generous. I ate a couple of chicken tacos with them while we communicated as best we could. Neither of them could be referred to as skinny and the thinner of the two made a mime of the larger one trying to ride a bicycle up a hill that brought laughs from all of us. I didn't want to eat too much of their food and, after a couple of tacos, I gave my thanks before returning to my tent and marveling at how kind the people living there had been to a foreigner who couldn't even speak their language.

I saw my hosts when I was leaving the next morning and thanked them again for their hospitality before descending toward Chihuahua City. I was on one of the main arteries into the city and the traffic was ridiculous. The three lane road was packed with cars that were barely moving. There was a wide dirt shoulder/drainage ditch where the drivers who were in a rush were practically jumping their vehicles into the ditch and driving along the bottom in an effort to get to where they were going just a little bit faster. Presently, there was a hole in the fence that lined the right side of the road; I went through it to try to escape the chaos and emerged onto a quieter side street that paralleled the main road. Some of the drivers saw me do this and soon, a line of cars was driving across the ditch and onto the parallel road I was on. Cycling the highway through the city would have been perilous and I got out my GPS to try to find a better route. Many of the numerous streets didn't have names and were built similar to a maze.

I wound my way along some quiet streets and eventually contented myself with threading my way along the sidewalk, close to the main road. A Mexican supermarket proved to be exceptionally well stocked and I resupplied before riding out of town. Later in the day, I reached 2,000 miles cycled. It'd taken me a day longer than my last thousand miles.

I wanted to stop for the day just short of the city of Delicas at around 60 miles (96 km), but there was nowhere to camp and so I had to keep going. I got closer and closer to the city without any luck finding somewhere to camp for the night so,

I had to ride through the city. It wasn't a big city like Chihuahua but, it was still several more miles of cycling. Outside the city, I found some abandoned buildings and, once I was confident they were unoccupied, set up camp for the night.

I was cycling through the desert again the next day. While I was resting in the shade, a man walked up to me and said he was a reporter for a local news station called 'TV Camargo' and that he'd like to interview me. His English was little better than my Spanish and he had to go get someone who spoke English. I told him which way I was heading and kept riding. About half an hour later, the reporter drove up next to me with his English speaking colleague. We pulled off into a turnout just ahead and I did my first ever television interview. It was recorded, not live, and they asked the usual questions they would in an interview: who, what, when, where, how and why of my tour. Why was I doing this? Just for fun; I love cycling and I wanted to travel. I managed to watch the interview at a later date and they called me 'El Aventurero', 'The Adventurer'.

After more than a week of cycling through the desert, I was finally approaching San Luis Potosi. I'd found another Warmshowers.org host to stay with in the city. I'd made a mistake in my estimated arrival date so, I rode a few long days through the desert as opposed to asking my host if I could arrive a day late. It wasn't exciting cycling, apart from a sandstorm. The highlight of the last week was probably the food; street food abounded in every city I rode through tempting me with tacos, burritos, and more.

In the city of San Luis Potosi, I went through my usual tasks, predominately buying groceries and finding wifi. Through a series of unfortunate events that I was uncertain about, my Warmshowers.org host cancelled on me at the last minute and I was left with nowhere to stay in a big city in Mexico. By the time I realized I didn't have anywhere to stay for the night it was getting dark and I was still well within the city limits. I found a wifi connection and located a hotel but it was almost

5 miles (8 km) across the city, through Friday evening traffic.

The ride was... exciting, to say the least. A truck stopped suddenly in front of me and I had to hit the brakes so hard that I lost my balance and fell over. Luckily, the beer I'd bought, to share with the host I no longer had, survived the fall.

I made it to the hotel in one piece. It cost me about $32 US, making it the second time I'd paid for a place to sleep and the most expensive too. When I arrived, the building looked abandoned; the sign outside said it was open and I walked in. Internet, a warm bed, breakfast included, and my first shower since Silver City, New Mexico; I was a little overdue. It turned out to be a really nice hotel. I practically had a whole suite to myself and they let me keep my bike in the room too.

I had originally planned to stay in San Luis Potosi for two nights and have a zero mileage day the next day, but, since my host fell through and I didn't feel like paying for another night at a hotel, I decided I'd just have an easy day instead. I devoured the complimentary buffet breakfast and then went for a walk to see some of the sights the city had to offer before coming back to the hotel and enjoying the air conditioning until checkout time.

After a few more days of cycling through the desert, I was finally getting into the mountains of central Mexico. Following one particularly trying day in the desert, during which I got six flat tires from pieces of wire, I woke the next morning in my camp by a lake in the mountains. Idyllic villages through a high mountain valley made for incredible cycling. I followed the road along a lake and marveled at the sights around me. It seemed a land that time had forgotten; farmers were out plowing their fields with horse drawn plows and women carried water from some of the many streams that skirted the fields. Next, the road began a series of winding climbs through forested hills and suddenly, a more modern world was present again.

I had a short descent out of the mountains the next morning before the madness began. Mexico City and its outlying areas were similar to the traffic that I'd experienced in San Luis Potosi and Chihuahua, except Mexico City was almost 50 times the size and it was not flat. Blaring horns and crazy drivers were the order of the morning. There was no sympathy for me while I pedaled 120+ lb (55+ kg) of bike and gear up incredibly steep hills, swerved around potholes, and dodged the less than courteous drivers. It was a relatively short day in distance but what miles I did cover wore me out more than a full day of riding. I found a hotel near the city center for a much better price than my last one and booked two nights. The following day was my first zero mile day since I started traveling nearly two months earlier. I spent the day exploring the city and eating tacos.

After my day off, I used my GPS to route my way out of the city and it worked surprisingly well. I still had some congested roads to ride on but, the GPS led me down some quieter side streets that made leaving Mexico City much less terrible than I thought it would be. My legs were feeling great after the rest day; I had to watch myself to make sure I didn't ride too hard.

Approaching the outskirts of the city, a driver of a van, full of people, passed me aggressively with his tires squealing and the engine full throttle. He lost control of the vehicle, sliding one way then another before slamming into the back of another passenger van on the side of the road. Bodies flew around the van and splattered blood on the windows. A crowd formed almost instantly around the wreck. Shocked by the incident, I didn't know what to do. Already, people were helping the injured and the presence of a foreigner on a bicycle would only be a distraction to those able to help; I kept cycling, feeling numb and helpless from witnessing the incident.

A few miles later, I arrived at the ruins of the ancient Aztec holy city of Teotihuacan. Standing among the stone pyramids of an empire gone by made life seem fleeting, especially after witnessing a probably lethal crash earlier in the day. I climbed the tallest structure, the Pyramid of the Sun, and looked off at the outskirts of Mexico City; nothing had changed and yet everything was different.

After riding away from Mexico City for a few days, I spent a night camped at just over 10,000 feet (3,030 meters) above sea level on the slopes of Pico de Orizaba; the third tallest mountain in North America and the tallest volcano on the continent, I wanted to climb it. As the rising sun lit the sky on fire over the volcano, I began riding up the mountain, or at least I tried to. I had all of 8 miles (13 km) to cover with over 4,000 vertical feet (1,200 meters) of elevation gain at an average grade of above 10%, and some of it was flat or even downhill.

I made it about 4 feet (1.3 meters) before I almost fell over. I pushed for a little over 1.5 miles (2.5 km) before the grade became so steep I could hardly move. I was near a well-forested area with grasses a couple of feet tall covering the undergrowth so, I cached my bike and all the gear I wouldn't need for the climb in a place where they would be invisible from the road, I shouldered my backpack, loaded with everything I needed, and I began to walk.

Not willing to be deterred, I climbed and I climbed; the condition of the road quickly deteriorated to a steep, rocky, rutted, and root-strewn jeep track. By the time I broke through the tree line at 13,000 feet (3,940 meters), I was stopping to rest every quarter mile (400 meters). My 60 pound (27 kg) pack, weighed heavily on my every step with all the water, food, and gear I had for the next two days. I made it to base camp after 2:00 pm; it'd taken me almost eight hours to cover as many miles (13 km).

There were several other groups at the base camp hut: some college students traveling over spring break, an American couple living in Mexico, a California father and son, and a Ukrainian climbing team; all of them had planned and trained to climb the mountain. Besides cycling almost every day for the last couple of months, I hadn't done any other training. I talked with various people for a couple of hours before retiring for the evening, at about 5:00 pm, to try to get some sleep before I started the climb in the dark.

Sleeping didn't go as well as I'd hoped; thanks to the altitude, I slept for less than two hours. I woke just after midnight, dressed, and shoved all the gear and supplies I'd need for the climb into my backpack. I'd tweaked both my knees the day before: the left on the climb up and the right almost falling down a ladder in the base camp hut. They were still sore but not too bad; some stretching helped loosen them up.

I started climbing at one in the morning with almost everyone who'd been at the hut. The mass start quickly broke up into smaller groups and I stayed with the fastest group. The moon was full and so bright that it was easy to climb without lights. I felt great leaving camp at around 14,000 feet (4,240 meters); I had no problem with the elevation then.

Near dawn, I approached the glacier at about 17,000 feet (5,150 meters) and began to get symptoms of altitude sickness; shortness of breath and a minor headache were my main ailments. My strength was disappearing quickly; I had to dig deep just to keep going. The college students I was climbing with weren't doing well either.

As we approached 18,000 feet (5,450 meters) one of them started talking nonsense, such as saying his kidneys were hurting, and showing signs of severe oxygen deprivation. The entire group of three I'd been climbing with turned around with him while I kept climbing alone. When I was within a few hundred feet of the summit, I had to stop to catch my breath every few minutes. If I sat down to rest and tried to look up to see how far I had to go, I'd get vertigo and almost fall over while seated.

I reached the summit, at 18,491 feet (5,603 meters) above sea level, after climbing for almost seven hours. I peered over the edge of a cliff, into the smoking crater of the volcano, while the shadow of the mountain cast a pyramidal shape across the landscape on the far side of the rising sun.

The view from the top of the volcano was like looking down from an airplane. Pico de Orizaba (or Citlaltepetl,

Mountain of the Star) rose over 10,000 feet (3,030 meters) above the surrounding ground in every direction. Only the volcano Popocapetl, on the distant horizon, came close to matching its dominance. On a clear day it's possible to see the Gulf of Mexico 100 miles (160 km) away while standing on the summit; I wasn't sure if I could see it. After taking some pictures and resting for a couple of minutes, I began the descent.

Climbing down took less than half the time going up did. Of the nine people who'd started the climb that morning only three had reached the top, including myself. I caught a ride back to my bike; because it was an out and back, the car ride didn't jeopardize my goal of traveling only by my own power overland and, after eating, I promptly fell asleep.

CHAPTER 4

Day 55, March 26, 2016

Veracruz, Mexico

Unfortunately, I was exceptionally sore from climbing that volcano for the next several days; I had to stretch every morning and throughout the day just to be able to keep riding. My knees had developed the habit of locking up suddenly and painfully, at random intervals, which made progress slow and exhausting.

I descended off the high plateau of central Mexico and down to the coast where I'd camped less than 20 miles (32 km) away from Veracruz. With the descent had come heat and humidity; I sweated all night long in my tent. All this combined discomfort had me feeling overwhelmed and unable to continue. I was seriously considering finding somewhere to store my bike and then fly home for a break. My sister's wedding was a couple of weeks away and I felt conflicted about missing it.

Previously, my logic had been that my tour had a start date for over a year before she got engaged; it seemed to make sense at the time but I was having second thoughts. I called home from a Carl's Jr. and while I was spilling all my troubles to my mom, and before I got to the part about flying home, she encouraged me to take it easy for a while to recover.

Taking it easy for a while sounded way less complicated, and also far cheaper than flying home, so I resolved to make sure I could at least video-call into the wedding. I shopped around for hotels in Veracruz with the idea of taking a day or two off the bike but, all the prices were inflated for spring break; I camped at a deserted construction site instead.

After a couple of shorter distance cycling days, I got to a small city called 'Alvarado' and took a day off the bike. A couple of easy days with a day completely off the bike seemed to do the trick; my knees didn't lock up at all after that.

Almost a week later, I was about 10 miles (16 km) away from Heroica Cardenas when a Federal Policeman pulled off in front of me and told me to stop. He didn't speak English and we had the conversation about where I'm from and where I'm going. I'd had enough practice with that particular exchange that I could get people to think that I could speak Spanish for a minute or two. The policeman wanted a picture of my bike before he sent me on my way. I thought that was the end of it, general curiosity and people asking for photos was common, but he started following me with his lights on. I pulled over to see what he wanted but he waved for me to keep riding. I continued riding with him following close behind and he continued to tail me for several miles.

When I felt like it was time for a snack break, I pulled over in the shade; the policeman got out of his car and asked me for my identification. I gave him my driver's license; he took it back to his car and took a picture of it before copying some of the information. He gave it back to me, and then he drove off. Looking back, I think asking for my ID was a way for him to get a glimpse inside my wallet to see if I had money for a bribe. I also had a growing suspicion that I was supposed to have a stamp for entering Mexico even though the border guard in Juarez had told me I didn't need one when I entered the country.

Nearly a week after the incident with the Federal Police, I was eating breakfast one morning when I saw two cycle tourists ride by. I was hidden at my current camp, in the jungle, and they didn't see me. I figured I'd be about 30 minutes behind them and I packed quickly to try to catch up to them. I rode for a little over an hour before stopping at a gas station to refill my water. Just outside the convenience store, I saw two bicycles. Their owners appeared soon afterwards and they introduced themselves as Sarah and Bruno, from Canada and Switzerland respectively; they were also heading towards Merida and said I could join them.

They were the second and third cycle tourists I'd met so far and, seeing as I hadn't ridden with anyone for my entire tour, I jumped at the chance to have company. I rode with them for a little more than 30 miles (48 km). They'd been on tour since the beginning of January and were finishing up in Cancun, Mexico in a couple of weeks, after riding through most of the Central American countries. They were traveling light with only two panniers each, compared to my four panniers and 65 liter backpack strapped to my rear rack. Their riding days were similar to mine in distance but, they were in the habit of having almost as many off days as riding days. I was able to glean some excellent information about the roads ahead and they gave me much to look forward to over the coming weeks. I enjoyed riding with them; we were already in Merida and parted ways far too quickly. They planned to cycle northwest out of the city, to find somewhere to spend four or five nights, while I headed east.

The next morning I reached 4,000 miles cycled on my tour before I stopped for my first break; the days were passing quickly! That afternoon, I got to Chichen Itza. The entrance fee was high for Mexico (about $12), and it was quite obviously a tourist trap, but it was an impressive testament to the ingenuity of the Mayan civilization and worth a visit. Intrigued, I walked around the entirety of the ancient city over the course of a few hours, taking it all in: temples, astronomical observatories, roads, houses, and an aqueduct. There was a ball court where competitors were supposed to have played; the stakes were that the losing team was sacrificed to the gods.

The following day, I rode into Valladolid and checked into a hotel for a couple of nights. I was able to attend the entire ceremony of my sister's wedding via video-call. The next item on my list, for my rest day, was going swimming in a 'cenote'; a water-filled limestone sinkhole that was common in the Yucatan peninsula. Cenotes were considered by the Mayans to be passages to the underworld. It was an incredibly beautiful spot hidden away in the city of Valladolid. The water was lukewarm and I had the entire spot to myself. After swimming for a while, I sat and admired the beauty before doing some cliff diving off the walkway. Luckily, I never entered the underworld.

A couple of days' ride from Valladolid were the Mayan ruins at Tulum on the Gulf Coast of Mexico. At the entrance to the ruins, I met two men from Poland who were on a bicycle tour of North America. Their names were Patryk and Kuba. Kuba, they said, is Polish for Jacob, same as my name. They wrote their names down for me to make sure the spelling was correct. They'd been on tour for 10 months and had covered about 12,400 miles (20,000 km). We got to talking and, when I said I'd started in Idaho, I was somewhat surprised when they asked me if I'd had any issues with bears. They had heard that there were bears in Idaho and chose to avoid that region of the US because of them.

I thought about this for a while after we parted ways, and came to the realization that, while their fears were grounded in facts, I couldn't think of anyone I'd ever met who'd been attacked by a bear. I further decided that fears about any particular area, although they may be based on facts, are generally of similar irrationality. As with many ideas, there are exceptions; some of the countries in the Middle East probably have a higher chance of dangerous incidents, compared to other regions.

The ruins at Tulum were gorgeous, surrounded by palm trees and right on the beautifully clear Caribbean Sea. It's easy to see why the Mayans built a city there. The remnants of the buildings were all grey stone, but supposedly, they were painted in gaudy colors when the city was inhabited.

When I rolled through the town of Limones, the next day, I caught up to two bicycle tourists from Germany. Their names were Olaf and Johanna; they'd started out of Cancun four days earlier and were traveling for a year or two along the Pan-American Highway, going south on a similar route to mine. The Pan-American Highway stretches all the way from a town called Deadhorse, in the far north of Alaska, to the southern end of South America, but it's interrupted by the Darien Gap; a road-less swamp, between Panama and Colombia, that most people take a boat around or fly over. Olaf and Johanna were having trouble adjusting to the heat and were about to stop for the day when I saw them; they were riding much slower than I was. Meeting them meant I'd met more cycle tourists in the last two days than I had in the previous 70. I rode for a couple more hours before coming to a break in the fence that lined the road, just as I hit my goal for the day of six hours riding time. It turned out to be a good spot to set up camp and I was less than 30 miles (48 km) away from the Belize border.

I was at the Belize border by midday. Crossing was a confusing process, even though it's considered straightforward as far as borders are concerned. I was fairly confident I would figure out border crossings before too long. On the Mexico side, I got waved away from one building and told to keep going. There was a kiosk right next to the road so, I stopped at the window and handed my passport to a bearded guard with a high pitched voice; apparently there was something wrong. He told me to park my bike by the kiosk and wait for him. I did so and, after eating a bit and still seeing no sign of the guard, I walked around to the door to see what was happening.

After waiting a while longer, I walked into the office. There were two guards inside; both of them were doing something with their smartphones. I tried to find out what was going on. The guard I'd talked to first said that there was a problem because my passport hadn't been stamped when I entered Mexico. He offered me a chair and began to explain that he was trying to find out what to do with the situation; more waiting followed while both guards played on their phones.

Eventually, I was told to go to the office across the street. They had me pay $20 worth of Mexican pesos for the exit fee and write a letter explaining why I didn't have an entry stamp and what I'd been doing with my time in Mexico. Thanks to the border guard in Juarez not stamping my passport, even though I'd asked about it, my entire stay in Mexico was done illegally. They explained what would have happened had I been 'caught' at a checkpoint. I would have been arrested, done a lot of waiting and answered a lot of questions before being extradited; oops.

Upon learning this, I was surprised that I'd made it through the country without being checked; I'd ridden through at least ten checkpoints throughout my stay and was waved through every single one. I'd even been stopped by the Federal Police without ever having my passport checked. After taking a photocopy of my passport and stamping it as exiting Mexico, they added my letter to a suspiciously large pile of letters. The Belize side was much simpler: follow the signs to immigration, stop at the office, fill out a form, answer questions about only having an exit stamp for Mexico, gush about how nice I've heard Belize was, explain what I was doing, and get the Belize entry stamp, before getting back on the road.

The first thing I noticed in Belize was a reduction in the amount of vehicles on the road. The second was the relative lack of the road signs that were everywhere in Mexico. The third was that there were very few fences; camping should be easy.

I followed the Northern Highway to the south and chose to stay inland instead of detouring toward the coast. I bumped along the broken pavement, dodging potholes, and saw a car about once every five minutes. Now that I was getting closer to the equator, the tropical sun beat down on me. There was a serious deficit of shade; I took breaks at bus stops rather than in the sun.

My front tire was flat the next morning. On top of that, I

didn't get as much water before camping as I should have and I had to ration it all evening to have some left for the morning. Getting the tire off was more difficult than usual; I struggled with it for a long time before I was successful, albeit bleeding from a few places on my hands. I located and patched not one, not two, but three holes in the tube, before setting about the tedious task of picking everything out of the tire. I found at least twice as many bits of thorns in the tire as I had punctures.

Getting the tire back on wasn't any easier than getting it off. I can usually get it on in two tries, this time it was closer to eight, with the last being a Herculean effort to get the last couple of inches of tire over the rim while I fought for grip with sweaty palms in the already oppressive heat and humidity. After sweating even more from pumping up the tire, I got on the road over an hour later than planned.

The city of Orange Walk was only a few miles away; I was pleasantly surprised to find that the car traffic was light compared to many of the cities I'd ridden through in Mexico. I was on the hunt for wifi and I checked several of the less rundown-looking places without any luck. At the southern edge of the city, I'd almost given up hope when I came to a hotel/restaurant that advertised having internet.

Belize was pretty cool; almost everyone spoke English and they used the imperial system of measurement, which means mile markers instead of kilometers. It was almost like being back in the US. The restaurant really did have wifi and I ate a breakfast of scrambled eggs, bacon, beans, and "fry-jacks" (some kind of puffy fried pastry), with melon juice to drink; in the US we'd call it cantaloupe juice. By the time I finished eating, called home, and got around to leaving, it was approaching 10:00 am and I'd only ridden 7 miles (12 km). A stiff headwind awaited me outside and I rode into it all afternoon.

CHAPTER 5

Day 76, April 16, 2016

Belize

My front tire was flat again in the morning. I guessed that it was a slow leak and I pumped it up before I started packing my stuff. Because it seemed close to the same pressure when I was done packing, I started riding on it without fixing the leak; it was too much work to fix a flat that didn't absolutely need it for the second morning in a row. I started riding at dawn and, thanks to the humidity, I was back in what had become my normal state of being drenched in sweat right away. Throughout the day, I checked a few stores to see if I could get some famous Belizean rum. None of them took debit cards and I had no local currency, an unfortunate bust.

When I was about 5 miles (8 km) away from the border of Guatemala, the road began to follow a river. There were people swimming in it and I joined in, albeit at a different spot along the beach where I hoped I would be left alone. The water was perfect, cooler than the air but not cold; it was an excellent escape from the tropical heat.

I arrived at the Guatemala border a few hours later; the process was simple, I walked into the Belize exit office, paid the exit tax, and got stamped out. Next, I crossed a bridge and walked up to the Guatemala border control office; the guard took a quick look at my passport before stamping it and handing it back. It was done so quickly that I asked if I had to do anything else; I didn't.

On the other side of the border, the buildings were more run down and everything was in Spanish and metric again; it's amazing how quickly things can change. I stopped for the day, just outside of the border town, in the first open field I came to. The flies were numerous, but at least they weren't the biting kind; I'll take non-biting flies any day over the mosquitoes that had been plaguing me almost every evening since I got to Veracruz.

Over the course of a couple of days on the road, the landscape had transitioned from the gentle rolling hills I'd encountered in Belize to mountains. Occasionally, the main roads were dirt and poverty was more evident; some people lived in ramshackle structures that were crammed next to each other wherever there was flat ground. Streams that were colored dark from waste trickled down the mountains; piles of plastic wrappers and bottles lined the roadsides which turned stretches of road into makeshift rubbish dumps. Yet, between the towns, the mountains were incredible! Jungle and undergrowth, so dense that it was nearly impassable, covered the almost sheer walls of the mountains like something out of a Jurassic Park movie and I cycled by in awe.

The roads going up the mountains matched the exceptionally rugged terrain; some of them were so steep they resembled walls of pavement. My speedometer would read zero for a few seconds when my speed dropped below 2.5 mph (4 km/h) because, apparently, you're not supposed to be able to ride a bicycle slower than that; but that was the best I could do pedaling up those grades.

Some of the rivers didn't have bridges and the ferries I rode on to cross them were so packed with cars that I was nervous that they wouldn't make it across without breaking apart or sinking from all the weight. Amazingly, they held together, but it was always an exciting ride, even though they went less than a few miles per hour.

I started buying ice cream throughout the day for a temporary relief from the heat. Sitting on the shaded steps of the small shops in the villages, I ate and watched the small crowds that would gather to stare at me and my bike. The Guatemalans added a whole new element to the stares and picture taking that I had to put up with in parts of Mexico. Apparently, it's absolutely hilarious to see a sweaty foreigner drenched and struggling to pedal up an exceptionally steep hill; people laughed, sometimes even when I just rode by. I liked to think that they were not laughing at me, per se, but at the unusual sight that my recumbent bike was to them. Still, when I was already sweaty and tired, being laughed at wasn't helpful to my general good nature.

After a few days of cycling through the mountains, I had one of the hardest riding days since I started my tour. Right off the bat, I had a climb that gained 800 feet (240 meters) in 1 mile (1.6 km) which would be an average incline of above 15%. I had to walk most of it but was able to ride the last quarter mile (400 meters), so most of the grade was probably closer to 20%. That hill set the tone for the rest of the day; incredibly steep climbs followed by equally steep descents.

There were no shops all day and I needed water. Spotting a group of men building something along the road, I asked them about getting some water; one of them led me around the side of his house to ask his wife if they had water. He came out again and gave me a cup of something that looked like muddy water and was warm; I asked what it was and he said it was cacao, it turned out to be quite tasty and I hoped that the water had been boiled previously to kill off some of the germs. The man had said something about a water source up the road and walked with me while I pushed my bike. There was a gravel turnout and a path leading into the jungle. I followed him down the path to what appeared to be a spring, a stream of water running out of a wooden pipe stuck into the side of the mountain; I gladly refilled my water there.

Toward the end of the day, I was too exhausted to ride up anything steep which meant I was walking up almost everything. My average speed for the day was less than 4 mph (6.4 km/h) and I only managed to cover 32 miles (52 km) before I found a small grassy area with room for my tent. Some people who lived nearby came by while I was cooking dinner to see what I was doing; they were more curious about my bike than anything else and I was too tired to care about the attention. There weren't any bugs out so, I slept on the groundsheet of my tent to try to stay a little cooler. A couple of hours later, I was awakened by some curious locals; once I explained that I was trying to sleep and that I'd leave in the morning, they left me alone.

Two mornings later, I bumped along a rough dirt road for the last mile to the Chixoy river crossing. On the other side of the bridge, the road was paved. It began to climb and I slowly worked my way out of the river canyon that I had descended into the previous day via a steep and rocky dirt track that would have been better suited to a full suspension mountain bike rather than my overloaded touring bike.

The drivetrain of my bicycle had worn enough over the last several thousand miles that it began to skip whenever I was trying to muscle my way up a steep section of road; it happened repeatedly and at inopportune times that caused me to fall over. Soon, I had bruises covering both sides of my body from the impacts. Having a less than functional bike was driving me crazy and I needed to find a solution.

I rode what sections I could and passed through a couple of hamlets without seeing anything that resembled a bike shop. Hoping on a random chance that I'd see a bike shop wasn't getting any results, so I asked a man I saw working outside and he told me there was one in the next town. Eventually, I found it, though not without having to ask a few more people for directions. They had some kind of knockoff Maya Tour branded derailleur that I bought for $3 and swapped out its upper cog with the one on my higher quality derailleur and saved the other cog for a later date. By some miracle it fit perfectly. One of the employees at the shop spoke English and told me that the cog was the cause of the problem and that my chain was still good. He was a mechanic by profession so I took his word for it.

I rode out of town and began going up a steep hill when, lo and behold, my chain skipped and, before I could catch myself from falling, I was lying on the pavement for the umpteenth time that day. I tried climbing in my second easiest gear and it skipped less often. In my third easiest gear it didn't skip at all so, I figured the problem was the cassette. The skipping chain had worn enough material off of the cassette teeth to where it would no longer mesh properly. I decided that I was going to get a new chain at the next opportunity, regardless of whether the mechanic there thought I needed it.

A 2,000 foot (600 meter) climb greeted me the next morning. My chain was still working in my third easiest gear and I climbed slowly, mashing the gear as best I could. Not being able to stand up to pedal on my recumbent bike made climbing similar to doing thousands of repetitions of leg press. Over the 7,000 foot (2,120 meter) tall pass, I had an exciting descent down to about 3,800 feet (1,150 meters) to the city of Sacapulas where I found a bike shop and bought a new chain. I tried to buy a new cassette as well but, they only had a six speed cassette; this confirmed my fear that I had just installed a six speed chain on my eight speed drivetrain. I started riding and it worked for the most part; I could use the four easiest gears without issue, no skipping in any of them, the fifth gear only worked in my largest chainring, the other three were a lost cause. Shifting between the cogs didn't work well, but it did work.

I climbed out of the city and, over the remainder of the day, had a rolling climb up to about 7,000 feet (2,120 meters) in elevation. Being able to use my low gears again made climbing much easier. Closer to the summit, the road deteriorated into broken pavement and, eventually, become a gravel road; it was moderately well-maintained gravel rather than the rough, uneven cobble-sized stones interspersed with gravel that I had climbed a few days ago. Joyfully, after about 5 miles (8 km) on the rough surface, the road turned into a blissfully smooth pavement that passed over some rolling hills. I made camp in a forest and, about an hour before dark, it began to rain. The evening was pleasantly cool thanks to the elevation and I had to use my sleeping bag for the first time since before I got to Veracruz.

The mountains were refreshingly cool when I woke up in the morning. Some light rolling hills started off my day, and compared to the significant amount of climbing over the past several days, my first 20 miles (32 km) or so passed relatively easily. After riding through Sanata Cruz de Quiche, I had several steep descents and climbs; the road would descend steeply for 500 feet (150 meters) or more into a canyon before climbing up an equally steep and serpentine road up the other side. The roads were so steep that I had to stop to readjust my brakes a couple of times from the amount of wear they would incur while I was trying to stay in control on the descents.

One of the climbs was so steep that my rear tire lost traction, going uphill, on damp pavement, and I almost fell over. This was frightening because the roads were plagued by the craziest bus drivers I had ever seen; they drove brightly painted school buses called "chicken buses" that were among the largest vehicles on the road and they drove like it too. I quickly learned that chicken buses have the right of way, no matter the situation.

The final climb topped out at almost 9,000 feet (2,720 meters) in elevation and I had an inconsistent descent to Lago Atitlan; a body of water surrounded by volcanic mountains on all sides and supposedly one of the most beautiful lakes in the world. Since I arrived during the sugar cane harvest and subsequent burning, the ever present shroud of smoke gave the area less appeal.

I found a relatively cheap hotel in the lakeside town of Panajachel. Within an hour of checking in, I twisted my left knee going down some stairs; I was unsure of the exact cause, but my left kneecap slid painfully over to the outside of my knee and it took me an excruciating minute or so to get it to pop back into place. I had already planned for a day off and I hoped my knee wouldn't keep me there for too much longer. Later in the afternoon, my knee was feeling strong enough to walk on and I went for a stroll around town to see the colonial architecture and sat quietly out by the lake.

CHAPTER 6

Day 86, April 26, 2016

Pan-American Highway, Guatemala

At the end of the day, when I'd just finishing setting up my tent on the edge of an empty field, two men carrying machetes came walking across the field toward me. Anywhere else their machetes may have been cause for concern but, in Central America, almost every working man carried a machete. I walked a short way in their direction and greeted them. From what I could glean with my very limited understanding of Spanish, I think they were asking me if I wanted to move my tent into the trees near where they lived. It was already raining, and I had all my gear set up inside my tent, so I told them I would be fine where I was. I thanked them for their offer and they left.

It rained most of the night. Even though rain meant slightly cooler temperatures, I was still sweating in my tent while trying to sleep as I had been almost every night for over a month. My knee was sore again when I started riding the next morning; not as bad as the day before though, and after an hour, it'd loosened up enough that it was feeling relatively normal.

I'd climbed away from Lago Atitlan a couple of days earlier. Over that pass, I descended almost all of the way to the Pacific coast, a region made up entirely of rolling hills. I'd climb at less than 4 mph (6.4 km/h) up the steepest hills before descending at close to 40 mph (64 km/h) down the other side. Rinse and repeat for the entire day.

Around midday, I came upon two people on a bicycle tour along the Pan-American, heading north. Their names have since escaped me, but they were from Chile and France; they'd started in Chile about 310 miles (500 km) south of Santiago and were riding all the way to northern Mexico. While I was talking with them, another cyclist showed up, Jesse from Oregon. He was heading in the same direction as I was and on a similar route. Just as we were about to part ways, I found my rear tire was flat; the rim tape had slid over and the tube had been punctured by the spoke hole. Jesse waited for me to fix it, then we rode on together. Jesse was carrying about 40 pounds (18 kg) less weight with his setup and was a strong cyclist; to the point that I was having difficulty keeping up. The last I saw of him that day, he was going up one of the longer, rolling hills, but I didn't blame him at all. If our roles were reversed, I likely would have done the same thing. I rode along, alone once again.

My knee was feeling much stronger the next morning; within 15 minutes of riding, it was back to about normal. I camped about 20 miles (32 km) before the border with El Salvador. About 5 miles (8 km) away from the border there was a line of semi-trucks waiting to cross into El Salvador. They were lined up, bumper to bumper, for the entire distance. My border crossing went smoothly; I received an exit stamp for Guatemala with no charge, then across to the El Salvador side which was also free, but no stamps as their system is entirely electronic. Taking my Mexican border experience into consideration, I double checked with the border guards just to make sure.

Just over the border, I went to a restaurant for breakfast and got beans, scrambled eggs, cheese, and bread with a wifi connection for $1.50 US; El Salvador uses the US dollar as their currency. The temperature was already up to 91 degrees F (33 C) with 65% humidity and I was sweating like crazy.

After breakfast, I was making my way up one of the gentle rolling hills when I saw a cycle tourist in my rear view mirror;

it was Jesse, one of the cyclists I'd met yesterday. Last night, he'd stopped about 10 miles (16 km) ahead of me but had started riding about two hours later this morning. We rode together for the remainder of the day. It was great having company and someone to talk to in English after being alone on the road for so long.

I hit 5,000 miles cycled! There was a tamale stand a short way up the road and I bought a couple to celebrate the occasion. Once again, I was having difficulty keeping up with Jesse. I drafted (followed closely so that I was in his slipstream and not working quite as hard) when possible so I could keep up and matched his pace the majority of the time on the flat roads. The miles passed quickly and soon we arrived at the ocean.

Houses lined the oceanfront and made it nearly impossible to camp in that area. There was a sign for beach access; we took it and, a quarter mile (400 meters) later, we were on a beautiful beach made up of black volcanic sand. We hung around the beach, swam, and ate dinner.

Over dinner, Jesse mentioned he'd be down to zero food after a light breakfast the next morning and would need to stop right away. The idea of running out of food was appalling to me; I regularly carried a several day supply regardless of my location. Jesse's explanation that there were shops almost every day made sense and, because I'd seen the proof of his words from how much faster his lightweight setup was, I ditched some of the pasta I'd probably bought in New Mexico and had been carrying ever since. It might have been only a few pounds compared to the 40+ lb (18 kg) lower bike and gear weight he had but it was a start.

Jesse and I started early the next morning. I still wasn't keeping up with him; I'd ride along at my own pace while he sped up the rolling hills that lined the El Salvadoran coast and waited every so often for me to catch up. At one point, he got a flat tire. He had everything he needed so I kept going and he caught me within an hour; he was quick at fixing flats too.

The rolling hills kept up for about 35 miles (56 km) before leveling out near Las Libertad. I saw Jesse's bike outside a gas station convenience store and found him inside. The air conditioning and an ice cream came as a blessed relief from the heat and humidity.

That evening, Jesse introduced me to the concept of camping at fire stations. We found a fire station and he asked the firemen if we could camp there; they showed us a flat grassy area behind the station where we could set up for the night. Jesse had been asking for a place to camp almost every night of his tour and had been staying at churches, random people's houses, fire stations, and other government buildings as well. While a free place to stay was nice, I didn't like the part about being dependent on the local population for a place to stay when it wasn't an absolute need.

The firemen in the city we stopped at the following evening were not as friendly as the previous ones. They made up several excuses for why we couldn't stay there before telling us "no"; they recommended that we try asking at the military base up the road. We did, but had no luck there either. Jesse was getting discouraged from the failed attempts at asking and was going to find a cheap hotel for the night. I didn't want to spend the money on a hotel so I rode out of town to try to find somewhere to camp. We swapped routes before parting company with the intention of meeting up later.

While I was riding out of the city, somebody on a bike came by and started talking to me in Spanish; they asked where I was going and after I said, "Honduras", they told me I was going the wrong way. I was confused by this and checked my GPS, it looked fine to me. Once I reached the outskirts of the city, I found that I had plotted the wrong direction on my GPS. Even with a GPS telling me where to go, I had managed to get lost and I'd have a difficult time getting anywhere without it. I did not want to ride back through the city, so I found an alternate route to get back to the correct road. It would add a few miles but that was much better than riding back through the city. I found an abandoned airstrip with a broken fence and spent the night there. It was nice having the time alone after being whistled, yelled, honked, and laughed at all day by the locals while I cycled through the intense heat.

My wrong turn in the city cost me dearly in sweat and blood the following morning; it was steep rolling hills the whole way with roads as steep as any I'd seen in Guatemala. After a few miles, the road turned to dirt and continued to wind steeply up and down. There was a stream crossing; my front tire slid on a submerged rock causing me to fall in, and I came up bloody with the palm of my right hand split open. Immediately after the stream, there was a steep and very roughly cobbled climb; I had to push my bike the whole way up and my wet shoes had little grip on the cobbles, it was a struggle just to keep moving. A steep, winding, and sandy descent awaited me at the top and I had to descend at barely 5 mph (8 km/h) to stay in control. When I finally reached the road I was supposed to be on, it'd taken me over 2.5 hours to go 15 miles (24 km).

Once I was on pavement, getting to the border only took a couple more hours. I didn't see Jesse all day; he must have gotten ahead while I was trying to get back to the main road.

Border formalities passed easily; the only difference from the last few was that they had to scan my fingerprints. Then it was on to my fifth country, Honduras. The landscape was much more arid compared to the lush forests of Guatemala and parts of El Salvador, at least in this part of the country. The population density was also much lower than in El Salvador where houses had lined almost the entirety of every road.

Camping wasn't difficult; I found an unused field and made myself at home. The nights hadn't been cooling off much and I was sweating profusely while trying to sleep. My air mattress had been punctured by thorns, and the like, several times over the last months; that night, just as I was starting to fall asleep, all the patches failed from the accumulated sweat. I'd already used all of the included patches and so I tried a vulcanizing patch for an inner tube. It held for ten minutes before all my sweat worked it loose again.

I lay sweating, on my flat mattress, on the hard ground, trying to think of how I could fix it. I tried a combination of super glue and the glue-less patches that I'd never gotten rid of; this worked! It took me close to an hour to find all the holes and patch them using this method; all the while I was being eaten by mosquitos.

I fell asleep exhausted and still sweating.

CHAPTER 7

Day 93, May 3, 2016

Nicaragua

I crossed into Nicaragua the next day and camped a few miles away from the border. The Hondurans had checked my fingerprints again as I left, to make sure they hadn't changed overnight. I'd only spent one night in the country. There wasn't much to see in the southern part of the country that I cycled through and the north, with its major cities, was becoming increasingly dangerous and politically unstable.

Nicaragua was green and flat, except for the volcanoes that rose dramatically out of the otherwise featureless landscape. Roughly 30 miles (48 km) in, I had something of a surprise when Jesse caught up to me. After comparing notes, we realized we'd missed meeting up earlier by less than an hour on several occasions over the last couple of days. Jesse had spent the night at a restaurant about 20 miles (32 km) ahead of me but had a later start and was about 10 miles (16 km) into his day when we met.

The winds of the day were neutral to favorable which, coupled with mostly flat roads, made for fast riding. We stopped in Chinandega for groceries and, when I came out of the store, my front tire was flat. It initially appeared to be a failed patch but, after fixing the patch, filling the tire, and re-installing the wheel, it was going flat again.

With the wheel and tire taken apart again and the aid of a

sink in the grocery store, I found two holes. Both punctures were on the inside of the wheel; my rim tape had slid over and the tube had been cut open by the edge of a spoke hole. I removed the old tape, then replaced it with a couple of rounds of electrical tape. It did the job and, with a new tube, I was ready to roll. We ended the day in Leon where another fire station graciously hosted us for the night.

It rained overnight, though I stayed dry in my tent. I had my bike leaned up against a tree at the fire station and, in the morning, I went through my routine of checking and packing my gear. I reached into a pannier for my water reservoir to check how much water I had left. When I pulled the reservoir out, it was covered in biting red ants. I shook the ants off my hand and dropped the reservoir. My entire pannier was filled with biting red ants. I shook everything out of the bag. My sleeping bag, spare tire, allergy medicine, and crampons for mountain climbing all fell on the ground, covered in ants. I removed the ants as best I could before repacking the bag.

Jesse and I got a later start that morning; we didn't really get around to riding till almost 9:00 am. He tended to start a couple of hours later than I did. We rode towards Managua on mostly flat roads. The weather was overcast and therefore cooler than the last couple of days; it drizzled some in the afternoon.

As we were getting close to Managua, I told Jesse that we had a left turn in about 2 miles (3.2 km). Jesse started off at a slower pace, but soon began riding faster; by the time I reached the turn, he was well past it and out of earshot. He must have heard me shouting or remembered about the turn and began to slow down but, when I caught up to him, we were close to half a mile (800 meters) past our turnoff. We decided to take a different, though slightly longer, route into the city. Then it happened again a few miles later. I told Jesse we had a turn coming up, but he was well ahead and passed the turn, so we took yet another detour, adding almost another mile. It was at this time that we realized that it did not make sense to have the slower rider be the navigator and I handed my job as navigator over to him.

Finally in Managua, we checked one of the fire stations to see if we could stay there for the night; we were turned away from that one but they told us there was another one a short distance away. We stopped by a mall to get online on our way over. Jesse tried to see if he'd heard back from a friend he had in the area; no luck with them either.

We stopped by the second fire station but they turned us down as well and recommended the first station we tried. It was getting dark when we tried asking at a church but they said it wasn't safe and that's when I noticed just how rough of an area we were in. Plastic waste fires burned along the streets and somebody had set a tire on fire too. In the distance we heard an audible series of pops that could have easily been gunfire.

We made a last ditch effort back to the mall to see if any of Jesse's contacts had replied. They hadn't, but we found a hostel a few blocks away. By then it was dark, and the hostel was up one of the biggest hills in the city. Once we had pedaled up the hill to the hostel, we discovered, much to our dismay, that the hostel was no longer in business. Not to worry, there was another hostel a few more blocks away, down the other side of the hill we had just climbed. The price was very reasonable, considering the circumstances. I walked by a street food stand after we were settled in and got some fried taco things for dinner; they really hit the spot after the somewhat stressful evening.

CHAPTER 8

Day 99, May 9, 2016

Limon, Costa Rica

I'd cycled on alone after the night in Managua. My plans were different from Jesse's for the next week or so and we intended to meet up later.

It took me a couple of days to get to Costa Rica. Once there, I rode to the Caribbean coast over the course of a few days, camping in the jungle each night. I'd planned to take a rest day in Limon as; when I researched it, it had seemed like a picturesque town on the shores of the Caribbean. Expectation, however, did not match the reality.

Like many other towns in Central America, Limon was rundown and dirty. I rode to the waterfront and it didn't have a decent beach either. Some internet research revealed a town called 'Cahuita' that was only 25 miles (40 km) away, close enough that I might be able to make it before dark.

After less than two hours of cycling, I took the turnoff toward the town and checked my GPS to find out where I needed to go. While navigating in the failing light, I suddenly came upon a pothole and, with no time to swerve out of the way, I slammed on the brake with my free hand. I hit the pothole and flew over the handlebars. Thankfully, the handlebars were right under the seat on my recumbent bike and my flight was short-lived. After untangling myself from my bike, I inspected it for damage. Nothing was broken and both wheels were still true; I made it to a hotel without further incident.

Even though I had the luxury of a safe, clean, and comfortable hotel bed to sleep in, I was up with the sun; after months of wild camping with sunrise wake-ups, it'd become a habit. I ate the included hotel breakfast of deliciously fresh fruit, with toast and jam, and some local coffee, before heading across town toward Cahuita National Park.

I followed a trail near the beach, shaded by the dense jungle, and wound my way into the park. After reading about the park the previous evening and becoming paranoid about the pit vipers with necrotizing venom that were native to the region, I was spending more time watching my step than the jungle around me. Small colorful lizards were the most frequent sight and, farther along, there were some burrows inhabited by a species of blue crab. I also heard several howler monkeys during my walk but the thick canopy of the jungle prevented me from seeing any of them. I walked along for a few miles and scouted some spots with access to the coral reef for the following day, before working my way back.

I put the inevitable sunrise wakeup to good use the next morning by heading back out to Cahuita National Park for a swim. Snorkeling in the reef in the national park was prohibited without a local guide but I didn't have a snorkel and the signs didn't say anything about not swimming there. I had bought goggles in town; I was carrying enough gear as it was and the few additional ounces of weight were added to the list of things I carried but rarely used. This list included: my ice axe (I'd used it since I'd gotten to the tropics, but not for axing ice), -65 F (-48 C) rated boots, and crampons; I had more mountain climbing planned for South America.

I walked a few miles along the trail and found somewhere to stash my stuff, just before the path turned deeper into the jungle. I waded out into the warm waters of the Caribbean and swam away from shore. The visibility was limited to a few inches; it'd been raining frequently and the runoff from the rivers caused the poor visibility. I continued swimming in hopes it would improve farther out. To some extent, it did;

about a quarter of a mile (400 meters) offshore, visibility was up to 4-5 feet (~1.5 meters), though there was still no sign of a decent coral reef. Soon afterwards, I came upon a sandbar where the water came up to about knee level for me. Waves were breaking over the sandbar and, with the visibility as poor as it was, I wasn't going to see much even if I found the reef. I swam back to shore and walked out of the park, still not seeing any monkeys, though I heard several once again.

My GPS recommended straying off the main highway the next morning as I pedaled through a small surfing town. I'd just had two days off the bike in Cahuita and I was feeling adventurous so I took it, figuring, "How bad could it be?" It turns out, it could be pretty bad.

The road was graveled with river rocks which acted like marbles whenever I'd try to climb a steep hill and there were several steep hills. I ended up pushing much more than expected. Roadworks were also present and that caused a few delays too. Eventually, I made it to the main road and then it started to rain; not too much but enough to send the humidity through the roof.

I reached the Panama border after about 30 miles (48 km), around midday. Leaving Costa Rica took a while; after filling out a form detailing my trip, I had to go down the road to pay the exit tax of $8, and then go back to the immigration office to get my passport stamped. Panama wasn't too bad: a $4 entry tax at one office, then over to another office for the stamp. At the last office, they asked for a plane ticket; I gave them one that I had made online that said I was flying to Paris from Panama City in a few days, which I wasn't. I tried my best not to sweat bullets while they were looking at it, but it was good enough for them. Supposedly, I would have had to pay a $100 tax if I didn't have proof of transportation out of the country within three days. Some people said the tax was made up by the border officials to line their own pockets, but I don't know the truth of it.

The side road that I took away from the border soon

turned to dirt and then there was a rickety bridge I had to cross. I pushed across it and, after riding away, arrived at another bridge, then another, and another. There were a total of 4 bridges with steel and wood, slick from the rain, none of which were particularly safe for riding a loaded bike across and each in worse condition than the one before it, but I made it back to the main road alive.

The road wound along the coast quite nicely and was mostly flat before it turned inland; it then began to remind me of the steep hills of Guatemala. Some were so steep I had to push my bike; many were so steep my speedometer would read zero from how slowly I was climbing. The steep roads made the cycling all the more difficult, especially because of the view through the trees of a nice flat coastline where the road could have been flat if it was a mile closer to the coast.

I camped in a small clearing, in the rain. It continued to rain most of the night and I was having stomach trouble. I had to make several emergency dashes to the bushes in the rain and, by morning, I was weak and dehydrated. The hills were not quite as steep as the day before but, in my weakened state, I had to push up a few of them that I would have been able to ride up normally.

The temperature wasn't too bad but the humidity was high again and, by midday, I had a pounding headache from all the electrolytes I'd lost from sweating. This was in addition to the stomach troubles that had me dashing off the road and into the jungle on a few occasions. It took me another hour to reach a gas station with a mini-mart where I stopped for an electrolyte drink and some cheese puffs, to try to replace some of the salt I had lost being sick. I felt much better afterwards. I camped in yet another clearing that night; it was raining again and I had a second consecutive night of stomach troubles.

I'd been working my way toward the Pacific coast over the last couple of days, and had camped on the climb going over the mountains that stood between me and the Pacific Ocean; I still had a few thousand feet of climbing (~1,000 meters) left to get over them in the morning. Weak from lack of sleep and loss of electrolytes, I ended up pushing my bike much of the way up. The road wound its way up through a spectacular rainforest with frequent waterfalls but, the intense effort of climbing made it difficult to appreciate the scenery.

Finally, at the top of the climb, I had a descent that lasted for a little over 15 miles (24 km) before leveling out the rest of the way to the Pan-American Highway. I stopped at a gas station/mini-mart that had wifi, and, after checking some maps, I realized I had less than 300 miles (480 km) to go to get to Panama City. I was about to log off and continue riding when I got a message from Jesse. He was at a hostel in David, about 12 miles (20 km) west of where I was. The distance was in the opposite direction from Panama City but, I had some extra time so I decided I'd go a bit out of my way for the prospect of having company.

I checked into the hostel and soon met some other cyclists: Johnny from Ireland, who'd been riding for about a year with most of his time in North America, and Mike from Australia, who'd been on the road for over three years and had cycled as many continents in that time. In addition to the cycle tourists, there were also several other people there from various countries in Europe and a few from Australia. I spent the evening socializing and was up till well past midnight. It made for a pleasant change of pace compared to the quiet evenings spent reading in my tent before going to bed early; especially after a challenging few days of cycling.

CHAPTER 9

Day 112, May 12, 2016

Panama City, Panama

The day after I'd reunited with Jesse at the hostel in David, he cycled off uncharacteristically early. I had already booked a spot on a sailboat to Colombia and had given myself plenty of time to get there, but Jesse wanted to try to find an earlier sailboat to Colombia and avoid sitting around for a few days.

I cycled the 310 miles (500 km) to Panama City over the course of five days, then stayed in a hostel for a few nights and explored the city. I had a leisurely start when I left Panama City; I had two whole days to get to Puerto Lindo, the gulf-side town where the sailboat that I'd booked to get to Colombia would depart from.

I took a detour along the Panama Canal to see it up close and in person. Once I was on one of the main roads out of the city, I noticed the left lane was sectioned off with traffic cones. After riding a little farther, I saw cyclists riding in the blocked-off lanes. Apparently, Panama City blocked off portions of the main roads on some Sundays for bicyclists. I was quite surprised and I had a much more pleasant ride out of the city than I could have hoped for.

The road closely paralleled the Panama Canal but, seeing it was another thing; most of what I saw was either trees or cranes for moving cargo to and from the ships in port. The road opened up to an excellent view of the canal, a few miles up the road, and I stopped to watch a container ship pass through the locks and begin its way to the Caribbean. Just as the ship came up next to me, I started riding faster to see if I could keep up with it; the container ship moved slowly along the canal and I kept pace without difficulty. The road turned inland a little over a mile later and I lost sight of the ship. I'd heard from Jesse that camping was difficult along the main road so, I stopped early at a quiet spot in the rainforest to avoid any troubles.

I was on the road at a normal hour the next day and I got to the highway shortly after. The toll road promised wider shoulders, less traffic, and flatter riding than the side roads did, plus, I'd never had to pay the tolls and there were no signs saying I couldn't ride my bike there. The toll road was all I'd hoped it'd be: flat, fast, and low traffic. 5 miles (8 km) later, a police truck traveling in the opposite direction started honking and flashing their lights; the driver was yelling at me saying what I can only assume was that I wasn't supposed to be on the toll road. I stopped briefly but, thanks to a barrier dividing the highway, they couldn't get to me. They soon drove off to turn around and I took off sprinting to try to get to an exit to avoid having to put my bike in the truck and break my rule of traveling only under my own power.

While I was pedaling furiously down the highway, I checked my GPS to see when the next potential exit was. I made it almost 2 miles (3 km) before the police pulled off in front of me. The policemen stepped out and after realizing that my Spanish was very limited they said that I was not allowed to ride the toll road and would have to put my bike in the truck. I showed them on my GPS that there was a crossroad less than a mile away. They discussed the possibility and, perhaps realizing that my bike wouldn't fit in their small truck, they allowed me to leave the highway at the crossroad. I was overjoyed at not having my line of cycling interrupted and happily rode to the bridge and exited the highway. The side road was, as I expected, hillier and more crowded, with little to no shoulder. I made it to the turnoff to Puerto Lindo just the same.

The road to Puerto Lindo had significantly less traffic and grew quieter as I progressed. It was then that I realized that that day would be my last riding day in North America for who knows how long. It'd been a great journey so far and I believed it would continue to be so in the continents to follow.

I rolled into Puerto Lindo, in the rain, that afternoon and found Jesse eating at a restaurant. I'd been in contact with him in Panama City and found out that he'd been unable to find an earlier sailboat so, he would be on the same one as me. Our sailboat wouldn't leave until the next evening and the afternoon consisted of sitting around the open air restaurant for a few hours before taking advantage of the free, but slow, wifi at a nearby school. We camped in the sheltered area of a church by the waterfront.

We didn't have to ride much of anywhere the next morning, our boat would depart about a quarter mile (400 meters) away from where we slept. I was unable to sleep past dawn, again, and took my time getting ready. A few days ago, one of the joints on my tent poles had fused together from the humidity and salt in the air; I devoted an unsuccessful couple of hours to trying to get it apart. Jesse and I went back to the same restaurant as yesterday for breakfast; it appeared to be the only restaurant in town that was regularly open. There was little to do after eating; we waited on the restaurant patio for the majority of the morning.

Approaching noon, I gave separating my tent pole another try. I tried using chain lube to no effect; levering a small gap in the joint apart with a screwdriver had the same result. Next, I heated the affected area with a lighter in an attempt get the metal to expand and loosen, but that didn't work either. My attempts degraded in sophistication from there coming down to trying to knock it loose on the ground using a rock. The last resort came when the owner of the restaurant saw my efforts and was kind enough to lend me two pairs of pliers. The risk of damage was high but, riding around with a tent pole sticking perpendicularly out of my backpack had become a great bother. I carefully picked the placement of the pliers before the utilizing combined efforts of myself and Jesse in a twisting motion. On the first try, it just barely budged and, after a few minutes of effort that left us both drenched in sweat, the pole came apart with little visible damage. I got a few drops of grease from the restaurateur and applied a film of grease to all of the joints on all of the poles before stowing them.

We waited on the restaurant patio the rest of the day, not doing much of anything. Time slowed to a crawl from the inactivity and it was a struggle to not check my phone every ten minutes. The scheduled meet time of 3:00 pm came and went without anyone else showing up. Two people of the ten that would be on the boat showed up around 3:30. The captain and crew arrived shortly after. An hour later, the 4:00 pm deadline came and went and still we were short six people. They finally showed up after 5:00 pm, but, by then the passport control office had closed. After spending a significant amount of time on the phone, the captain was able to get an appointment to get our passports taken care of. We boarded the boat after 10:00 pm and it was after 11:00 by the time the safety briefing was done. We motored out of Puerto Lindo around midnight and I went to bed shortly after.

Technically we hadn't left North America yet; the coast of Panama was occasionally visible over the horizon. We spent a couple of days island hopping through the most picturesque Caribbean islands I could imagine. White sand beaches and palm trees covered every island; the Kuna tribes who lived on the islands sold us coconuts from dugout canoes. We spent every day snorkeling among coral reefs, relaxing, or exploring the islands, and every night we feasted on fish that was fresh caught by the crew or natives.

A couple of hours before dark, we began the 40 hour sail towards Colombia; I sat outside and watched another brilliant sunset and saw the light fade next to the coast of North

America. Stars appeared, much to the wonder of most of the Europeans I was sailing with; some of them had never seen that many stars before. The hills of Panama were silhouetted against the night sky and I wondered how long it would be before I saw North America again.

The next morning, I began my project for the day, swapping my rims front and back. The rear rim had begun to crack near some of the spokes; the front, with its lighter load had not. The idea behind the swap was to extend the life of the rims by rotating them in the same manner as rotating tires. I started shortly after breakfast and worked consistently until I had the back wheel disassembled.

Because the captain was concerned about getting grease or similar compounds inside the cabin, I worked while sitting on the bow of the boat; that end also happened to be the most exposed to the sun. I had to stop after the first wheel to change into long sleeves; I was already starting to get sunburn after less than an hour of exposure, while wearing sunscreen.

The second wheel was taken apart in a similar timeframe and I began the process of lacing the front rim onto the rear hub, but, I'd never built a wheel before and I was having some trouble figuring out the lacing pattern. In addition to that, the strain of the increasingly equatorial sun was beating down on me and I was beginning to get nauseous from sea sickness; I stopped for a break with some concern about whether I'd be able to get my wheels put back together. I took some sea sickness medication and sat inside trying to cool down.

After 20 minutes or so, I was feeling better and I began studying the pictures I'd taken of the spoke lacing pattern before taking my wheels apart. When I thought I had it figured out, I went back to work. I had to redo most of my work a few times before I got it right. Pushing noon, I still didn't have the first wheel done when I stopped for a lunch break. Once I finally had the first wheel assembled, I asked Jesse's opinion on my work; he noticed that while the spokes were laced correctly, the cross pattern was wrong. I had to undo and reattach half the spokes to get the correct cross.

I started the second wheel and was about halfway through lacing it when Jesse spotted a whale breaching about a mile off the bow of the boat. Everyone on board rushed to get a position where they could see the whale, even the captain. The captain of the boat identified it as a pilot whale and said it was the first one he had seen on this route in over six years of sailing it a few times a month. We were able to sail within 100 yards (90 meters) of the whale and saw it swimming just below the surface and breaching again.

Evening brought another spectacular sunset and darkness a multitude of stars. We watched the bioluminescence from plankton in the water, then spotted several planets and con-stellations, with some help from the captain.

PART TWO

Cartagena, Colombia to San Pedro de Atacama, Chile

CHAPTER 10

Day 119, May 29, 2016

Cartagena, Colombia

We were sitting in the Cartagena harbor when I woke at sunrise. It was strange seeing South America; another city on another continent with tall buildings and people everywhere. It didn't look too different from Central America, but, that'd probably change soon.

It was time to play the waiting game; we sat on the boat while the captain went ashore to take care of the immigration paperwork. I worked on getting my panniers organized in preparation for riding. Once our captain got the okay from immigration for us to disembark, he began ferrying everyone to land on his small motorboat. My bike and gear were not quite ready so, I was the last to get to shore. After I had my bike loaded up, we headed over to a grocery store to wait for our passports and the entry stamp for Colombia. I worked on truing my wheels and reinstalling my chain while we waited. The passports arrived just before I finished. Normally, we would have had to stay in Cartagena for up to 24 hours to wait for immigration to process our passports, but, thanks to our early arrival, it was done the same day.

The convenient location of the grocery store where we met to collect our passports made the decision on what to do next an easy choice. Prices were a bit higher than Panama but, from what I could tell at another grocery store I went to in the afternoon, the stores seemed to have a price fixing agreement. Cartagena was a tourist town and it was made obvious by the amount of westerners in the streets. As much as I would have liked to begin riding right away, I had other responsibilities to take care of; mostly updating my journal and calling home to let my parents know I made it to Colombia. Jesse and I rode by the fire station to see if they would let us stay there for the night. They had a rule against hosting people so we looked for a cheap hostel instead. After a couple of hours of being redirected by people trying to be helpful, checking out some of the most expensive hostels in town, and myself getting a flat tire, we found one in the Gethsemani district that fit our budget at a little under $7 per person, with wifi and air conditioning. It also happened to be my cheapest non-free accommodation for the tour.

Once most of my tasks were completed, I went out to get dinner. The hostel we were at had the vibe that someone was just waiting to steal something, so, Jesse and I took turns going to eat. Once Jesse was back, I began wandering the area in search of food. After walking in a large circle, I came to a square with a church that was crowded with people and street vendors. I had a few empanadas at one before walking towards one that had a large crowd gathered. They had a few options from hot dogs to hamburgers and something called 'plato de carne' or plate of meat. It looked appetizing enough and I ordered one. It was indeed a plate of meat. It was piled high with potatoes, various sausages, and other forms of meat.

Jesse had the same problem I had of my wheels falling apart, though his were much worse than mine had been. He'd ordered some new ones while cycling Panama and, when he checked the tracking number he, found that they would not arrive for several days, so, he would have to wait in Cartagena. We discussed a plan to stay in touch; with him being the stronger rider he'd catch up to me eventually.

I left the hostel early the next morning and began riding out of Cartagena. It felt good to be back on the road after almost a week off the bike and I was excited to see what Colombia and South America had to offer. The humidity was at 95%; you can sweat all you can at that level and it will do almost nothing to cool you off. High humidity and the increasingly equatorial sun made for hot riding; I took breaks in the shade frequently. Out of Cartagena, there was a 600 foot (180 meter) climb. It was a consistent climb and not too steep; I wondered if all the roads were graded decently in Colombia. I rode down the highway in a southerly direction, after a gentle descent, and I found myself on a relatively flat road.

The miles passed fairly quickly and, later in the day, the terrain became low rolling hills. About 5 miles (8 km) away from San Onofre I saw somewhere to camp but since that was my first day back on the bike and I was still almost 30 minutes short of my goal of six hours of rolling time I kept going. It began to rain shortly after and the temperature dropped enough that I had to use my rain jacket for what I think was the first time since Mexico. It'd always been too hot before.

I hit my six hours of riding time in the city of San Onofre. There was nowhere to camp and I didn't feel comfortable trying to ask for a place to stay. I rode out of town with high hopes for finding a campsite in short order but Colombia seemed to have the best maintained fences of any country I've ridden through. They were so close to the road that there weren't any spots in between the road and the fence either. Any ground I could have camped on was flooded from the rain. After an hour of continuing down the road without seeing anything, I started feeling more open to asking and I tried asking at a couple of different places without success. Maybe it's my Spanish.

Still riding along the road, I saw a lake that was entirely surrounded by fences. There was some ground that I checked between the fence and the outside of a bend in the road but it was utterly infested with mosquitos and all I got for my efforts was bug bites in at least a dozen places. A couple more miles up the road was a soccer field with a concrete grandstand like structure. Thanks to the mud, no one would be using the field and I set up camp on the concrete pad at the top of the grandstands. My riding time for the day was 7.5 hours.

Dawn came earlier in the morning than I was used to; part of traveling so far to the east without a time zone change. With an early wake up came an early start an hour later. The morning was blissfully uneventful. Just when I was beginning to wonder what I was going to do with my afternoon, there was a police roadblock. On the other side was a group of protesters blocking the road. It was peaceful at the moment so, I pulled off into the shade of a tree to wait. There was a civil war going on in Colombia; it started in the 1960s. The anti-government group called 'FARC' was made up mostly of workers who were being exploited with low wages and long hours in a dangerous work environment; they were fighting to provide social justice through communism. On the other hand, the government claimed to be fighting for order and stability but, both sides had engaged in drug trafficking, terrorism, and numerous human rights violations. Armed battles were now rare in all but a select few areas and, despite the conflict, the tourism industry continued largely unhindered. Not 30 minutes after I got there, the police launched tear gas grenades and the protest quickly dispersed. I know it was tear gas because there was a headwind and some of the gas reached me. The police gave me the okay to continue 20 minutes later and I cycled off. Some of the tear gas was still hanging around the road and I rode through while coughing with my eyes watering, but the effects of the gas wore off quickly.

After the previous day's grossly extended search for a campsite, I decided I wasn't going to be very picky that evening. There was a large parking lot, complete with shade and a grassy area, which would've been a great spot to camp. I asked the owner of the lot but he said it was car parking only. About 15 minutes later, there was a bus stop with a brush covered area that had a clearing large enough for my tent. It was good enough for me but, I had to wait until dark to set up. I read for a while and ate dinner then read some more before darkness finally arrived. My tent was only a few yards away from the road but I slept fine.

CHAPTER 11

Day 124, June 3, 2016

Puerto Valdiva, Colombia

It was raining again that morning: it'd done so most every day since I rode out of Cartagena several days ago. I'd camped near the base of a massive climb into the mountains. This was a day I had looked forward to since soon after my arrival in the hot humid locales of Central America; I would finally get high enough into the mountains that it wouldn't be hot anymore.

When I was riding through the town of Puerto Valdiva, barely more than a mile away from where I'd camped, my back tire went flat. The tire had been cut by a piece of glass that had sliced through the tire, deep enough to get to the tube. While there was a sizable cut in the center of the tread, it was not bulging at all when I pumped it up to operating pressure. I added it to the growing list of things to keep an eye on. When I was reinstalling the wheel, I heard a metallic ping; my axle was broken. My heart dropped and I immediately began to think of ways to get a new axle, ranging from seeing if Jesse could bring one from Cartagena to taking a bus to a city with a decent bike shop then returning to reconnect my line. Luckily, there was a bike shop not 50 yards (45 meters) away; but, it seemed unlikely that a rural shop would have a quick release skewer in stock. I knew none of the Spanish words for the part I needed but when I showed the owner of the shop the broken skewer and pointed to the hub he got the idea. After rummaging around through various shelves he came up empty handed but then he turned to a parts bin and pulled out the axle I was looking for. The only problem was that it was just barely too short. He had a thru axle and offered to change it out but I declined as politely as possible; I didn't like the idea of swapping out the high end hubs I'd invested in before I left or any part thereof. The owner turned away to help another customer and left me to look through the parts bin. I found a flanged nut that had the correct threads and tried it out. It fit and threaded all the way through. It was a bit of a jury rig but, I couldn't have been happier. I would have been willing to pay a high price for the parts but when I asked the owner how much it was going to cost me he flatly refused any payment, regardless of my offers.

With my bike in working condition again, I began pedaling up the road into the mountains and continued to do so all day. There were a few overly steep sections where I lost traction in my rear wheel on the wet roads and had to push my bike up a paved road. It rained most of the day and that kept me cool while I worked my way into the mountains. It was a beautiful climb; frequent waterfalls lined the roadside and spectacular vistas waited at almost every turn, but it was also heavily populated. Every bit of ground that was even close to being level was taken up by houses of some kind. I expected to have to pay or ask for a place to sleep.

I rode until I got six hours of pedaling done and made it to about to where I expected to make it, around 7,000 feet (2,120 meters) in elevation. I camped at 500 feet (150 meters) the night before and, with a few short descents thrown in, it'd been a strenuous day. My goal came and went but no hotels appeared; it came down to the question of just how badly I wanted to stop. I found a clearing on top of an 8 foot (2.4 meter) cliff and decided that yes, I dearly wanted to stop. After making a few trips to get my bike and gear to my campsite, I camped at about 6,850 feet (2,075 meters).

Morning broke clear and cool; the air was fresh from the

rain overnight and I was happy. The mountains of Colombia boasted a climate of eternal spring that I vastly preferred to the endless summer of most of Central America. I climbed a few hundred feet and then had an unexpected descent down to 6,700 feet (2,030 meters) before climbing again. The scenery was gorgeous and made for excellent riding. The temperature was mild and the sky was clear. I descended through a mountain town before going up another climb all the way up to 9,100 feet (2,760 meters). The weather was as close to perfect as I could have asked for and I was surrounded by mountains, covered in green vegetation, and the occasional waterfall cascaded by the road.

Just as I reached my distance goal for the day, there was a hotel. It seemed as if I was supposed to stop there with such incredible timing. I walked in and asked the price, about $5 a night. The low price made me somewhat wary and I tried to ask to see the room. The woman in charge looked to be around 80 years old and she would not let me see the room before I paid. I thought that perhaps I did not get my point across and tried to ask again. Once again she refused before she went on a rant of what I think was about how rich Americans travel to other countries and don't have the courtesy to learn the local language. I disagreed somewhat; every word I had spoken to her was in Spanish. It was an unfortunate mar to an otherwise awesome day and I decided I'd take my business elsewhere.

I rode a few more miles before I saw an inactive construction site; a bunch of dirt had been moved around with no construction going on yet. It was Saturday, however, and the likelihood of being told to leave was low. I hung around and waited for darkness to fall. Once I finished setting up my tent, I noticed something I hadn't seen in a while, stars. It was strange looking up and not seeing any of the constellations I was used to seeing at home. There'd been views of the stars on the boat from Panama but it was a very different experience alone and it made me feel like I really was far away from home, but that's what makes an adventure. My camp was at about

8,100 feet (2,450 meters), the highest I'd slept at since I was near Pico de Orizaba in Mexico.

In the morning, I descended away from my camp down to about 6,600 feet (2,000 meters). This was promptly followed by a climb to 7,700 feet (2,330 meters) then it was down again on a steep and winding descent to 4,500 feet (1,360 meters). There were a number of cyclists going up and down the mountain that I was descending. Several of them were found to be lacking in skill at descending and I passed some of the riders who were on high end racing bikes and a few semi-trucks on the way down too.

The city of Medellin sat in a large canyon with sides that rose steeply for several thousand feet; I was now at the bottom of this canyon and had a rolling climb to get to the city. A couple of the cyclists slowed down to talk to me but, none of them spoke English and our conversation was limited to what little Spanish I knew.

While I was connected to an open wifi signal at a supermarket in the city, I found out that Jesse's wheels had arrived a couple of days earlier than expected and he'd been putting in some high mileage days to try to catch up with me. After the excessive climbing of the last couple of days, I felt like I could use an easier day and ended the day at a hostel on the southern end of the city. The afternoon was restful and made for a pleasant break; I felt like I would have been ready to be on the road again in the morning if I wasn't waiting for Jesse. I went to look over my bike the following evening to make sure everything was in an acceptable condition for riding and found my front tire was flat.

Jesse showed up at the hostel a couple of days later and we left the city the morning after he arrived. We pedaled south through Medellin with rush hour traffic. The road began to climb as we left the city. After a few hundred feet of climbing was a slightly shorter descent and the cycle continued a few more times before we got to a consistent part of the climb that continued for the last 2,000 vertical feet (600 meters). A mile or two into that section of the climb, it began to rain and continued to do so until shortly before I reached the top. Jesse was still faster than me and he'd ridden ahead then waited at the top of the 8,000 foot (2,420 meter) pass. After a short break at the top, we began the descent. The road descended inconsistently, just like the climb had; it would level out from time to time and there were several uphill sections. There was a long section of road construction on the way down; the road turned to grooved pavement that made for some sketchy riding. All that descending took its toll on my brakes and I had to stop a few times to readjust them.

All the way down at 2,500 feet (760 meters) was the town of La Pintada. Jesse had seen a church on the way in and we stopped to see if we could stay there for the night. We had to wait 30 minutes for a service to end before Jesse went in to ask; meanwhile I waited with the bikes. They said "yes", we could stay, and showed us to a room with two beds. After we showering, they asked us to come eat with them and they shared dinner with us! We helped where we could with a few different chores before heading back to the room for the night.

As if cooking dinner for us wasn't enough, our hosts insisted on making us breakfast in the morning too. Following that, we gave our thanks and started cycling. The road rolled along through a beautifully green river canyon with steep mountains on both sides that rose several thousand feet above us. The people at the church had been so kind to us that everything felt right with the world and I had a renewed faith in the goodness of humanity. As usual, Jesse was riding much faster than me and we did a leapfrog sort of progression for the majority of the morning. Jesse would ride ahead then take a break until I caught up, then he would wait behind for a while before catching up to me and riding ahead again.

After lunch, we chose our goal for the day, a town called Chinchina, and arranged a place to meet up near the edge of the town. Jesse took off and I continued at my own pace. As I was taking a break at the top of one of the larger rollers, I was suddenly surrounded by a mostly female group of about ten mountain bikers. They were doing a few hours spin on some of the gravel roads and trails in the area. All of them looked on in awe of my bike and the ride I was doing. After talking with me in mostly Spanish for a while, they all wanted pictures with me and my bike and a photo shoot followed.

The mountain bikers were heading in the same direction as I was and I passed most of them on the downhill before keeping pace with all but the fastest riders in the group on the following hills. After a few miles, they turned off onto a dirt road and I was on my own again. There was an inconsistent climb for the last 15 miles (24 km) into Chinchina.

A couple of miles away from the city, I saw a touring cyclist coming down the road towards me. We stopped to chat and his name was Jose. He was from Brazil and spoke excellent English. Jose had ridden north from Ushuaia on a very similar route as the one I planned to take southbound and he gave me some good information on the road ahead. We talked for a while before exchanging contact information and he invited me to stay with him in Brazil if I made it that far before we parted ways.

I met Jesse at the gas station as arranged and we set off in search of a place to stay for the night. We were unable to find anyone to ask at the three churches we checked and, after being turned down for lack of room at the town's fire station, we found a cheap hotel that we split at the cost of about $3.30 US each. It was a surprisingly nice hotel for the price; our room had three beds and there was wifi. After checking in and showering, we went out to get dinner. I'd ridden for a little over seven hours and went to bed early; I'd be surprised if Jesse had much more than five hours of riding time.

CHAPTER 12

Day 131, June 11, 2016

Puerto Tejada, Colombia

Jesse and I had been hosted by fire stations the last two nights in a row and it was from them that we learned that the FARC and the Colombian government had signed a ceasefire only a day earlier to begin brokering for peace after nearly five decades of conflict. Good news for us too, we'd been concerned about cycling by the city of Cali as it'd been one of the most volatile conflict areas in the whole country for the last several decades.

The road past Cali towards the city of Popayan was a rolling climb; it was littered with burned out tires, broken glass, and sandbag machine gun placements. Although there were no longer any guns, bullet casings were littered all around. At the top of the climb, a group of locals had gathered along the road with signs and banners. When we asked what was happening, they said they were getting ready to block the road for a protest so we left quickly.

Less than a mile away from the fire station in Popayan, someone pulled up next to us in a car and, after telling us that he had hosted touring cyclists before, asked if we needed a place to stay and we said we did. I don't remember his name, but he owned a car lot nearby where he had to grab something first. We followed him there and after he took care of a few things we followed him to his house a block away. Adjacent to his house was a studio apartment with one room and a bathroom. It was being used to store some building materials and after we helped him move it out he asked us how long we planned to stay in Popayan. We told him two nights then he gave us the keys to the room and said we could stay as long as we wanted.

Like most "rest" days our day in Popayan was just as busy as a day of cycling. Between hand washing laundry, buying food, eating, and trying to get online for a while it wasn't a very restful day. That evening, our host brought us dinner! Fried plantains, fried yucca, fried chicharrones (pig skins), and spiced cane juice. Jesse was absolutely disgusted by the idea of chicharrones even though they taste similar to bacon and I ate most of them while he ate most of the plantains.

Jesse and I had come up with a simple plan on our day off to make it so we finish the day around the same time. I liked earlier starts while Jesse liked to sleep in. I left Popayan at 6:30 and Jesse left around 8:00. Jesse named the road out of Popayan "death by rollers;" small but steep hills again and again that lasted for mile after mile. Although it was slow progress, the scenery was great; quaint farms surrounded the road and high mountains rose dramatically in the distance. I'd been riding for most of five hours straight and had only covered about 39 miles (63 km) when Jesse caught up to me; we rode together for the rest of the day. Our accommodation for the night was a hotel near a town called El Estrecho at the price of a few dollars each; we got dinner at the hotel restaurant for a few more dollars.

I started early again the next morning and, after a few miles of flat roads away from the hotel, it was back to rollers. If the road north of Popayan was death by rollers this was roller hell, constant steep undulations and tons of climbing. The day culminated with a 4,000 foot (1,210 meter) tall climb. About a quarter of the way into the climb, Jesse coasted past me, yes, coasted; he had grabbed on to the back a passing truck. I was utterly baffled by the idea and asked him why. "So I could catch up with you sooner" he replied. His answer did not help with my befuddlement as catching up with me sooner almost defeated the purpose of me starting early. Although catching rides by grabbing onto the back of slow moving trucks was a relatively common practice among cycle tourists, to me, it would break my rule of progressing only under my own power; we rode together most of the way up the climb. Despite starting two hours later after eating a big breakfast, Jesse was tired; this was also entirely beyond my comprehension as he was also putting far less effort into riding.

During a water break somewhere close to the top of the climb, I noticed that the tube in my rear tire was beginning to push through the slice in the tire that I had gotten a couple of days before arriving in Medellin. I took the wheel off and booted the inside of the slice with some cardboard from an inner tube box. When I started riding again, my brake pads were making a tinkling noise and that meant they were worn out and we stopped again so I could change them. The new problem was that the brake pad adjustment screw was stuck and would not move for anything. However, I was able to change the more worn pad and that was good enough for the time being. At the summit of the climb, the noise was getting worse and we stopped again to try to fix it. We were near someone's house and they walked up right as we were approaching. I asked if they had some pliers I could borrow after looking up the Spanish for pliers, aclicates; they did, and I loosened the brake pad adjuster as much as I could. It still wasn't enough and I ended up shimming the brake on one side with a couple of washers to align it properly; this worked and we did a 3,000 foot (900 meter) descent without further issue. At Jesse's admonition, I also removed the stump of the kickstand that had broken in the first hour of the first day of my tour and promptly disposed of it at a gas station. Previously, I'd kept it without thinking about the weight as it reminded me that you can still keep going even if you're a little broken, but in reality it was a few more ounces of weight that I didn't need to carry.

After the descent was another climb; we found a spot in a field with a few trees that would work for my tent and Jesse's hammock then we wild camped for the first time in over a week. Before that, we'd either been hosted by locals or stayed in hotels since we met up in Medellin. We camped at about 3,500 feet (1,060 meters) and maybe a mile up the road from the bottom of the descent.

Jesse and I started riding at the same time the next day, about 6:45. The road continued to claw its way out of the deep canyon we had camped near the bottom of and the views of the Colombian Andes were spectacular in all directions. Ahead of and behind us the road cut a scar into the side of the canyon; to the right was the wall of the canyon where it was possible to see the layers of rock pushing upwards at 45 degree angles and to the left of the road the canyon dropped away in a near vertical face to a river thousands of feet below.

After about an hour and a half of riding for me, we had covered barely 7 miles (11 km) and we arrived at a hotel/restaurant/gas station sort of place the style of which had been common throughout Colombia; we stopped at the restaurant to refill our water and eat breakfast. The meal consisted of a potato and chicken soup, the meat portion of which was mostly giblets and feet; I'd never tried chicken feet before and, perhaps unsurprisingly, it tasted much like the rest of the bird. Jesse didn't like the chicken so I ate it all. In addition to the soup, they gave us a platter each of eggs, rice and fried plantains all for less than $2. The climb was somewhat less inspiring following breakfast but quite pleasant nonetheless with the cooler temperatures from the elevation. The road topped out at about 9,300 feet (2,820 meters) above sea level having gained well over a vertical mile (1.6 km) in elevation from where we camped. We descended into Pasto where we stayed the night at the fire station on the east side of the city.

We were on the road out of Pasto around 7:00 the next morning. The road began to climb right away, a 2,000 foot (600 meter) climb over 9 miles (15 km). Immediately following the 10,600 foot (3,210 meter) pass was a 5,000 foot (1,510 meter) descent over 14 miles (23 km) then there was a 4,000 foot (1,200 meter) climb that took around four hours as it was spread over about 25 miles (40 km). That one topped out around 9,500 feet (2,880 meters). Wow, that was a ton of climbing!

Some flat to rolling roads into Ipiales made a nice change of pace after the last pass; we rode through town and directly to the border of Ecuador. The border crossing was quick and easy; we didn't have to pay anything on either side. A nasty little climb took us into the city of Tulcan at 9,700 feet (2,940 meters) in elevation where we tried asking to camp at the fire station. The firemen there weren't allowed to host cyclists but one of them very kindly hopped in their truck and drove slowly to a church run place a couple of miles away while we cycled behind them. We were able to stay the night at no cost, but, the situation seemed awkward since the fireman had asked for us and the managers weren't really in a position to say no. We tried asking if we could help with a few chores, but they wouldn't let us.

CHAPTER 13

Day 137, June 16, 2016

Tulcan, Ecuador

After a long hard day of riding through the mountains to get to Ecuador, a lie in was in order, I slept till almost 7:00. I was up before Jesse, as usual, and I looked over the route for the day on my GPS. For the first time in a while there was a good option for a side road. It wasn't really any longer than the Pan-American route and it would be a nice change from riding on the main road as we had been for the last couple of weeks. On the GPS it appeared to be a secondary road and after discussing it with Jesse we decided we'd take it. The turnoff was just outside the city and the pavement ended immediately. It started out as a two lane dirt road and began to deteriorate slowly. After a few miles it was down to one and a half lanes. A few miles later it was one lane and slightly muddy from the light rain that was falling. About 10 miles (16 km) in a large mud bog covered a 10 yard (9 meter) section of road and I, not wanting a mud bath, carefully walked my bike around it. I made it to the other side unscathed and the road had changed again, this time to a rocky track. Jesse's bike was much better suited for riding rough roads and he pedaled ahead then waited every few miles. I bounced along behind him while having to put as much effort into pedaling as balancing. I was going little more than 4 mph (6.4 km/h) and the road continued to climb; it made for miserable progress, I was putting as much effort as I could into riding and I was barely moving.

It took me well over four hours to cover the 20 miles (32 km) of dirt roads to the top of the 12,200 foot (3,700 meter) pass. Jesse was waiting at the top and we began the descent after vowing to avoid such bad roads. The descent wasn't much better than the climb had been. The road was still so rough that I had to keep my speed low to maintain a modicum of control. When the road finally started to improve it changed to rough cobbles and the 7 mile (11 km) descent into the town of El Angel took close to an hour. The roads were paved again past El Angel and I don't think I'd ever been so happy to see a paved road. We still had several hours of daylight left so we kept going until the next town; a few mile descent followed by a 2 mile (3 km) climb ended with a fast descent into a town called Mira. There was no one at the fire station when we stopped by, so we went to a market to buy food then rode back to the station; the firemen were back and said we were welcome to stay the night there.

After climbing out of the short but steep hole that the fire station was in, we had a fast descent from 8,000 feet (2,420 meters) down to 5,500 feet (1,670 meters) during which I broke my top speed for the trip by going 49.1 mph (79.2 km/h) We covered our first 12 miles (19 km) with an average speed of over 30 mph (48 km/h). The road leveled out then began to trend upwards after meeting with the main highway and a few miles later my rear tire was punctured by a large shard of glass. Jesse was far enough ahead that he didn't hear me shouting that I had a flat tire so he kept going while I pulled over to fix it. The side of the road was exposed to the sun and there was no shade within a reasonable distance; in addition to being exposed to the scorching equatorial sun, the spot was infested with biting sand flies. All I could do was try to ignore the biting and change the flat as fast as possible while being swarmed by the flies.

Once the puncture was fixed, I was back on the road and going up a gentle incline. Compared to the difficulty of the previous day's ride on rough tracks through the mountains, the miles flowed by easily. The gradient increased for a few miles before topping out, around 8,000 feet (2,420 meters), where I met Jesse waiting for me near the top of the climb. A rolling descent brought us into the town of Ibarra.

Jesse's phone had quit working and the cause appeared to be a software issue. After a run by a grocery store to buy food, we found a cell phone place that said they should be able to fix his phone, though the estimated wait was two hours; we settled into wait it out. We started waiting around 2:00 pm and came back at 3:45; they said they needed another 30 minutes so we waited yet again. We came back and no luck; Jesse's phone still didn't work even after they'd supposedly reinstalled and updated the operating system. We pedaled out of town and got to the next town, Otavalo, just before dark.

We asked about a place to camp at the fire station in Otavalo but they weren't allowed to host cyclists. It was getting late and we stopped at one of the many Chinese restaurants in town for dinner; it seemed odd that there were so many since we were in Ecuador but the food was great. We asked some policemen if there was anywhere we could camp for the night and they said we could stay in the park; sleeping in a public park, in the middle of town, seemed to be too high of a safety risk so we found a cheap hotel instead.

After a late night to get to Otavalo, we didn't get on the road until after 9:00 am then rolled out of town on the highway, a rolling climb for the first few miles, then a more constant grade that peaked at 10,200 feet (3,090 meters). We descended a couple thousand feet before the road leveled out and we stopped in Cayambe for lunch, then reached the equator soon after. It was an anticlimactic event; some of the locals had fenced off the area around an elaborate marker and were charging $2 a person for entry. The equator marker was quite visible from our vantage point and seemed to be a waste of money so we contented ourselves with some pictures with the sign outside the fence.

Rolling hills trending downward followed the equator sign and we reached the casa de ciclistas in Tumbaco that evening. The idea of a casa de ciclistas or 'house of cyclists' started in Trujilo, Peru when a local, who hosted cyclists frequently, came up with the name; others followed suit and soon there were several casas de ciclistas all over Latin America, network of local cyclists who opened their homes as a place to stay for anyone traveling by bicycle. We met Tom, from France, whom Jesse had ridden with in Mexico, and two women, from Belgium; all of them were traveling by bicycle and heading in a southerly direction.

Jesse and I took a couple of days off at the casa de ciclistas in Tumbaco. Our first day involved a visit to Quito, the capital of Ecuador. We'd considered riding our bikes into the city but the owner of the casa, Santiago, recommended taking the bus. After seeing the roads by bus, we were glad we did. Most of the roads were steep, narrow, and crowded with reckless drivers. Once we were in Quito, we began walking in the general direction of the Old Town. We walked for the better part of the day and stopped at every bike shop we passed in search of decent tires. The hunt for tires was unsuccessful but, I bought new Simano brake calipers and a new spork. My rear brake was no longer adjustable and the front wouldn't stay properly adjusted so I'd have to stop to readjust them every few miles if I used them on descents; I think my original brakes, Avid BB7, had overheated and the plastic parts had melted on a steep descent. My original plastic spork had broken and I bought an aluminum one. We made it to the Old Town later in the afternoon and took lots of pictures of the colonial-era buildings, then ate at few different places. Once it was beginning to get dark, we caught the bus back to Tumbaco. Upon our return to the casa de ciclistas, we found that three more cyclists had arrived, an English/Mexican couple and another Frenchman. Introductions to everyone were followed with lengthy discussions about routes and the like.

I'd looked up some stuff to do in Quito at the end of our first day off but, once morning rolled around, the more I looked at things to do, the less I wanted to do anything that involved going back to Quito. Instead, I installed my new brakes, and then took a freezing cold shower since there was no hot water heater, and hand washed laundry. Later in the day, I made a grocery store run and the rest of the afternoon was spent doing normal things like scrolling through social media. All the cycle tourists staying at the casa de ciclistas returned by dark and eight of us went out for dinner at an excellent Italian restaurant a few blocks away. We ate a ton of delicious food, drank a few bottles of wine, and had a grand old time.

Our late night out with all the cyclists the previous evening made for a late start in the morning; goodbyes to our new friends and exchanging contact information was a significant part of the delay and we didn't start riding till after 9:30. We took some hilly side roads from Tumbaco to get back to the Pan-American Highway. Once on the highway, the road trended gently upwards. As we approached the top of the pass, Jesse and I began to discuss our options for a place to stay for the night. Camping would have been easy but Jesse, having only a hammock with limited protection from the weather, was concerned by the dark clouds and wind near the 11,600 foot (3,515 meter) pass.

The winds were favorable at the top and we kept riding. Tailwinds and a steep road made for a fast descent and I broke my top speed for the trip again going 52.2 mph (84.2 km/h) down the long straight road. There were more options for wild camping but, the weather wasn't looking any better so, we kept riding. We rode into Latacunga that evening and began searching for a fire station. The city had a confusing layout and we had to ask for directions, multiple times, before we finally found the fire station. When we asked about a place to sleep there, we were shown to an area where we could set up our air mattresses for the night.

Several alarms went off at the fire station over the course of the night and they were not the gentle kind either. The alarms were so loud they caused me to wake up almost instantly with my heart pounding in my chest and adrenaline coursing; the result of these repeated wake ups was that I slept terribly, but that's a risk of sleeping at a fire station. I woke up, tired and sore, around seven. My back was hurting from being violently awakened by the alarms. We got on the road a couple of hours later and headed south, out of the city, on some roads that ran parallel to the highway for a while, then met up with the main road. The firemen at the station where we'd spent the night had said that the tap water was potable and I'd refilled my water without filtering it. Within an hour of drinking some of it, I began having stomach cramps; I told Jesse of my plight and we exchanged our water for filtered water at a gas station. Jesse was lucky enough not to have drunk any before we changed it out.

The road began to climb just as we were leaving a town called Ambato. A couple of hours into the climb, we met two southbound cycle tourists: Neil from Ireland and Vicky from England. We talked with them for a while and discussed a plan to stay in a town called Mocha that evening; Jesse and I were riding faster than them and continued climbing. My stomach cramps hadn't gone away and I threw up a few times on the way up the climb.

We made it to Mocha by late afternoon; a steep climb at a roughly 20% grade into the town center greeted us. It was slow enough that my speedometer read zero as I was riding up it. Fireworks were going off as we made our way into the town; a festival was going on. I was unable to figure out the reason behind it, but almost everyone was dancing around. Some people dressed as old fashioned doctors were giving out free shots of an exceptionally strong green colored mint flavored liquor from bottles that were so large that the people carrying one wore it on a sling. It would have been a nice way to spend the afternoon but, it was raining and the temperature was in the low 40s F (~5 C) thanks to being at almost 11,000 feet (3,330 meters) in elevation.

We asked at the church to see if we could stay there but they said, "no". Next, we asked a few people about directions to a fire station, but everyone said there wasn't one. We were standing next to a building, trying to figure out what to do, when the cyclists we met earlier in the day showed up; we told them our situation and realized that there was in fact a fire station in town. It turned out that Jesse and I had been watching the festival from right in front of the fire station without noticing it; but to be fair, it was a discreet looking station. We asked about somewhere to camp there and, although there appeared to be more than enough room for the four of us, they said there was a better one only five minutes away. Five minutes away didn't sound too bad so, we rode out of town following a car that was driven by one of the firemen. The major problem now was that we were going down the hill we had fought so hard to get up, but, they had said it was only five minutes away so we continued following them. Five minutes came and went followed shortly after by ten minutes. When we finally arrived we had traveled over 3 miles (5 km) back down the mountain which was exactly what we'd wanted to avoid but we were already there so we made the best of the situation; we had a free place to stay that was warm and dry so, it wasn't all bad. I was still having stomach cramps throughout the evening and went to bed early; hoping the extra rest would help me feel better in the morning.

My stomach cramps continued to afflict me throughout the night and I was running a fever by the time morning came. I slept as long as I could but, I wasn't feeling any better when I got up. I told Jesse about my situation and decided it would be best to take a day off to recover as opposed to pushing through the sickness. The firemen said I was welcome to stay at the station for another night and I settled in. Neil and Vicky, the other cyclists, took off around nine while Jesse left a little over an hour behind them. Jesse had planned to take a day off with some family friends in a town that was a few days ride away and didn't want to be late in arriving there. I spent the entire day laying down and doing my best to sleep while moving as little as possible.

The night passed slowly. At one point, I woke up with a burning fever and my stomach distended from the incredible amount of pressure in my gut that was caused by gas buildup from whatever disease I'd contracted; the pressure was relieved substantially by an extended period on the toilet. When morning dawned, I was feeling a little better and, not wanting to overstay my welcome at the fire station, I departed around 8:00; also, I was almost out of food. I decided I'd take it easy and find a hotel in the next town to rest for another day or two.

The road began to climb immediately; a 2,000+ foot (600+ meter) climb topping out at over 12,000 feet (3,630 meter) above sea level was made all the more difficult by the knowledge that I'd had to backtrack to get to the fire station, so much for riding easy. I felt weak and sick riding, but I was producing a good amount of power and I was at the top of the 8 mile (13 km) climb in less than two hours of riding. At the top, I took off the shirt I was wearing and wrung it out which left a puddle of sweat on the ground. I then bundled up in dry clothes for the descent into the city of Riobamba. I went to a supermarket and resupplied before beginning the hunt for a decent hotel; I was being picky, setting my standards too high, and soon found myself on the other end of the city with nowhere to stay. No matter, I asked someone about a hotel to the south and they said there was one in the next town, only a couple of miles away. I was in the next town in short order and inquired about the location of the hotel. There weren't any hotels according to the local I asked but there was one in the town after that. Well great, that would be another 4 more miles (6.4 km) and 700 feet (210 meters) of climbing. I didn't want to backtrack so I began riding. Approximately 40 minutes later, I reached the center of the next town and asked about the elusive hotel; the man I asked said that there was one in the town I'd just left. At that point, I absolutely refused to ride back down the way I came, but, it looked like I was out of options for a hotel. I was contemplating my situation while sitting in the town square when the same person I had asked about the hotel came by and invited me to lunch. Whatever disease I had from the water had caused me to lose most of my appetite, but I could still eat something light so I went with them. They gave me a delicious bowl of chicken soup, complete with the feet and gizzards of said fowl. A plate of rice, potatoes, and a chicken leg accompanied the soup. Because of my sickness, I wasn't able to finish it all but there were no less than five dogs at the house that were being fed leftovers by the other guests so I followed suit. I really didn't want to ride any farther so, I hung around and answered the usual barrage of questions about where I was from and what I was doing in hopes of getting an invitation to stay for the night. I admit to it being a selfish motive but, I really wasn't feeling up to riding anymore. After an hour of waiting I got the idea that I wasn't going to have somewhere to stay there so I got back on my bike. I thanked my hosts for their hospitality and began riding again with everyone at the house gathered to see me off.

The next known location for a hotel, according to the map on my GPS, was a place called Guamote; almost 20 miles (32 km) away, with an additional 1,300+ feet (400+ meters) of climbing in the first few miles to the top of a pass near 11,000 feet (3,330 meters). I began riding and lost part of my lunch within ten minutes and I threw up the rest of it a couple of miles later. While I can say with confidence that the scenery was beautiful, I was not enjoying it. I survived my second 2,000+ foot (600+ meter) climb of the day and followed the road down into a river canyon. Instead of contouring the canyon along a gentle upriver incline, the road clawed its way up and down the side of the canyon in a manner that was better suited to a roller coaster, but, it had a distinct lack of the excitement present when riding a roller coaster. I was barely able to cycle at 4 mph (6.4 km/h) going up but, I descended at over ten times that speed going down. There were options for camping along the road but, at that point, it seemed better to push through the sickness to get to a hotel than to stop a little earlier and have to ride again in the morning. It was dusk when I rode into Guamote. I checked into the first decent hotel I found and, coincidentally, it was the same price as some of the ones I'd turned down in Riobamba. I'd accumulated nearly seven hours of riding time and I fell asleep exhausted following a hot shower.

Even after the grossly extended ride to Guamote, I felt much better after a decent night's sleep. I was curious if my ailment had a name and an online symptom checker showed that my sickness matched remarkably well with Cryptosporidiosis - a disease contracted by drinking water that was contaminated with fecal matter but generally not serious or fatal. It was either that or cancer, according to the online symptom checker. The only treatment was rest and staying hydrated. I spent most of the day in bed, trying to plan my upcoming route for the next few weeks. My appetite came back and I went out for lunch and dinner. I felt well enough to get back to riding the next morning but stayed another day at the hotel, just to make sure I didn't relapse right away, and went for a walk that evening. Now that I was in the rural parts of Ecuador, the local culture was much more apparent; women wore dresses with brightly colored shawls and topped off the look with bowler hats. Men usually wore suits or more western style clothes.

When I left Guamote, it felt good to be back on the road after two days off the bike; after being sick and in such a low place mentally for the last several days, the freedom of riding was amazing. Ecuador really was pulling out all the stops. The riding was incredible, cooler temperatures from the high elevation, gorgeous mountain scenery, and a nice tailwind had me feeling great. The contrast from being sick made me feel that much higher. Cycle touring is an emotional roller coaster, the longer the time on the road the lower the lows and the higher the highs are and that day was one of the highest days for a while. On one of the steep descents, I finally achieved my lifelong dream of going faster than a mile a minute on a bicycle; I could hear my tires singing on the pavement and the wind raging as the road zipped by as I went my highest speed ever on a bicycle, 60.2 mph (97.0 km/h).

The road undulated continuously; I was either clawing my way up a serpentine climb on a steep mountainside or flying down a winding descent. A fog descended, once I was outside of the town of Chunchi, and I climbed out of the small mountain town; the fog that gave a dreamlike aura to the ride until some dogs came charging at me while barking fiercely; they grabbed at my panniers and tried to pull my bike down to the ground while I hammer fisted and kicked at them while still trying to pedal. Once I got to the end of what they considered to be their territory, they left me alone. It was already late enough in the day to camp but, I rode a few extra miles to make sure I was far enough away from the dogs before ending my day at a level clearing that was surrounded by trees and elevated above the road.

I was sore when I woke up the next morning; I'd ridden too hard because of how great I was feeling. My muscles were exceptionally tight when I started riding and I had to pedal slowly for the first ten minutes or so before I loosened up. Jesse had said that the road between the towns of Chunchi and Cañar was tough riding and I agreed with him; I pedaled along steep roads through the mountains with tons of climbing, all day long.

After two hours of riding, I stopped by a gas station to fill up on water and have a snack; while I was eating, the wind began to pick up. When I started riding again, I had a tailwind, but, the road soon turned 180 degrees and I was climbing into a strong headwind. The wind quickly became strong enough that it was all I could do to stay on the road and then it continued to get even worse to where I got blown off the road a few times by the powerful gusts. The gale only continued to get stronger and stronger until, eventually, I couldn't ride at all. I got off my bike and started pushing in hopes the wind wouldn't be as strong over the top of the climb. I pushed my bike for maybe a quarter mile (400 meters) before the wind blew me over while I was pushing; I fell on a rock and lay where I'd fallen, in pain, feeling utterly defeated. It didn't matter how hard I tried to keep going; the wind would just blow me over again. By then, it was blowing so hard that it was threatening to move my bike while it lay on the ground. I waited for a break in the wind before picking up my bike again and pushing it across the road to a more sheltered area on the inside of a turn, almost getting blown over again in the process. I couldn't ride in that wind; I couldn't even push my bike it was so strong. I had no choice but to settle in to wait until it stopped and that might be a while; it was only 10:00 am.

I put on most of my warm clothes and settled in to wait in a sheltered ditch by the side of the road. The wind only continued to get stronger and I was surprised that passing cars weren't getting blown off the road; some of the buses and trucks would have one wheel come off the ground while they were going around the turn I was sitting in, but none of them tipped over. I did my best to take a nap and eventually just started thinking about life. The process lasted several hours but, eventually, I decided that, even with how much cycle touring sucked sometimes, there was still nothing I'd rather be doing.

When 5:00 pm came and went, I'd been waiting for seven hours and the wind was barely starting to slow down. I'd have to ride in the dark if I wanted to get anywhere.

Half an hour later, the wind had finally slowed enough that I could push my bike; I pushed it the rest of the way up the hill; when the wind gusted, it brought my progress to a temporary standstill until it backed off again. I don't know how long it took me to get to the top, but I did. The sun was beginning to go down, by the time I got over the pass, and I had to pedal going downhill to keep moving. I wound my way towards Cañar, in the dark, and began the climb into town. Many of the houses had dogs and several of them escaped to chase me but, none attacked like they did yesterday. I went by a bakery in town for some pastries, and then continued climbing up the pass towards the city of Cuenca. I started falling asleep while riding at around 9:30 which meant it was time to stop. I was still a mile or so away from the top of the pass when I rode by an open field and camped there for the night. I felt too lazy to set up my tent so, I just laid out my air mattress and sleeping bag on top of my groundsheet.

I woke to a drizzle pattering on my face. Unfortunately, it was still dark and I covered my face with my rain jacket before going back to sleep. When dawn finally came, I hadn't slept very well and my sleeping bag was soaked from the rain. I wormed my way out my sleeping bag and into the cool mountain air, then dressed quickly. I'd slept at around 11,000 feet (3,330 meters) in elevation and the temperature was around 40 F (4 C).

I started riding an hour later and I was feeling weak and sore from my late ride the previous night. I made it over the top of the pass and began the descent towards Cuenca. The pass happened to be South America's continental divide with the east side of the pass being part of the Amazon River basin while the other side drained into the Pacific Ocean. The road leveled out, after about 15 miles (24 km), and I had gentle rolling hills the rest of the way into the city of Cuenca.

While I was at a grocery store that happened to have wifi, I received a message from Jesse saying that he was waiting for me at a fire station on the south end of town and I met him there an hour later. He'd stayed a few nights with his family friends near Cañar, then was hosted for a night at the fire station. We rode out of the city right away. Jesse understood how far I'd already ridden so, we rode to Cumbe; a short day for him and a longer than average day for me. When we arrived in town, we asked some policemen about a place to camp. They said to check at the church; failing that, we could sleep in the square/park outside the church. We found said building and asked to speak to the Padre but he was in Cuenca and would not return for a couple of hours. We waited around and had some kebabs at a street food stand nearby. A couple of hours later, the Padre was back but he went straight from getting there to doing a service at the church. The service lasted around 30 minutes, then we went and talked to the Padre. He wasn't the nicest person and said we'd have to find somewhere else to stay. We'd exhausted several options by waiting and, while we were trying to decide what to do, a man who had attended the church service came up and asked us if we needed help. We told him we were looking for a place to sleep and he walked with us to a building in the square. After some discussion, he handed us a key and told us to follow him with our bikes. We walked a few blocks away from the square and ended up at what appeared to be a school; the man unlocked the door, showed us around, and asked us to lock up when we left in the morning. While it was often a nice experience staying with locals, it usually took a lot more effort than camping. Jesse liked asking people and, since he usually did most of the leg work in the asking part, I was fine joining in on it.

CHAPTER 14

Day 153, July 3, 2016

Saraguro, Ecuador

The last few days had been challenging riding through the mountains with beautiful scenery and constant, steep grades; I'd pedal up the mountains at 3-4 mph (5-6 km/h) while Jesse rode a little faster. I finally made a few more cuts to drop some weight, such as emptying the 100 ounce (3 liter) water bladder that I'd previously carried full of emergency water. I'd probably only used it twice in the last five months and that was only because I hadn't paid attention to gaps between water sources. Carrying less weight made the climbs a little bit easier.

The previous night had been our fourth night in a row of being hosted by locals. After the school in Cumbe, we lucked out with places to stay at fire stations for three nights in a row. The most recent one had an unusual addition, a cock fighting ring, complete with roosters stored in cages throughout the premises; animal rights aren't a thing outside of most western countries. Neither is noise pollution; almost every restaurant we'd been to had music videos, playing on a continuous loop, as loud as the TV would go. The roosters at the fire station had crowed all night long, though it was a free place to stay. The crowing of the roosters had been especially difficult for Jesse; earplugs worked well enough for me but Jesse had been up most of the night. Despite his being up earlier than normal, we didn't get going any quicker. After another beautiful day of cycling through the mountains, we rode into Loja and found another fire station that would host us.

Jesse's phone had finally broken and he wanted to get a tablet to replace it functionally. We spent part of the day riding around Loja looking for a fairly priced electronics store. After looking for a while, and not finding anything, we rode by the other fire station in the middle of the city to see if we could stay there for the night. They referred us to the one at the north end of the city where we'd stayed the night before so we ended up getting a cheap hotel ending the five night run of staying with locals; that was definitely a record for me. I hung around the hotel while Jesse went out on foot to look for a tablet and he returned successful a couple of hours later.

My afternoon was spent planning the route ahead, among other things, while Jesse worked on getting his tablet set up. We'd realized that many restaurants in Ecuador were cheap enough that it costs about as much to eat out as it does to cook a decent meal. Obviously, if we ate nothing but rice, or its nutritional equivalent, it'd be cheaper to cook our own food but for a moderately nutritious meal, the price was comparable. We went out to a Chinese place near the hotel for dinner and toasted the 240th birthday of the United States with a beer.

A couple of days later, we were getting ready to leave the fire station where we'd spent the night at when one of the firemen came by to talk to us; he said it was flat to downhill the rest of the way to the border of Peru, with only a few small hills; I did my best not to laugh; thankfully, I knew better. The road began climbing right out of Vilcabamba, for 1,400 vertical feet (425 meters). A little over an hour of riding brought me to the top where I met up with Jesse, and then we descended nearly as far as we had climbed.

Another climb followed, though this one was closer to 1,300 feet (395 meters) tall and there was another descent after it that was about 800 feet (242 meters) down. Somewhere around there, Jesse asked how long it'd been since we had rain. I didn't know off the top of my head and guessed about a week so we agreed that the part of Ecuador we were in must be pretty dry; not one hour later it began to rain. A long and very inconsistent climb brought us to almost 9,000 feet (2,730 meters) in elevation. Vilcabamba, the town we started from that morning, was at barely over 5,000 feet (1,520 meters) and the fireman had said it was flat to downhill all the way to the border. According to Jesse's app that records his bike rides, his total vertical ascent for the day was just over 7,300 feet (2,220 meters), about the same elevation change as a moderate Tour de France mountain stage, but in half the distance. We'd only covered 40 miles (64 km) and I was hauling an extra 85+ lb (38+ kg) of bike and gear compared to what a racing bicycle weighs. Somewhere in the mountains, surrounded by mist and rain, I hit 8,000 miles cycled. We descended out of the mountains into a small town called Valladolid and asked to camp at a church; they showed us to a nice covered area, adjacent to a garden, where we could setup for the night.

My back tire was flat the next morning; I didn't realize it at the time but, it was an omen of things to come that day. My brakes had come close to failing a few times on the descent towards Valladolid but, I'd repaired them last night. It was still raining; we tried to wait out the worst of it, and then started riding around 10:30. My brakes lasted a few miles before they quit working completely; I tried to fix them and got the rear brake in decent working order but the front was a lost cause, the pads were already worn out and, stupidly, I didn't have any spares.

The road trended downward and we had an easy ride into a town called Polanda. The previous evening, Jesse had noticed some chipped paint on one of his chainstays and was worried that it could be a crack in his frame. We got online at the library in town and Jesse was able to send a picture to a frame expert he knew back home and found that it was indeed a crack in his frame. This complicated things significantly; the frame expert said it was deep enough that it could fail at any time, however, it was a steel frame and therefore capable of being repaired so we began riding around Polanda looking for someone who could weld Jesse's frame back together. We were in luck and were able to locate a welder within 20 minutes of riding in circles. The welding shop happened to be located on top of one of the steepest roads in town; it was so steep that there was a set of stairs lining the road instead of a sidewalk. Neither of us were able to ride up it and we pushed our bikes up with great difficulty. Once Jesse had everything taken off his bike, and removed his rear wheel, he found that the drive side dropout had cracked all the way through to where the chainstay and seatstay would move independently of each other. The welder expertly repaired both problems for the sum of $5.

The total time for the repair, from getting to the library to the repair being done, was about three hours. It was early afternoon when we finally left Polanda. We only had 30 miles (48 km) to go to the next town and it paralleled a river so, therefore, it should have been relatively flat. The road was flat to rolling for the next 5 miles (8 km) after which we stopped for a lunch break. Right after we started riding again, the road dropped quickly then clawed its way back up the side of the canyon on a dirt road with a grade in excess of 15% and climbed about 1,100 feet (330 meters) in the space of a few miles and I was just barely able to ride up the climb. There was a short, gentle descent afterwards; during the descent, my brakes stopped working almost completely. A dirt road then contoured the canyon for a ways before gaining an additional 400 feet (120 meters) in a rolling climb, then came to a village at a pass, between some mountains, in the jungle. We had a couple of hours of daylight left by the time we reached the village near the pass and we only had 8 miles (13 km) to go to get to the town of Zumba; that was our goal for the day. Since half of the road was supposed to be downhill, we chose to push through it.

Jacob Ashton

My brakes were almost useless on the descent and I had to drag my feet down the hill to keep from going too fast; the road began to get steeper as we neared the bottom and I stopped again to try to fix them. After close to 30 minutes of working on my brakes, they squealed loudly but had enough power that if I dragged my feet I could keep my speed at a safe level. Right when I finished the brake repair, Jesse had a flat tire; we mutually agreed that I should begin the climb and he could catch up. My brakes were rubbing horribly and I readjusted them so they wouldn't rub at the bottom of the descent but this meant I had almost zero braking power. Next was the climb, only 4 miles (6.4 km) left to Zumba; I was about a mile up the insanely steep climb when Jesse caught up with me. We continued climbing and soon darkness fell. With a little over 2 miles (3 km) left on the climb, the road became slick from the rain and resulting mud. I lost traction from my tires slipping in the mud and fell over; I picked myself up and tried to start riding again but, without brakes, I had no way of keeping my bike from rolling backwards while I tried to start pedaling. I ended up jamming my right foot behind the front wheel while putting my left on the pedals and then, while maintaining this balancing act, tried to start pedaling. It took a few attempts and subsequent falls into the mud but eventually I was rolling again. I made it a quarter of a mile (400 meters) before my rear wheel spun out again and I was on the ground, covered in even more mud. This cycle continued a few more times with me riding progressively shorter distances until I spun out and found myself lying on the ground after making it barely 30 yards (27 meters). At that point, I opted for pushing my bike until the road leveled out; I wasn't going much slower pushing than I was riding but it put enough strain on my back and neck that I had to stop a few times to keep them from going into spasms. I pushed while Jesse rode slowly alongside.

It was so dark by then that, without lights, the road would have been almost invisible. We continued our progress at a

94

snail's pace and, after a few hours of effort, we were at the top. It was after 9:00 pm when we reached the pass; the road had climbed 2,200 feet (670 meters) in less than 3.5 miles (5.6 km); an average grade of about 13% and there were a few flat sections. The pass was not the end of our ride however; we had a short descent into Zumba during which I had to drag my feet most of the way to keep my speed in check; most of the roads in Zumba were steep and made of cobblestones. I tried to zigzag down the deserted roads, like a skier going down a mountain, while dragging my feet on the cobbles to keep from going too fast. There was no fire station in Zumba and it didn't take much contemplation to start looking for a cheap hotel. The last downhill to the hotel was exceptionally steep and paved with stones that were slick from the rain. Jesse went to the bottom to make sure the roads were clear before I tried to zigzag down. On the first turn, I slid out and put a nice scrape on my shin from it being ground along the edge of a curb while I was being dragged down the hill by my bike. I got my bike up and tried to walk it down the hill but it was too steep and I got dragged down the hill by my bike for several feet before ending up in heap with a few more scrapes in various places. Jesse jogged up to help me and we walked some of my bags down the hill before coming back up the hill to get my bike; with both of us trying to hold it back, we were just barely able to control the descent and make it to the bottom. It was 10:00 pm by then and all the restaurants were closing. There was one small grocery store that was still open and we bought some stuff to add to our pasta dinners before checking into the first hotel we saw. By the time we'd cooked, eaten, and showered, it was almost midnight and we were definitely taking a day off in Zumba; it was that rough of a day.

I slept till 8:00 the next morning. Shortly after getting up, Jesse and I went out for a breakfast of steak, rice, beans, yucca, and vegetables; yucca was usually boiled and had a taste similar to potato. Next on the day's agenda was fixing my brakes; upon disassembling them, I found that the rear brake pads were worn down to the metal. The brake pads were still the stock resin pads that came with the calipers I'd bought in Quito. Resin pads, while being an effective braking surface in dry, clean conditions, wear at an astonishing rate when in less than ideal weather. This explained the frequent stops required to keep them working as long as they did. Now to find new brake pads; I started by asking the hotel owner if there was bicycle shop in town and he said there was one just up the road, while pointing for emphasis. I walked a couple of blocks and didn't see anything so, I asked someone and was directed further along the road so, I kept going, still not seeing anything that resembled a bicycle shop. The road curved downhill and it looked like the edge of town so, I asked someone else and they pointed me up a different road in the general direction of the hotel. Another person told me to go up another road and I found myself less than one block away from where I started and still unable to find a bike shop. The process continued with me walking in several circles while following directions from many different people. After almost 90 minutes of looking, I reached my last straw when two people tried to tell me which way to go then pointed in opposite directions before realizing what they'd done and both being indecisive about which way I should go; eventually, they agreed on an entirely different direction. I gave up on finding a bike shop and walked back to the hotel. Luckily, Jesse's brakes used the same kind of pads; he had a few extra sets and was kind enough to loan me a set until I could buy new ones.

The front brakes were another story; the cable housing on the front brake had fallen apart, even though I'd replaced it at about the same time as I replaced the brakes. Although it was the best cable housing I could find at the time, the resistance was high enough that it was keeping the brake from working properly regardless of how hard I pulled on the brake lever. Neither of us had any spare housing so I lubed the housing as best I could. It helped some and gave me better power in the front brake than before. All that mechanic-ing worked up an appetite and I went by a bakery for some snacks, then spent the rest of the afternoon resting. I did my best to expend as little energy as possible and not move for the rest of the day. I was successful at that endeavor until dinnertime when hunger finally convinced me to get up and get something to eat.

We got on the road around nine the next morning and, although Zumba was a small town, we had some difficulty distinguishing the correct road out of town as all of them were dirt and in equally poor condition. After consulting my GPS a few times, we were confident of our direction and set off towards the Peruvian border.

It'd been sunny for most of our day off in Zumba so, it made perfect sense that it was raining that morning. The dirt road wasn't too rough but, the rain created mud and that made for slick roads. I was sliding around a bit, even going slowly, and gained some confidence on a descent until my front end slid out going more than 15 mph (24 km/h), by far the highest speed crash of the trip so far. My bike seemed okay but, my handlebars had been knocked loose to where they had a few degrees of play and wouldn't stay at the correct angle; I made an attempt to tighten them but it was ineffective. My left side had taken most of the impact with the brunt concentrated to the underside of my wrist, near my palm, where I had another patch of road rash that added to the collection of wounds I'd accumulated over the last couple of days; I washed out the scrape as best I could, then rode much slower after that. The rain and high humidity kept the exposed nerves on the scrape near my palm moist so it stung for the rest of the day.

The descent I'd crashed on was followed by a steep, but rideable, climb. Jesse was waiting at the top at a bus stop that seemed out of place for such a remote area and a woman was talking at him, nonstop, in a language that wasn't Spanish; she wouldn't stop talking for anything. We rode off down another descent that was followed by an even steeper climb; I made a valiant attempt to ride up it but, my effort was in vain and I had to push my bike most of the way up. Near the top was a military checkpoint where I had my passport checked at a spot that was not a border for the first time on the trip. They also wanted a look inside one of my bags though they only checked a couple items at the top of one pannier.

The road followed a ridge for a few miles before climbing steeply for a few hundred vertical feet, then turning into the final descent down to the border. The dirt road wound gently down the mountain for a time, then, a mile (1.6 km) away from the border, it dumped into a 30% or more descent down to the river that makes the border for Ecuador and Peru. It took me over three hours of riding to do the 18 miles (29 km) from Zumba to the border. We rode up to the immigration office, but, the border official was nowhere to be found. We checked the few buildings close by and found him eating at a small restaurant a couple of buildings down. It was past noon by then and we were hungry so, we ate lunch too. When we were finished, we went back to the office, filled out a form, got our passports stamped, and rode across the bridge to Peru. The Peruvian immigration office was closed for lunch too and we began asking around to try to find out how long it might be. We found out, from a restaurant across the street, that the official was on a lunch break and would not be back until 3 pm, over 90 minutes away, and we had no choice but to wait it out. The Peru side was paved beautifully smooth and we aired up our tires in preparation while waiting. The official came back early and was surprisingly friendly; he had us stamped in and on our way in a little more than five minutes.

The paved road on the Peruvian side rolled gradually along a river, then climbed about 1,000 feet (300 meters) over a pass before dipping towards a small town at the bottom. As it was getting later in the afternoon, we tried looking for a place to stay for the night, but found nothing. We began climbing out of the town and, after more than an hour of climbing, came to the town of Nuevo Esperanza. There was a municipal building there and when we asked if there was anywhere we could camp for the night they said there was not. The sun had set already and we began discussing our options; Jesse was fine with pushing through the 11 miles (18 km) to San Ignacio where there was supposed to be a fire station while I was leaning towards stopping sooner. While we were talking, one of the employees at the municipal building came by and said we could sleep in an uncompleted portion of the building. It was free, though spartan, accommodation; a concrete floor and no lights, but it was a roof over our heads and we agreed to stop for the day.

CHAPTER 15

Day 160, July 10, 2016

San Ignacio, Peru

J esse had two flat tires in the morning; thanks to that, we had a slow start. While he was fixing his tires, I tried to figure out the mystery of my floating handlebars; I started undoing the bolts that held them to the stem and saw that the faceplate holding the handlebars into the stem was cracked. There was nothing I could do about it without special replacement parts so I tightened them up again and added it to the list of things to buy at the next bike shop. The mechanical problems delayed our start until almost 10:00.

The road climbed out of town to a false summit and then continued up for a few more miles. We were riding relatively quickly and were in San Ignacio in about 70 minutes. In town, we stopped by a bakery and had a slice of the best passion fruit cake in the world before going to a restaurant for lunch. It really was some incredible cake. I ordered what I thought was a pork stew for lunch; it was pork but the meat was heart. It still tasted alright and was served with rice and yucca as sides; they paired well with the remnants of the stew. We tried to find a grocery store but, after being told there was nothing more than mini-mart like shops called tiendas, we went to another bakery instead.

A short climb out of San Ignacio brought us to a gradual, winding descent that was about 14 miles (22 km) long and it went down to a river canyon around 1,600 feet (485 meters) in elevation. This was the lowest we'd been since Colombia and the temperature was significantly higher, about 80 F (27 C) and somewhat humid since we were in the Amazon Basin.

A rare treat awaited us there, a flat road. It'd been so long since we'd ridden on a flat road that we'd forgotten just how easily the miles could pass. The road was mostly flat with a few gentle rollers the rest of the way into the village of Perico, our stop for the day. In the village, we began looking for a place to stay; there was no fire station in town and, it being Sunday, the municipal building was closed. There were a couple of people nearby and we asked if they knew of anywhere we could stay; in response, one of them hopped on a motorcycle and told us to follow them. After chasing the man on the motorcycle for a few blocks, they stopped at someone's house. The owner came out and, after conversing for a while, they gave the man on the motorcycle the keys to a building. We followed him back the way we'd come and to the building. He unlocked it, showed us around a bit, and then left. The place smelled absolutely terrible; the toilet was full from previous use and there was no water to try to get rid of it. In addition to this, the bathroom was not entirely closed off so the smell permeated the entire floor. There was an upstairs, but it appeared to be locked as the handle did nothing. I pushed on the door a bit and it opened to a wall-less area covered by a metal roof. After locking our bikes downstairs, we brought our bags up, and made ourselves at home; it didn't stink on the roof.

Like Ecuador, the restaurants in Peru seemed to be relatively cheap so we went out to eat at one of the many restaurants in town. We both tried ordering a beef dish but, something got lost in translation and, we ended up with fish that was similar to trout; but, were still hungry after that and we went to another restaurant; it only cost a couple of dollars anyways. While we were deciding which restaurant to go to, a local cyclist named Milton rode up and asked if we had somewhere to stay. After we told him we were staying at the municipal building, he invited us to stay at his house about half a mile (1 km) away. This was an excellent option to escape the smelly municipal building so, we went back to get our bikes and gear, then met him at one of the restaurants; the restaurant happened to be a bar too and Milton and his friends insisted on paying for some beers. The Peruvian style of drinking was quite unique; everyone at the table used the same smallish cup that was passed around the table with a large bottle of beer. One person would fill the glass and drink it quickly then dump the remaining foam on the ground before passing it to the next person. After several large beers had been consumed by the five of us at the table, we went across the street to eat at another restaurant. When we were done eating, we walked our bikes to Milton's house; his wife and children were away in a city for a few days so he had us use his kid's beds that were complete with mosquito nets. I didn't know if there were insect borne diseases in Peru.

After talking for a while the next morning, we left Milton's house around 8:00; I found it amusing that we had almost the exact same conversation as the previous night. Back in Perico, we stopped by a small shop to get enough food to get us to the city of Jaen. We had flat riding for a few miles before getting into some gentle rolling hills that took us past some terraced rice fields. After 10 miles (16 km) or so of riding, we began pedaling up a gradual climb on a quiet road. The road climbed about 1,000 feet (300 meters) before it leveled off into some rollers for another 10 miles (16 km). Towards the end of the rolling section, we stopped for lunch; we both ordered beef and, while the meat we were given was probably beef, it had similar taste and texture to jerky. Several houses along the road had had lines of thinly cut meat drying in the sun and there was a good chance that that was the kind of meat we were served. After lunch, the road trended downwards into a valley then began a shallow climb towards Jaen and we rode into the city after midday. Suddenly, we were on busy roads and surrounded by traffic, primarily motorcycles and brightly painted tuk tuks called 'mototaxis'. Mototaxis were three wheeled vehicles with a partially enclosed cabin that may or may not have doors with large windows; the driver sat on a motorcycle style seat in front and there was a bench seat for multiple passengers plus whatever cargo they had with them, sometimes chickens or even goats.

We kept seeing signs for a shopping plaza and decided to follow them in hopes of finding good prices for food at a grocery store. The plaza was on the very south end of the city and, unfortunately, the prices were no better and, in some cases, were more expensive than the shops/tiendas we'd been going to in rural areas.

Jesse and I both needed parts at the bike shop and we backtracked into the city, once we were done at the supermarket. The bike shop we went to had a decent selection of parts and sold them at better prices than the US. I was able to buy brake pads but, the stem on my bike was one of the few recumbent specific parts and they didn't have just a faceplate to replace the one that cracked during my crash in the mountains of Ecuador a few days prior. The owner of the bicycle shop recommended going to a nearby machine shop and getting one custom made. The bike shop operated on Latin America time, no one was in a hurry to do anything, and it took the rest of the afternoon to get things done but, they let us use their wifi while we waited. We met a few other cycle tourists at the shop: a French couple and a solo female cyclist from Brazil; all of them were northbound. The cyclists told us that the fire stations in Peru almost never hosted cyclists but, there was a fire station barely more than a block away so, we decided to give it a try anyway. After asking, they let us stay for the night, under a covered area in the back of the station, next to several 110+ pound (50+ kg) sacks of dried, unroasted coffee beans.

Over the last week or so, I'd realized that I had only used my thermos a few times the entire trip and, when I did, it was only because I made coffee. I hadn't been drinking coffee much at all for the last few months and I had only drank it because it was served with breakfast, so, I gave my thermos away to the firefighters at the station we were staying at in Jaen. It was a couple of pounds of weight that I didn't feel like carrying through all the mountains that I had left to climb. The firemen were grateful for the gift and I was glad to be rid of it. Supposedly, one kilogram (2.2 pounds) of weight adds roughly one minute per hour when riding uphill on a bicycle. It was something.

We'd planned for a rest day in Jaen and, after we left the fire station, we rode to the bike shop. The owner of the shop had mentioned a machine shop nearby where I might be able to get a new faceplate for my stem made and I asked about directions that morning. His response was to hop on his motorcycle and lead me there while I followed him on my bike. He was aware of just how fast I could go on a fully loaded bicycle and I didn't have to try too hard to keep up. When we got there, he explained to the machinist just what I needed and, after telling me it'd probably take a few hours, I thanked him and he left.

The machinists tried to convince me that a plastic replacement would work fine but I insisted on metal for the durability and, eventually, they conceded. It did take a few hours, including the time it took for them to get started on actually working on it and several long breaks to stop and chat with anyone who walked in. I found the cutting, grinding, hammering, and drilling of the piece, interesting and the waiting wasn't too bad since I didn't have much else to do anyways. The resulting piece was functional and had the silvery look of machined steel. It cost me a bit less than $10 US and, since that was probably a quarter of the cost that a new stem would have been, I didn't try to negotiate a lower price.

I pedaled back to the bike shop afterwards and met Jesse there. The owner of the bike shop was on the Warmshowers.org hospitality site and he offered to host us now that the other cyclists had left. After using the wifi at the bike shop for a while, his son led us to where we'd be staying. It turned out that we would have an unfurnished apartment, entirely to ourselves, that had electricity and running water. We got settled in, then I went by a bakery to get some stuff for lunch; I'd planned to save some of the pastries I bought for a snack later but, they were so good that I ate them all in one sitting. I took the rest of the afternoon to use the wifi at the bike shop and finally got caught up on some things that had been piling up for the last week or so.

We went to a Chinese restaurant for dinner; they tended to have excellent portions at good prices and great food every time we'd gone to one in any country and, like most restaurants, it was relatively cheap too. Back at the bike shop, the owner, our host, invited us to have coffee with him. We rode in a mototaxi/tuk tuk to the coffee shop and he told of some sights nearby that we then planned to incorporate into our journey through Peru. Upon finishing our coffee, and a few tamales, our host paid for everything before we could protest otherwise. Neither Jesse nor I drank coffee regularly and the Peruvian coffee we had that night was exceptionally strong. By the time midnight rolled around, my heart was still pounding and I didn't feel tired at all because of the caffeine; try as I might to go to sleep, it just wasn't working. The last time I checked the time it was after three in the morning and I happened to get up at dawn again.

The next day, Jesse needed to replace his cassette and chain as he'd been unable to do so during our rest day. The bike shop didn't open till 9:00 so, we went by a bakery for breakfast. We arrived at the bike shop at the same time as the owner. What should have been a quick process of simply swapping a few parts took much longer; Jesse's bike wasn't ready for a couple of hours. By the time a photo shoot of us and our bikes finished, and we had said our goodbyes then gave our thanks, it was almost noon. We still had to buy food before leaving Jaen and we had an escort to the grocery store composed of the owner and his son, with most of the bike shop employees, plus a few customers, all riding bicycles with us. After the 15 minute ride to the grocery store, and some more goodbyes,

Jesse and I went to the store while everyone else headed back to the bike shop. The checkout lines at the grocery store were incredibly slow and we finally got on the road after almost an hour at the supermarket; most of that time was waiting in line while the cashiers chatted at length with every customer they helped.

The road climbed gently out of Jaen, after which there was a nice gradual descent for several miles. During the descent, we saw four cycle tourists headed up the hill; we stopped to talk for a while and exchanged information about our various routes. The tourists were two couples: one couple from Argentina and the other from Spain. Jesse was closest and started talking to the Spaniards who happened to speak English and I talked with the Argentineans who did not. After talking with them, we hit the road again and I realized just how far my Spanish has progressed. Although I was still a very, very long ways from fluent, I was able to have a decent conversation.

The road rolled gently up a river gradient, past some rice paddies, and we moved along at a good pace. We were over halfway done with our planned distance for the day when Jesse's back tire went flat, after being punctured by a piece of wire. There was no decent shade along the road; the only vegetation was desert scrub and a few scrawny trees. He fixed it in the sun while I waited with him. A few miles later, Jesse's front tire went flat. We were a little more than 12 miles (20 km) away from where we planned to stop for the day, Bagua Grande, and we decided I should ride ahead while he fixed his tire so we could arrive in town at a decent hour. I rode off and I found a tree to sit under, just before town, and began to wait. Jesse showed up almost an hour later. He had gotten three more flat tires from the ineffective glue in his patch kit failing on separate occasions on the way in and had been going at a time trial pace in between. We then began our search for somewhere to stay for the night and asked at the fire station, municipal building, and two police stations, without any luck, so we split the cost of a cheap hotel room that only cost a few dollars each.

Because of our caffeine fueled and unintentional late night in Jaen, we slept in a bit and got started around 9:30 which was actually a pretty normal start time. We followed a gently rolling road, along a river that trended upwards, which took us into a deep canyon. There was a section where the road turned inland and climbed for a ways before descending almost as far so, we chose to take a dirt side road that would cut off much of the unnecessary climbing and was only passable by four wheel drive vehicles thanks to a ditch blocking the road. The shortcut took off almost 5 miles (8 km) and who knows how much climbing. The cutoff road climbed steeply on pavement before turning to dirt and continuing to climb. Most of the dirt road was rideable for me, though I had to push a couple of short sections, and, over the top, we had a spectacular view of the Andes Mountains.

We descended on dirt for a short ways before the road became paved again. There was a restaurant a few miles after the cutoff road met up with main road and we stopped for a delicious lunch of steak, rice, beans, and yucca. The road continued to follow the river, after lunch, and began to climb steeply, shortly after we started riding again. An hour later, it began to rain but, it was warm enough neither of us wore our rain jackets and long portions of the road were carved into the canyon to where the overhanging cliff protected us from the rain. We made it to our goal of Pedro Ruiz, then asked at the police station for a place to camp and they let us stay on the paved soccer field behind the station. It was still raining but, I had my tent and Jesse had a tarp, so we stayed dry.

There was about 10 miles (16 km) of gentle rolling hills, the next morning, before we reached the base of the climb to the village of San Pablo. We turned off the main road and began the climb towards the small village. It was about 1,600 vertical feet (485 meters) up a scenic road to get there and I met Jesse at the top an hour later. In the village, the tourist information office told us we could leave our bikes there while we hiked to Gocta Falls, a waterfall that was one of the places the bike shop owner in Jaen had recommended we visit.

The hike was about 4 miles (6.4 km), one way, to the falls and trended upwards, though not too steeply most of the time. We hiked along the well maintained trail, through the jungle, to the upper part of the falls and enjoyed spectacular vistas of the surrounding mountains on the way up. After taking a break, and some pictures, at the upper section of the two-drop waterfall, we took a side trip to the top of the lower section of the falls that cascaded off the mountainside in a drop that was more than five times the size of the upper falls. It took a bit of scrambling to get near the edge of the almost 2,700 foot (820 meter) drop but, we could not safely get close enough to see completely over the edge. The second drop makes Gocta falls the 5th or 16th tallest waterfall in world depending on who you ask. If you add both drops together it's the 5th tallest but, if you only consider the drop of the lower falls, it's the 16th. Some weeks later, we learned that one of a group of two tourists had died falling off the edge of the lower falls. Perhaps surprisingly, the waterfall had only become known to the outside world around the beginning of the new millennia because the locals feared that the beautiful blond haired mermaid spirit that lived in the falls would curse them if they revealed its location. After the hike back, we asked the people at the tourist office about somewhere to camp and they showed us to a covered area, a block or two away, where we set up for the night.

While I was packing my gear in preparation for the day's ride the following morning, I felt the call of nature; that shouldn't have been a problem, except that the water had been turned off all night so the toilet we had access to wouldn't flush and it had been filled by someone else the previous evening. I saw somebody working across the street and asked if they had a restroom I could use. They didn't know of any besides the aforementioned toilet, but, they went to show me where it was anyways while I followed along asking them to stop so I could attempt to explain the problem of the in-operable toilet in Spanish. I was unsuccessful and, when they saw the situation in the restroom, they went to turn the water on. They'd been gone less than a minute when the water began to flow out of every tap in the building at full force. It'd been turned off all night and Jesse's bike was parked right in front of a sink. Jesse happened to be stuffing his sleeping bag into a pannier on his bike when the water turned on and it sprayed all over him and his sleeping bag. It was a down sleeping bag and, since it would be detrimental to the longevity of the bag to put it away wet, he started the process of attempting to dry it out in the sun. With the amount of water saturating the bag, it was going to be a while. We started riding a couple of hours later. A few mile descent from San Pablo took us back to the main road and we had another day of beautiful scenery along the stunning canyon. The riding was incredible and more than made up for the hurdles of the morning.

Around noon, we caught up to some cycle tourists who were also heading south; they were taking a break on the side of the road and we met Tyndall and Liz from Alaska. They were both on mountain bikes with lightweight bikepacking style setups. They'd started near home and had ridden south, on mostly dirt roads, over the last 13 months. We all had the goal of making it to the town of Nuevo Tingo that evening and we rode together for parts of the afternoon. After we passed the turnoff to the city Chachapoyas, the road went down to one and a half lanes and the traffic on the already quiet roads dropped off even more. A perfectly paved road followed a river until the turn for Nuevo Tingo where it changed to dirt and climbed 500 feet (150 meters) up to town.

In Nuevo Tingo, we chose to get a hotel for the night. Jesse and I went out to look for something to eat later on and we saw a mountain bike with bikepacking style bags outside a restaurant and met Scott from Washington. He'd been riding for two years from Alaska and was heading south on almost entirely dirt roads. Jesse went back to the hotel to get Tyndall and Liz and we all had dinner together. Scott mentioned hearing about Jesse and I riding for the last week or so, thanks to my unusual recumbent bike, and he had met Tyndall and Liz earlier in his journey.

The next morning was the day we'd planned to go to Kuelap; the ruins of an Inca city on top of a mountain above Nuevo Tingo. We got up at dawn, packed our gear, and arranged a place for our bikes with the hotel owner; then, we left around 7:30 and began looking for a ride to hitchhike to the top. Tyndall, Liz, and Scott, the other cyclists we met the day before, had woken up early and they planned to do the 5.5 mile (9 km) 3,500 foot (1,060 meter) vertical hike. Jesse and I had considered riding our bikes up to the ruins but it was a 20 mile (32 km) climb that gained over 3,000 feet (910 meters) on a poorly maintained dirt road and, since it was an out and back, that seemed to be too much effort to go see some old buildings. We walked to the road going up to the ruins and tried to hitchhike. One vehicle came by right away but the driver wanted four times the price we were told it should cost in town and would not negotiate. About 45 minutes later the first tour bus that we'd seen all morning drove by but it appeared to be full and it didn't stop anyways. About 20 or so minutes later, a truck heading uphill went by and we tried to flag him down but he pretended we didn't exist. After seeing only three vehicles in two hours of waiting, and only one that might have taken us to the top, we gave up on seeing the ruins and walked back into town to get ready to ride.

Scott, the cycle tourist we met the previous evening, had a philosophy that I was inclined to agree with. His idea behind archeological sites was that they really didn't do anything on a satisfactory level. We go to such a site and the train of thought is, "Wow, that's really old and it must have taken a lot of work with the tools they had. Now we have better tools and it isn't so hard. Okay, let's go." The better option is natural wonders such as Gocta Falls. It took a hike to get there but, when we stood at the bottom of the falls and looked up while hearing the roar of the falling water and feeling the wind and spray, it created a sense of awe that an archeological site could never match. Even the cycling through the canyon that we'd been doing for a few days was at least as good, if not far better, as any archeological site I'd ever seen. I'm sure Kuelap would have been an interesting site but it's likely I'd have found the view from the top of the mountain it sits on at least as intriguing as the site itself.

A dirt descent took us out of Nuevo Tingo and back to the main road. The hike up to Kuelap started in that area; we didn't see the other cyclists bicycles around but, we weren't about to walk all the way up the mountain anyways. We climbed along a rolling river gradient and slowly gained elevation. Around noon, we stopped for lunch in one the larger hamlets that dotted the road and had duck served over fried rice with yucca. It'd been a long time since I'd had duck and I thoroughly enjoyed it. A drink called 'chicha', which was made from purple corn, was included with our meal and it tasted similar to kombucha. Like the other countries in South America, there was a TV in the corner with music videos playing at full volume the entire time.

After eating, we rode slowly out of town at a 'digesting lunch' pace; we had a headwind most of the day and rolled into Leymebamba a couple of hours later. We both wanted to get online and went looking for wifi. Once we found a restaurant near the town square that had wifi, we hung around for a couple of hours. Just as we were getting ready to go, it started to rain. We'd considered riding out of town and camping but, with the cooler temperatures up at 7,300 feet (2,200 meters) in elevation, and because of the rain, we chose to split a hotel and soon found one for less than $5 US each. While we were walking around town in search of an after dinner ice cream, we saw Scott, Tyndall, and Liz, the cyclists we'd met a day earlier. They'd been unable to find somewhere safe to keep their bikes for the hike up to Kuelap and had also chosen to skip seeing the ruins too; that information made me feel better about our failed attempt at hitchhiking. We talked with them for a couple of hours before heading back to our hotels.

While I was walking around town looking for breakfast to next morning, I saw Scott at a restaurant and stopped by to talk for a bit. He started riding around 7:00 am. I packed all my gear up and got on the road an hour later. There was a big climb out of Leymebamba and Jesse left later than me. I was feeling good climbing and pushed it right to the limit of what I could sustain for the duration of the climb. It was a little over 18 miles (29 km) to the top and it went up 4,400 feet (1,330 meters) to a pass that was at almost 12,000 feet (3,640 meters). Jesse caught me when I was a bit over a mile (1.6 km) away from the top and then waited for me at the pass. Next, we had an 8,800 foot (2,670 meter) descent over 38 miles (61 km) that we'd been calling "the chasm" ever since we learned about it in Jaen. The entire descent was only interrupted by a couple of flat portions and some small humps that could easily be coasted over. It was possible to do the entire descent without pedaling at all. On the way down, I caught up to Scott and after meeting up with Jesse, all three of us stopped in the small town at the bottom of the descent for lunch. It'd gone from being cold at the top of the descent to being oppressively hot at the bottom. Next was yet another climb and we began our way up the 10,000 foot (3,030 meter) climb.

Jesse and Scott rode ahead while I continued at my own pace; the lighter weight of their setups really showed on the climb and had me wanting to get rid of my excess gear but I had one more mountain climbing expedition planned, so cutting more weight still wasn't an option. I found Jesse and Scott about 9 miles (15 km), and several thousand feet up the mountain; when I met them there, they'd been there for almost an hour. I was exhausted from all the climbing but the idea of dinner and beer was enough motivation to ride for another hour to get to a restaurant in the next village. We all ate dinner and had a beer at a restaurant on the main road, then continued into the village of El Limon and camped on a soccer/basketball court in town; my riding time was just under 8 hours. Dinner at the restaurant hadn't been enough food for Jesse or me, so, we cooked up some sausage and rice to eat before bed. Scott had learned how to survive on less food and didn't eat anything else.

We broke camp after dawn the next morning and began riding the rest of the way up the climb; we'd done a little more than half of it the previous day and, once again, Jesse and Scott were going faster than me but, they stopped to wait a few times. I made it to the top but, I'd run out of water on the way up and I was too tired and dehydrated to care about how long it'd taken me to get there. There was a shop/restaurant at the top where I got some more water. Scott and Jesse had made it up well ahead of me and they began the descent into the next town, called Celendin, while I was still eating and trying to hydrate.

As planned, we met up at the town square in Celendin and got lunch shortly after. Scott wanted to continue riding, and did so, while Jesse and I went to look for somewhere to stay. The fire station a few blocks away had a covered area we could camp under. Jesse and I were hungry again a few hours later and we wanted to find wifi too; we left, stopped by a bakery for some snacks, then began looking for wifi. Every person we asked about wifi directed us to some computer labs. While these places had computers connected to the internet and could be used for a nominal fee, they did not have wifi which almost entirely defeated the purpose of getting online as we wanted to upload photos and call home so, our search for wifi was unsuccessful.

Back at the fire station, a puppy living there had stolen our socks and scattered them around the yard. Thankfully, they weren't damaged, but we weren't so fond of that puppy anymore. We hung around the station for a couple more hours before going to get dinner. While we were out, a woman who taught English stopped to talk to us. Both of us were about 6' 6" (197 cm) and we stood out from the generally shorter Latinos a little bit. We talked for a while and she mentioned a full moon festival was going on that night; one of the events was dancing and there were groups from several countries in South America performing. She said it started at 8:00 pm and admission was free so we decided we'd go. Although it was supposed to start at 8:00 pm, some of the groups were running late and it didn't start till after 9:30. Then, they gave a long speech, presumably apologizing about the delay and, after some pomp and circumstance, the performances finally began. Many of them had obviously put a huge amount of effort into their performances, others, not so much. Jesse and I were falling asleep in our seats around midnight and left early; almost half the audience had left before us.

Jesse was feeling sick the next morning; he decided it was some of the food he had eaten the night before, but I'd eaten the same thing and was feeling fine. While we were getting ready to ride, I was checking over the spoke tension on my wheels and saw that one of the cracks in the rim that had been there for thousands of miles had progressed to the point that one the spoke nipples was bulging out of the rim on my front wheel. It looked like it could quickly transform into a serious situation but, for the moment, the spoke was still pulling tension. There was nowhere in town where I might have been able to find a new rim so all I could do was watch carefully for bumps in the road on the ride to the next city, Cajamarca, and hope I could get it replaced there.

A gradual climb started before we left Celendin. The road rolled gently and worked its way upwards over the course of our first 28 miles (45 km) or so. Jesse was feeling weak and lightheaded for much of the ride so, we took frequent breaks; for once, I was riding faster than him but he was sick so there wasn't any satisfaction in it. We stopped for lunch, a couple of miles away from the top, at a food stand that was serving some excellent roast chicken with potatoes, topped with a mild pepper sauce. While we were stopped, I checked my rim and it didn't seem any worse. Jesse felt stronger after eating and rode without issue for the rest of the day. The climb topped out around 11,600 feet (3,510 meters) and we began a gradual winding descent towards the town of Baños del Inca (Baths of the Inca). There was a hot spring in town that had been built up into a tourist attraction. It resembled nothing more than a resort with a hot swimming pool. Neither of us were interested in the expensive resort and we rode through town and on to Cajamarca. We got to the city with a couple of hours of daylight left and checked at the fire station to see if they'd let us stay there for the night. They turned us down but recommend the station in Baños del Inca, 5 miles (8 km) back the way we had just ridden. We weren't interested in backtracking so we found a cheap hotel in the city.

Apart from a visit to a nearby grocery store, Jesse and I had a lie in and relaxed all morning the next day. I headed out into the city of Cajamarca, a few hours later, in search of a bike shop, to find a replacement for my cracked rim. A quick internet search had shown that there was a shop less than half a mile (800 meters) away. I couldn't believe my luck, they even had a website saying that they aimed to be the region's premier shop for cycle tourists and it sounded too good to be true. I walked a few blocks and right up to the address I had but it wasn't there. It'd either closed down or moved away some time ago; it was too good to be true. I asked a mototaxi driver if there was a bicycle shop nearby and he said there was a shop two blocks away, perhaps I had the wrong address. I walked over and found what appeared to be a bicycle shop; by appeared I mean there was an open door with several bicycles inside in varying states of neglect. I tried pointing and asking about one of the rims on the pile of bicycles nearby. They didn't have any but said there was a shop that should have some near the city center. I had my doubts about the existence of said shop but a feeling of necessity took over and I started walking. The area around the city center was completely packed with people as school had just gotten out and walking on the sidewalk was like walking up a river of humanity. I got to a more open area and asked a policeman about the shop, he said it was only three blocks away. I followed his directions and found nothing. I walked a clover leaf pattern around the surrounding area to make sure I hadn't mistranslated his directions and was still unsuccessful so, I asked a few different people about the shop; some said it wasn't there and others said it was closed. It was around 2:00 pm so I was pretty sure it wasn't closed for lunch and took it to mean it was closed permanently; I gave up and headed back to the hotel. Supposedly, it's part of the culture of some countries to never admit that you don't know something when asked; that would explain the problems I had with directions to a bicycle shop in Zumba, Ecuador, and in Celendin, Peru.

Jesse had had a much more productive afternoon; he'd been lying in bed, watching movies, for the few hours that I was out on my wild goose chase. I tried searching the internet for a bike shop again but couldn't find anything else that suggested an open bicycle shop in the city. I looked over my damaged wheel; the cracked area didn't seem to have progressed at all and the spoke was still under tension; a good sign. Since I was unable to find anything to replace it, and taking a bus to another city and back would probably take several days, I'd have to continue riding on it and avoid putting any more stress than necessary on it.

I lazed the rest of the afternoon away; then Jesse and I went out for dinner. We didn't have a specific destination in mind when we set out walking and the restaurant we chose happened to have cuy (barbecued guinea pig, a popular local food in Peru) for a decent price and I gave it a try. The taste vaguely resembled pork, perhaps that's where the name came from. It wasn't bad but; it wasn't something I'd go out of my way to get either, another checkmark on the South American bucket list.

CHAPTER 16

Day 174, July 24, 2016

Cajabamba, Peru

After Cajamarca, we had a quiet few days through the mountains of Peru and police stations were proving very hospitable. We'd stayed with the police, or at some other government building, for the last few nights and, for two of those nights, we'd had actual beds to sleep in as opposed to floor space indoors or an area outside.

While we were riding through a small town, there was a sign saying the road was closed due to a bridge being out. The detour would have added a significant amount of distance so we gave the closed road a try. We pedaled uphill for another mile (1.6 km) and then we were faced with the lack of a bridge over a stream. Jesse took the shorter, more difficult path while I chose to backtrack about 50 yards (45 meters) to an easier path. It took me about 15 minutes of guiding my bike slowly down to the stream before carefully stepping across, then easing my bike through the shallow water, after which, I pushed and shoved my bike slowly up the other side. Back on the road, I started looking for Jesse. He was stuck with his bike on top of an 8 foot (2.4 meter) drop and trying to figure out how to get his bike down so I gave him a hand.

It was lunch time when we climbed a little farther and into another mountain village. There was a group of people gathered around a few houses and, when I asked about the location of a restaurant in town, they invited us to eat with them. We were given a hearty lamb and rice soup with a large bowl of steamed maize. Later, a woman passed us a giant basket of 'cuy', barbecued guinea pig. While we were eating, a man came by and offered us some homebrewed 'chicha', a purple corn drink. I tried some and the taste was slightly sweet with about the same alcohol content as wine. We were given several refills and it soon turned into the "get-the-foreigners-drunk game". After several cups of chicha, we were invited into the house for beer and more chicha. The room had a low ceiling; Jesse and I nearly had to bend over double to get to our seats. Our hosts began drinking in the Peruvian style of one glass passed around the table with a bottle of beer and we followed suit while talking with everyone in Spanish. Several beers were passed around the table and consumed; Jesse and I decided we'd better leave soon, if we were going to leave at all, before we got too drunk to ride. We excused ourselves and gave our thanks before getting back on the road.

Back on our bikes we climbed even more slowly and wobbled more than usual because of the food and alcohol. The scenery was incredible and the riding was so much fun for some reason. Thankfully, we were close to the top of the climb and soon we were descending the other side. After passing a lake, we heard some music playing nearby and, attracted by the sound, went to investigate. There was a concert going on and, as soon as we got close, somebody got excited about seeing foreigners on bicycles and escorted us past the long line of locals who were probably paying to get in and into the concert grounds, then showed us a place we could sit on the grass. We were still too drunk to ask for somewhere to stay at the next town so we stayed for a while and waited to sober up while we listened to the concert, a blend of traditional Peruvian music and pop. Once we were feeling pretty sober, we rode to a town called Huamachuco. That evening, we asked a police station about somewhere to sleep and one of the officers hopped in a truck and escorted us to an empty conference hall where we could spend the night.

One thing Peru didn't have much of is actual grocery stores; since entering the country we had been to two: one in Jaen and one in Cajamarca. Most of our shopping was being done in 'tiendas', small and usually poorly stocked mini-marts. More often than not, the items they sold did not have marked prices and, since haggling for better prices is not part of the culture of most of South America, we were at the whim of the shopkeepers and usually had to pay higher prices for being of Caucasian descent or better known as 'gringos'. Even though I was pretty tan by then, Jesse was paler with sun bleached hair, and the local population frequently felt it was obligatory to shout "gringo" at us whenever we cycled by.

Our route took an interesting turn the next day; the main road through the area went on a circuitous route through the mountains with a huge amount of climbing and descending. A few miles (~5 km) outside of Huamachuco, there was a dirt road heading south that would save an entire day of riding through the mountains. Not only was it shorter, there was also much less climbing as far as we could tell. When we got to said road, it appeared to be well maintained; appearances can be deceiving so, we planned on it taking all day to get through. There were few cars, as well suits a dirt road, and with my front rim still being questionable due to the many cracks around the spoke holes, I took it slow and chose my line carefully. The road climbed steadily as we had hoped but, not as expected from the elevation profile on my, often wrong, GPS, and topped out around 12,000 feet (3,640 meters) above sea level. There was a small mining town near the top of the climb and a restaurant appeared about the time we were thinking of eating lunch. We ate the common Peruvian meal of pan fried chicken, served on rice, with lentils, then continued on our way.

A few sections of washboard or sand made progress more difficult but, we made it over the top and began descending the other side. Once again, I had to pick my way down the mountain going little more than 12 mph (20 km/h) thanks to my damaged rim and lack of control on the loose and rough terrain while Jesse flew down the road. It was a process that I found tedious and frustrating but it could have been fun if I was riding a normal upright bicycle, one of the disadvantages of riding a recumbent; that, and the extra attention from its unusual design had me wishing I could switch to a normal bike.

We made it to the town of Cachicadan at a reasonable hour. Our mission of taking a more direct route had been successful and we inquired at the police station about somewhere to camp. The officer in charge directed us to the municipal building and sent an escort with us to explain our situation. An official with a high and mighty air about himself wrote a note and sent someone with us to a hotel with a large field behind it. Our messenger explained the situation to the hotelier and they had us set up camp behind the hotel, which was awkward because we were staying for free outside a hotel, but by then it was dark and there wasn't much we could do about it.

The next morning, we left the back of the hotel around 9:00 am, expecting to get to a paved road just outside town but, there was no pavement; the road continued to be dirt. Surely it would become paved through the next town a few miles away, but it didn't. A dirt climb continued for what felt like a very long time; I rattled up the road in a manner similar to a grocery store cart, even after I lowered my tire pressure. The return from the amount of effort I was exerting was minimal and I quickly grew frustrated. I met Jesse at the top of the climb and, after a short break, we began descending into Angasmarca. The descent brought no respite from my frustration. When we stopped for lunch in Angasmarca, I had reached the point of plotting mass murder. I thought it through a little more before I came to the conclusion that such a criminal conviction would create a serious problem in my travel plans so, I listened to some music instead. The music helped considerably and, by the time I was over that climb and down the other side, I was almost in a good mood. Jesse had bombed down the descent and I met him at the bottom of the next climb where he told me he'd caught a few feet (~1 meter) of air off the edge of a drainage ditch. After another snack break, we began our way up; this climb was steeper and sandy in some places. I made it about 100 yards (90 meters) before my back tire began to slide out. I did all I could to try to recover from the slide but it didn't work and I was lying in the dirt before I could catch myself; the fall didn't help my mood; I started pushing, there wasn't really any other option at that point. Once I got to a less sandy part, I was able to ride again. Most of the straight sections of the road were rideable but, many of the turns were entirely sand where my back tire would slip and I'd be pushing again. I found Jesse taking a nap in the shade at a small town near the top. He woke up soon after I arrived and was ready to get going right when he got up so I didn't get much of a break. The road climbed a few hundred feet (~100 meters) out of the town and, once again, I met Jesse at the top. A descent into the village of Mollebamba followed, after a few more miles of cycling, and we were still on dirt roads. The municipal building in the village had a small room they weren't using which we spent the night in. We were on almost entirely dirt roads that day; the only paved sections were through the few small towns and, consequently, my average speed for the day was about 6 mph (10 km/h)

After a short climb out of Mollebamba the next morning, we began descending on dirt roads. Right when we got to the next town, Mollepata, the road changed to pavement. It seemed too good to be true; I expected it to go back to dirt at the opposite side of town but it didn't; the road was paved. We rode a few miles downhill on the paved road, expecting it to go back to dirt at any second. Eventually, we were convinced that it was going to stay paved and we pumped up our tires back to normal levels in an effort to reduce rolling resistance on the smooth surface.

The view from the top of the next descent was incredible; the road snaked its way down a steep canyon in a series of countless switchbacks before working its way back up the other side of the canyon in a similar manner. Actually, there were about 52 switchbacks, so, not quite countless but, that's a lot of switchbacks. It was unlike any road I had ever seen in person and the kind of road I'd only dreamed of riding. Well, there I was doing the ride of my dreams and the experience was surreal. After a short ride along the river at the bottom of the canyon, the road began to climb up the other side. Not quite as cool as descending but, still amazing in its own way. The last few switchbacks were getting pretty steep but, then the grade became much shallower and the road contoured the side of the mountain while still working its way upwards.

In one of the small villages along the road, there was a woman soliciting business outside a small restaurant. She shouted that we could get lunch there as we passed by and, being hungry, we stopped to see what she had: barley soup and a potato and fish stew served with rice. We asked how much and she said it would be two Peruvian Soles or the equivalent of about $0.60 US. Of course we stopped. This was the record for the cheapest meal of the trip and one that was not likely to be broken any time soon. It was a good meal and a pleasant change from the constant barrage of chicken and rice that must be the most popular meal in Peru. We continued to climb, slowly, after lunch and another hour of riding brought us into Pallasca. It was a small town and we stopped to try to resupply after which we planned to continue riding. Past Pallasca, the road went back down to the same river that we had crossed earlier by a different route and we didn't expect to see any shops for a while.

The only kind of store in Pallasca was the small tiendas. We shopped around at the five different ones that we could find in the town square and the best we could come up with was cookies. That was enough for me to snack on throughout the day but, Jesse wanted to try to find something more substantial. At the police station, we asked about a market and they said the town only has one on Sunday. While talking with the police, they offered use of their showers and a place to stay for the night so we stopped earlier than planned. Also, we were hopeful we'd be able to find a decent breakfast in the morning before heading through the probably empty river canyon.

After riding a few blocks in the morning, we began descending out of Pallasca. None of the restaurants had opened that morning so we had cookies for breakfast. At the top was a spectacular view of the canyon we'd be riding through. The descent was paved, though it was steep and potholed. It became all the more treacherous when it would suddenly, and without warning, change to dirt, or be covered in gravel, through the sharp hairpin turns; to fall off the road could mean plummeting thousands of feet to the river below. The road changed to gravel through a deforested area that had subsequently become heavily eroded. The dirt sections were broken up by a few short, but very steep, climbs. Eventually, we made it to the bottom of the canyon after descending almost a vertical mile (1.6 km) from where we'd started the day in Pallasca. The canyon was incredible; multicolored walls rose steeply for thousands of feet on both sides while the road wound next to the river at the bottom. Sections of the canyon were as narrow as 50 feet (15 meters) across and some of the surrounding mountains soared over three vertical miles (4.8 km) above us.

We fought a strong headwind all morning until the road we were on met up with the main highway around mile 50 (km 80). The road turned inland and the wind we had been fighting all morning now aided our progress up the river gradient and back towards the mountains. Now we were in Cañon del Pato or Canyon of The Duck. Waterfalls cascaded off the sides of the canyon and across the road in some places. We didn't have a particular goal in mind and we just kept riding up the river, in awe of the canyon. Eventually, we stopped for a snack and discussed our options. We were both low on food and, although we did have enough to cook dinner, we would have very little food left for the next morning. Camping along the river was not ideal either because of a large population of biting sand flies; we chose to ride to Yurcamarca, the next town that was big enough to likely have some kind of services.

The incredible riding continued and, thanks to the tail-wind, we moved along fairly quickly. The grade kicked up to about 5% for last few miles into Yurcamarca and we arrived just as the sun was disappearing behind the walls of the canyon. We were both almost completely out of water and food that didn't need to be cooked; Jesse would call it, "a well-planned day" because we didn't carry much more weight in food and water than absolutely necessary. After a couple of ice creams, we were feeling much better so, we asked about camping at the same shop and they said that cyclists often slept under the covered area in the town square. Dinner was had at a street food stand serving fried chicken and fries, and then we waited around a while before setting up camp in an elevated gazebo sort of place in the town square, though not before posing for photos with several different people.

We rode down the quick descent out of Yurcamarca, back down to the river, then the road continued with yesterday's upriver grade. The first 9 miles (14 km) passed quickly and we stopped in Huallanca, a small town built around a hydroelectric plant, for a snack break. Past Huallanca, the road kicked up to a significant climb for about 5 miles (8 km) to get above the dam in the river and then wound its way along a steep canyon wall with many tunnels. We found out later that there were approximately 35 tunnels along that stretch of road. Most of them were less than 100 yards (90 meters), but some of them were long enough we should have gotten our lights out though we didn't realize that until it was too late.

On the way up, we met another cycle tourist heading the opposite direction; his name escapes me but, he was from Belgium and was also heading towards Ushuaia; after a quick chat, we were on our way again. A few more miles up the road, we caught up to some walkers: Regis and Jerome, both from France. Regis had been walking for over two years and had started in Haiti, then flown to Cuba, and later flown again and had walked through Mexico and Central America before flying to Colombia. He had an unbroken line of walking from Medellin, Colombia to where we met him. Jerome had met Regis in Trujillo, a coastal city in Peru, and was walking with him to Cusco before flying home. Both of them were traveling incredibly light; Regis said his pack weighed less than 25 lb (11 kg) without food or water. I was somewhat jealous of how little weight they were carrying but, neither of them had a tent. They'd been staying in places similar to those that Jesse and I had been. Darkness falls quickly for walkers and they had to continue after a few minutes chat.

Around mile 23 (km 37) that day, the canyon we were riding through became a valley and the grade leveled out. After one last climb, into the city of Caraz, we had a rare treat for Peru... a grocery store! It may seem odd to become excited about a grocery store but, after being overcharged in the poorly stocked mini-mart/tienda shops for weeks on end, a grocery store was a welcome change. It wasn't even a very good grocery store but, everything had marked prices, unlike the tiendas where we had to ask the price of every individual item while being watched like a hawk by the owner of a 150 square foot (16 square meter) shop. After the reveling in the delights of the grocery store, we began looking for somewhere to stay at the fire station; the person we talked to really wanted to let us stay there, and even showed us where we could stay, before we were turned away by his boss. We checked a few churches but, we couldn't find anyone to talk to. There were a few large vacant lots that could have worked for urban camping but, none that we felt confident about. All the cheap hotels were booked because of a patriotic holiday going on or they were just too expensive. We happened upon a guide shop, specializing in hiking tours through the nearby mountains, and went in to see if Jesse could buy a tent for our upcoming days in the high mountains. They didn't have anything for sale but they directed us to another cheap hotel that we chose to stay in for the night.

We were just walking out of the hotel to find dinner when we saw the French walkers we had met earlier in the day. They had similar luck trying to find a place to stay but, had met a priest in charge of one of the churches who had ended up paying for their stay at the same hotel we were in. We waited for them to change and drop off their packs before we all went out to dinner together. Neither of the walkers had blogs nor kept journals. Regis believed, and rightly so, that it is incredibly difficult to impossible to share even a small part of such a journey and that, with any attempt at writing, even the best authors can only produce the faintest idea of the kind of experiences that occur while traveling.

After getting dinner, we found a shop that sold beer, then walked around town with our drinks. There was some kind of a comedy show going on at the footsteps of a cathedral. Even though I couldn't understand everything that was said, there was some acting thrown in too. What I could understand was that it was a very vulgar performance. The location on the steps of the church made it seem sacrilegious but, almost everyone seemed to be enjoying it; especially Jerome; he hadn't adjusted to the rigors of exercising all day yet and his liver was absorbing the alcohol so quickly that he got drunk off of one large beer. The beers had required a significant deposit on the glass bottles and we walked back to the shop to get the money back in exchange for returning the bottles.

The next morning, we made a stop by an ATM and a visit to the grocery store, just because. About 9 miles (14 km) of a gentle incline brought us to Yungay where we turned our wheels towards the mountains. The road changed to dirt, just outside town, and was likely one of the busiest roads we'd ridden on in Peru. Jesse rode ahead and I worked my way slowly up the mountain while choking on exhaust fumes and dust from the many vehicles on their way up and down the dirt road. I was pedaling along the dirt road, trying to pick my way through on the smoothest line, when the road burst out of the trees. At first, there seemed to be some very straight edged clouds just above the forest ahead but then I realized they were mountains covered in glaciers and I stopped in my tracks, stunned by their beauty. About half way up the climb, I caught up to a couple of cyclists from Holland; they were heading north and planned to take some of the backroads on the other side of the mountains. We talked for a few minutes until they were ready to start riding and then rode together for a while. They were going slower than I wanted to and I rode ahead after a while. Jesse had already passed them several minutes before.

Jesse was waiting at the entrance to Huascaran National Park and, after we paid the entry fee, we continued the climb. The road surface deteriorated to exposed rock after entering the park and made for slower going. Jesse rode ahead again and, when I reached the first of the two lakes, it already felt like it was worth the effort that it took to do the climb. Mountains covered in ice surrounded the bright blue waters of the lakes. There was one unfortunate drawback; all the cars going up the road had come to see the lakes as well and a sea of humanity was crowded near the first lake. After taking a few pictures, I made my way towards the second lake. Right away, the amount of people dropped off and I was soon cycling along a quiet road. The second lake was incredibly beautiful as well and I met Jesse waiting across the road from a small waterfall. We'd planned on camping on the shores of the lake and Jesse had determined that this spot was our best option. After rolling our bikes down into the trees, we quickly changed out of our sweaty clothes; the sun was beginning to dip behind the mountains and the temperature was dropping rapidly from the high elevation. Our camp on the lake sat at about 12,500 feet (3,790 meters) in elevation. After cooking and eating dinner, we admired the alpenglow from the sunset and, later in the evening, the stars before we went to bed.

Explosive diarrhea hit me suddenly in the middle of the night and I barely made it outside my tent before my bowels began to vacate. Several more trips to the bushes were made through the course of the night. The illness, coupled with the exceptionally dry air, left me weak and dehydrated by the time morning came; I doubted my ability to make the rest of the climb over a high pass and I seriously considered heading back down the mountain to rest for a couple of days before continuing on. Jesse was patient and considerate of my situation so, I did my best to hydrate, then tried to eat something while I rested. A couple of hours later, I was feeling much better and, although I was still feeling weak, I decided I'd pace myself a little slower than usual up the climb and we got going at a relatively normal hour.

The views from the road continued to be incredible and they distracted me from the effort of pedaling up a dirt road at high elevation. After an hour and a half of riding, we caught up to the Dutch cyclists we'd met the previous afternoon; they had also camped by the lake but had started earlier than us and we rode with them for a while. Even though the surface of the road was bad enough that I was doing quite a bit of pushing, I was still walking faster than they were riding.

The rough and unpaved road turned into a series of steep hairpin turns that were nearly stacked on top of each other and I grew progressively weaker with the increasing elevation; I had to walk my bike most of the way up. I met Jesse, waiting at one of the overlooks, and we waited for a while for the Dutch cyclists, who we'd begun referring to as "the Dutch brothers", to catch up to us. After resting for a few more minutes, I started pushing again while Jesse rode ahead. There were a few sections closer to the top that were not as rough and I was able to ride much of the remaining distance to the top. Jesse was waiting at the 15,400 foot (4,670 meter) pass; it had taken me several hours of riding and pushing to get there. The pass was cut out of the rock and the road through a notch that was narrow enough that I could almost touch both sides of it if I stood in the middle with my arms spread out. If we looked carefully off the edge of the road, we could just see the Dutch brothers working their way up, several switchbacks down. We considered waiting for them to join us but it didn't take long for us to start getting cold so, we began the descent without them.

Going down, the road was just as rough as going up had been; I worked my way down slowly, trying to minimize the stress on my still cracked front rim, while Jesse took off ahead. I met up with him again farther down the descent and we raced against the remaining daylight to get to the town of Yanama in hopes of finding somewhere to stay there. The sun had set and darkness was falling when we rode into the small town. When we asked at the police station, about somewhere to camp, they went next door and unlocked the municipal building and said we could stay in an auditorium room for the night. We went out for dinner; there was a small restaurant a couple of blocks away. All they had was chicken and fries but, it was probably the best chicken in the world and you'll just have to trust me on this one.

Our plan for the next day was to ride to the town of Chacas. There were two ways to get there from Yanama and both of them were hilly, though one took more main roads while the other was mostly side roads. The side road was shorter and, after a discussion with the police, we found both ways were mostly dirt and thus chose the shorter road. The climbing started right away out of Yanama; the road was indeed dirt but in decent condition and I only had to walk a few sandy sections. It took more than a couple of hours to get up the 2,400 foot (727 meter) climb and we had spectacular views of ice capped mountains most of the way up.

A rolling descent wound its way through farmlands with sheep, cattle, and pigs, grazing all around. The road was in decent condition most of the way, though it had several very rough sections where my progress would slow almost to a halt. At the end of the dirt descent, we met up with a main road and our last 7 miles (12 km) into the town of Chacas were paved. The paved road climbed inconsistently up a river canyon and, after a crossing a bridge to the opposite side of a river, the final few miles of climbing into town began. Jesse had found an internet connection in Yanama the night before and was able to do some last minute research on Chacas. He found from another cyclist's blog that there was a group of Italian missionaries/woodworkers called 'the Don Busco' who had hosted that cyclist. We found the place he mentioned near the town square and asked about somewhere to camp for the night. They said they had a place for us to stay and showed us around the cooperative. There was some exceptionally impressive woodwork going on, all of it was completely hand-made with extraordinary detail and every piece of the wood-work on the building was covered in ornate designs. After a short tour of the compound, we headed over to the main building and, after parking our bikes, were shown to a room with bunk beds and a hot shower and then were told that dinner would be at 7:30 pm.

We had time to shower and rest for a while before we headed down to dinner. Dinner was a relaxed affair; although we showed up a few minutes early, it didn't actually start till almost 8:00 pm. It was worth the wait; we feasted on some excellent lasagna that was followed by oven fried potatoes with collard greens. After dinner, we stayed around and talked with our hosts for a while and later they brought out some champagne and invited us to have a drink with them too. There were a couple of other travelers there, mostly Italians, who'd come to volunteer at the mission for a couple of months. Even though we'd arrived only a couple of hours earlier, they welcomed us to stay as long as we liked, even for months if we so desired and would help out; they treated us like family.

The collective we'd spent the night with invited us to breakfast as well. It was a simple breakfast: bread and jam served with coffee, but very much appreciated. My front tire was flat when I got to my bike but, I'd noticed a slow leak the previous evening and expected as much. A significant amount of time was spent searching for the leak without result. Dunking the tube in a bucket of water revealed no holes in the tube but, there was a slow leak from the seal on the valve. I used some chain lube to try to fix the seal before pumping it back up and it lasted the rest of the day. After a stop by a tienda to get food for the next couple of days, we finally got out of Chacas at almost 10:45. The road descended gently out of town and down the river we had been following yesterday before returning to the upriver grade; 7-8 miles (11-13 km) in, the grade increased and we began a fairly constant climb towards Punta Olimpica, another high pass through the mountains.

Glaciers on the mountains came into view after a couple of hours of climbing and still the road continued to go higher in a series of switchbacks that passed by several pristinely blue lakes. Nearing the tunnel through the pass at the top, we saw a storm shelter about a quarter mile (400 meters) away from the road and, when we got to the trail to the shelter, we checked it out, then choose to stay for the night. We hauled our bikes up the trail to the small stone hut and collected water from a nearby lake and some dead wood for a fire later. After dinner, the colors of the sunset seemed to set the glaciers on fire; we retreated to the shelter as it got dark and built an actual fire, then watched the flames and waited for it to burn out before going to bed on our air mattresses that were set up on the rough stone floor.

The morning was freezing at 15,300 feet (4,640 meets) in elevation and made for a later start. We waited until the sun was shining on us over the icy mountaintops before walking back down the narrow trail with our bikes. After a mile (1.6 km) on pavement, we took the dirt turnoff for the old road that goes over the pass as opposed to going through the tunnel. The road was rideable at first but a few landslides had blocked several portions of the road farther on and it became more apparent that the road had been given up on where maintenance was concerned. It was bad enough in some sections that Jesse had to push his bike too, a rare situation. I worked my way up the road as best I could and met Jesse just over the top of the pass that sat at 16,174 feet (4,901 meters) above sea level and was an even narrower notch for the road to go through the mountains than the one we'd cycled through a couple of days earlier.

The dirt road going down the other side was not any better maintained, but the sight of the mountains was jaw dropping. We stood a vertical mile (1.6 km) above a narrow grassy valley that was surrounded by peaks in excess of 20,000 feet (6,060 meters) tall. Sections of the road had fallen away from landslides and required some careful pushing to navigate them safely. Soon, we reached the paved road on the other side of the tunnel and began the long descent. My cracked front rim had continued in its progression of slowly falling apart and it'd deteriorated enough from the bad roads that it was causing my bike to shake dangerously above 20 mph (32 km/h); I tried dropping the tire pressure to about 20 psi and it helped some. During the descent, I saw and stopped to talk to Scott, the bikepacker we'd met on the road a few weeks ago; he'd been around Huaraz for the last 5 days and was doing a day ride up Punta Olmpica. I found Jesse waiting for me at the edge of the national park. Jesse went on ahead while I took it a bit slower to try to keep my front wheel in one piece. We made a stop for lunch at a small roadside restaurant, most of the way down the mountain, and eventually we were back on the main road. At the bottom of the 8,000 foot (2,420 meter) descent, the temperature was almost hot compared to what it had been near the top.

A few miles after our lunch break and with only 20 miles (32 km) to go to the city of Huaraz, Jesse got a flat tire, then I started having trouble with my rear brake and was unable to get it to stop rubbing. It took longer than expected to get to the city but, we made it under our own power. Huaraz had a decent bike shop that was one of our first stops in the city. Lucky for me, they had a heavy duty rim on hand that was the correct size and spoke count to replace the one I had that was quickly becoming dangerous to ride on. I bought it; along with some much needed chain lube. There was a fire station less than a block away from the bike shop and, after asking, we had a place to stay for the night.

CHAPTER 17

Day 185, August 4, 2016

Huaraz, Peru

I was up at 2:30 am; the water had been turned off in the fire station last night and I ran out of water to drink; I was dehydrated and went to get some water and begin filtering it, then waited until I'd had enough to drink. Without success, I tried to go back to sleep afterwards and lay in bed for a long while; eventually, I decided I'd rebuild my front wheel with the new rim that I bought when we arrived in the city a day earlier, then go back to bed. After taking the old rim off and replacing it with the new one, then truing the wheel to an acceptable standard, it'd been over three hours and the sun had risen. There was no way I was going to fall asleep again so, I started fixing my brakes; they'd been rubbing on our ride into Huaraz the previous afternoon and I hadn't been able to fix them then. The pads were worn out again and I replaced them with some spares and got them properly adjusted. By that time, it was around 7:30 and I'd already finished my most dreaded tasks even though the day had just begun. Jesse was up by then and we left the fire station an hour later in search of a hotel where we could take a rest day. We checked at least ten different hotels before settling on one that was a bit more than we wanted to pay but, it had wifi and we were growing tired of looking. I spent what little was left of the morning, and much of the afternoon, accomplishing various tasks that I had been neglecting for some time, mostly laundry and my journal. As usual, the rest day ended up being busier than a riding day. Finally done with my most necessary tasks, I rested for the remainder of the day.

Just outside of Huaraz the next day, I had a close call with a driver who was driving recklessly; after passing me aggressively, he quickly pulled off the road and onto the shoulder right in front of me. I had to brake and swerve to avoid having my front end hit by the back of his vehicle. I was furious at the dangerous situation he'd put me in to save a few seconds and started telling him how I felt about it very loudly. Even if he couldn't understand what I was saying, his friends whom he had pulled off the road to meet seemed impressed by the volume and intensity with which I was voicing my opinion on being cut off. The driver seemed cowed as well and I was confident that I'd gotten my point across, in spite of the language barrier. There wasn't much else that could be done about it.

Jesse took off ahead and I climbed along a rolling river grade out of Huaraz. My bike was riding wonderfully smooth with the new rim. Farther along the narrow river valley we were in opened up to a wide expanse of rolling grassland. I found Jesse taking a nap on a bench, in a small park on the side of the road; he'd been nauseous yesterday and hadn't eaten much. He was feeling weak and unsure he would be able to ride much farther so, I waited with him until he was feeling strong enough to continue. Jesse rode along with me at my pace and was still having some trouble keeping up so, I slowed down to help keep him from pushing it too hard. Jesse had a couple of instances of coming close to passing out while riding and we camped short of our goal for the day so he could rest. We pushed our bikes off the road by a stream and soon saw a spot where we could stay the night. Jesse rested while I read a book the remainder of the afternoon. He was feeling better later in the evening, well enough to cook and eat dinner; a good sign since he'd had no appetite entirely earlier in the day. Our camp was miles away from the nearest town and the Milky Way was easily visible across the night sky once it got dark.

Jesse was feeling much better the next morning. His appetite had returned and he was no longer having dizzy spells. We'd camped at 12,500 feet (3,890 meters) in elevation; the altitude had likely played a significant factor in his illness. The road continued to climb gradually to the next small town before peaking at 13,500 feet (4,090 meters) and veering towards the coast. The next section of our ride was what we had been referring to as 'the descent', the road turned west and was downhill most of the way to the coast 80 miles (130 km) away. By the time we stopped for lunch, we'd ridden 65 miles (104 km) and my average speed was above 18 mph (29 km/h), even with the continuous headwind, and we still weren't at the bottom. It was getting hot again and the terrain had changed from mountainous grasslands to desert. Farmers had laid out giant tarps on the hills that were covered with peppers drying in the sun. The peppers were separated by color and made a patchwork pattern over many of the surrounding hills.

The road did level out eventually but, by then we'd descended nearly 2.5 vertical miles (4 km), almost all the way down to sea level. A strong headwind slowed our progress but, we pressed on and passed by numerous sugar cane fields. The road we were on met up with the Pan-American Highway right by the coast; we rode on it briefly for the first time since before Loja, Ecuador before turning off towards a town called 'Paramonga'. The town was run down: the streets were dirt except for the main roads and buildings were built of concrete and had laundry hanging from most every window. We checked the fire station but, they said they'd have to get permission for us to stay there from their boss and they didn't have a phone. It was a strange excuse considering almost everyone in South America had cell phones but if they didn't want to help us, that was their choice. The police station responded in a similar manner but, said we could camp in the town square. It was a weekend and people were everywhere in the town square. In addition to that, it seemed the kind of place where a robbery could happen in the blink of an eye; instead, we opted for a cheap hotel.

We spent much of the following morning online, trying to arrange a place to stay in Lima. Because of our efforts, we didn't get on the road until almost noon. A headwind picked up after a couple of hours of riding and slowed our progress on the flat to rolling roads. Farms and run down housing developments, along with the occasional few miles of sandy desert looking terrain, reminded me of the Mojave Desert in California, although without the oppressive heat. The temperature was cooler, high 50s to low 60s Fahrenheit (14-17 C), and actually dropped off enough in the afternoon that we stopped to put our jackets on; strangely, this was cooler than most of our recent days in the high mountains had been. In Huacho, we talked to the fire station about somewhere to stay; they were very generous and had a room with a couple of beds they let us use and even gave us toast and tea later in the evening.

Jesse and I, especially me, had a craving for bacon cheeseburgers. Unfortunately, the quality of cheeseburgers in Latin America was severely lacking compared to those found in the US. Latin American burgers generally had very little meat and an average amount of bun. Toppings were standard: lettuce, tomato, and onion, plus ketchup, mustard, and mayonnaise; but, the lack came from the deficit in meat. The patties were thin with minimal flavor and often dry and the bacon was similarly flimsy and paper thin with a taste that matched the physical description. The only burger place we could find in Huacho was called 'Fancydelicious.' It was trying to be like a classic American burger joint and it had signs in English scattered along the walls with American classic rock music floating from a couple of tiny and tinny-sounding speakers Some of the signs were rather strange including a picture of a burger with default text that read "simple text simple text, your text here your text here." Many such signs were scattered around; the actual meaning was apparently lost in translation by the mostly non-English speaking populace. The burgers left much to be desired; I'd be surprised if the dry and tasteless patty pushed 1/10th of a pound (45 grams) and it had a couple of strips of flimsy bacon topped with an inordinate amount of vegetables. It was a bacon cheeseburger nonetheless but, it only served to increase my resolve to cook my own bacon cheeseburgers in the true American style during our upcoming couple of days off in Lima.

Immediately after leaving the city the next day, the terrain changed to empty desert with the occasional shanty town scattered around at random. Because of another late start, the wind had picked up and we were fighting a headwind again. The road rolled gently through the desert, a barren wasteland compared to the mountains we'd been pedaling through only a few days prior. It was monotonous riding and time slowed to a crawl. Whenever we stopped for a break, we were attacked by a cloud of flies. The size of the rollers increased to being as much as 600 feet tall (180 meters) as the afternoon dragged on. We rode into Chancay, worn out and covered in dust, then checked at a fire station about somewhere to stay but, rather oddly, we were unable to find anyone at the station. The police station was the next stop, they said it would be unsafe to camp and recommended a hotel or checking the municipal building. We opted for the municipal building and, after some discussion, they said they had a spot for us at a sports stadium. They sent someone ahead of us and, after we pedaled our way over, we were shown to a sort of locker room area that was used by the employees of the stadium. After leaving our bikes inside, we walked towards the municipal building and the town square to find something to eat. There was a 'pollo a la brasa' or 'rotisserie chicken restaurant'; it was a good meal, though not the best chicken we've had, that prize goes to that little restaurant in Yanama. We walked to a bakery after dinner and I spent a little more than $1 on 36 bread rolls and I ate about half of them before bed. Although the city was deemed unsafe by the policeman we talked to, it didn't seem any worse than the other South American cities we'd been to.

One of the stipulations of staying at the stadium was that we had to vacate the building by 6:00 am; we were up at 5:00 and I ate the remaining 15 or so rolls that I'd bought the previous day as I packed up my gear and we were successful in leaving the building by the appointed time but, we stayed around the grounds a while longer to finish eating and use the bathroom. That morning was the earliest start time Jesse and I had managed in our months of riding together, a little before seven am. There was a turnoff near a small town and the road wound along the coast. It was a strange road, cut out of giant sand dunes in a manner that seemed it might slide the few hundred feet down into the ocean at any second. After following the ocean for several miles, the road turned inland and meandered past a military base; near the base was another rundown town that could have passed for a post-apocalyptic movie set and it had a strong scent of urine that lasted through the entire town.

The road into Lima was crowded with vehicles but, we were moving along quickly because of the vacuum created by the passing cars and trucks. We cruised along at nearly 20 mph (32 km/h) while dodging the buses that were continually pulling off the road to pick up more passengers, and the cars, that would swerve around them with horns blaring. Once we were well within city limits, we took an extensively potholed side street that was nearly devoid of traffic, to take us closer to our destination. Farther in still, there was a segregated bike path in the middle of the road that we followed while slaloming walkers that were completely oblivious to anything going on around them, including the fact that there was a designated walking path not 10 feet (3 meters) away that ran parallel to the cycle path.

Miraculously, we arrived intact at 'Specialized Peru'; Jesse was actually sponsored by Specialized and they were supposed to have sent him a new bicycle to replace the broken, but repaired, frame he'd been riding. The bike wasn't there and they hadn't heard that it was supposed to be there either. Jesse had a back and forth, by email, with Specialized that lasted all afternoon and ended with them saying they'd send him a new bike with two day shipping.

We had a late afternoon lunch stop at a burger place where they served an amazing bacon cheeseburger and I was happy. Once my craving was satisfied, we went by to pick up Jesse's new phone from some distant contact he had in Lima, then went back to the bike shop where I bought some new tires, Specialized Hemispheres. I'd grown tired of the slow rolling, Schwalbe Marathon tires that were, for some reason, exceptionally popular among cycle tourists even though I'd had two of them fail on me since I started. My front tire also had a bald spot from where it'd been strapped onto the back of my bike for many thousands of miles and I figured I was due for replacements anyways. The rear tire was still in decent condition and I kept it as a spare. It was almost dark when we headed back the direction we'd entered the city from for about 5 miles (8 km) to a church seminary that I'd been put in contact with through a friend back home. The pastor at the seminary had not received the email my contact had sent and we were almost turned away but, we were saved by the bell when the pastor went back to check his inbox for said email; upon seeing it, he welcomed us in and had someone show us to our room for the next couple of days.

CHAPTER 18

Day 191, August 11, 2016

Lima, Peru

I switched out my old tires for the new ones I'd bought when we arrived in Lima the day before; it took less than an hour. Jesse had enlightened me to lighter weight touring since I'd been riding with him and, after seeing it in action and, now having a good idea of what I did and didn't need, I went through all my gear to try to figure out what I could get rid of. The result was somewhat frightening, close to 20 lb (9 kg) of gear, or more than 1/3 of my original estimated gear weight, that could possibly be eliminated with little compromise in comfort or warmth. I was already committed to one more mountain climbing expedition since I'd been carrying my heavy boots, crampons, and ice axe for so long and I couldn't get rid of them yet. With that in mind, I had to keep the majority of it though I found about 5 lb (2.2 kg) worth of gear that had fallen into disrepair and worn out or had gone almost unused for the entirety of my travels; some clothes that I'd used a handful of times that were old or falling apart and things like sunscreen that I'd only needed on the San Blas cruise, plus a few other knickknacks that I'd never used and could not anticipate needing in the future. It was a work in progress and, after my mountain climb in northern Chile, I wanted to cut a significant amount of gear, whether by sending it home or otherwise.

Jesse and I went looking for wifi once mid-afternoon came

around and found a place with wifi at the seminary we were staying at and hung around until evening. Once we were getting hungry, we headed out to look for dinner. During our search, we saw a place making churros; they had just come out of the fryer and they were golden brown, covered in cinnamon sugar, and filled with dulce de leche, a milk based caramel. They were amazing and probably the best churros in the world too. I really wish that I could remember the name and location of the churro place but I can't, sorry. We walked around until we found a bakery and had a slice of cake each, then went to a mall where we'd seen a McDonald's, and consequently, where someone tried to sell us magic mushrooms, but we didn't buy any. My meal came with some coupons for discounted milkshakes and we had two each. There was a grocery store across the street from the mall and I bought some snacks later and stuff for breakfast the next morning. Back to the seminary afterwards where we rested in our room then went to bed.

I did almost nothing the next day, even though I probably should have, but, the day after that was actually a productive day. My bike was in desperate need of new cables and housing. The front brake would still stick whenever I used it and it'd been doing so since we were in southern Ecuador. To use the rear derailleur, I'd have to shift twice in any direction to shift one gear then shift in the opposite direction once to keep it from skipping. The housing on the front derailleur was the wrong length too; it'd get in the way every time I put my feet down too. I rode to the bike shop where Jesse would get his new bike from; the shop wasn't busy and they gave me almost free reign of their mechanic shop to re-cable my bike. It took a couple of hours, the most difficult part was the internal cable routing on the handlebars. The manager at the shop noticed how dirty my bike was and offered use of their bike washing station too so, I went through the tedious process of trying to get all the dirt and grime off my bike. After an hour of bike washing, and trying to get rid of all the dirt, I settled for just getting the heaviest dirt and grime off, then focused mainly on the drivetrain.

While I was there, I asked about Jesse's bike. They needed his passport number so they could get it through customs and said it should arrive in a couple of days, another waiting game. With a freshly washed and re-cabled bike, I rode back in the direction of the seminary. My previously sticky front brake had been rubbing on the way over to the shop, for how long it was rubbing I really didn't want to know; now that it was properly adjusted, and with faster tires, I was nearly flying through the city. I hit 25 mph (40 km/h) on a smooth, flat bike path and I still had power left to go faster. My bike felt close to being as fast as a road racing bike and I still had 26X1.95 inch wide hybrid tires. With that taste of speed, I wanted to switch to even faster tires after I dropped some gear.

After a couple more days of waiting, we'd finally reached the day that Jesse's bike was supposed to arrive. The plan was to ride to the bike shop and get it setup, then figure out a place to stay before continuing our journey south on the morrow. I was ready to go by 9:30 am, then Jesse got in the shower; two hours later we still hadn't left. We finally got away from the seminary, after a few goodbyes and thanks, around 12:30. It'd been a bit of an awkward place to stay and I was glad to be leaving. A bit less than an hour's ride brought us back to the bike shop and, when we inquired about Jesse's new bike, the reply came back that the bike was still in customs and would be stuck for another three or four days. Not only was the bike not there but, when we'd left the seminary, we told them we were leaving Lima so we had nowhere to stay. Hotels were expensive in Lima and even one night would stretch our budgets; three nights or more would leave a monstrous hole that would be difficult to fix. We asked at the bike shop if they knew of anywhere we might stay but, they had no suggestions so, we sent out a couple of last minute Warmshowers.org requests and began to wait. I was not looking forward to more time in Lima and was trying to think of what I was going to do with myself when I realized that there was a Brazilian embassy in Lima. The cruises from Buenos Aires, Argentina to somewhere in Europe that I'd planned to take had filled up without me ever buying a ticket but, a cruise from Brazil to Italy still had several open spots. As a US citizen, I needed to get a visa to enter Brazil and an embassy in Lima meant I could apply right away, then hopefully pick up the visa at another embassy in Bolivia or Chile. The embassy was only a couple of miles away and we rode by, after a late lunch, to see what I'd need. Brazil had recently gone to an electronic application process and I was told I could get most of it done online, then bring the printed form in the next morning.

Using the wifi back at the bike shop, I started working on the visa application, but the website was awful. I'd get most of the form filled out, six pages of information, then it would freeze and delete everything I'd entered. This happened multiple times but, eventually, I got all the information filled out and the form saved. The last step was uploading a passport photo and signature. I got the photo up but the page would freeze soon after and I'd lose the photo. This happened many times before I decided to wait until I visited the embassy in the morning; hopefully they would be able to help me.

It was starting to get dark by then and we were growing concerned about a place to stay when we heard back from John, one of the Warmshowers hosts we'd messaged a few hours ago. We'd messaged John on our original search for somewhere to stay in Lima and he'd been away on a business trip for a few days, but now he was back in the city and available to host. He was a school teacher, from the UK, who lived and worked in Lima. John happened to be working late that evening and wouldn't be off work till 8:00 pm but, said we could meet him shortly after; his apartment was barely 2 miles (3 km) away from the bike shop and we pedaled over as the bike shop was closing at 8:00. John rode up on his bike shortly after we arrived at his apartment building and we thanked him for the place to stay on such short notice; he welcomed us into his apartment and even made dinner for us. We talked over a dinner of rice, eggs, and avocados for a while before heading to bed.

I got to the Brazilian embassy right when they opened at 8:15 the next morning. I'd never been to an embassy or had to apply for a visa before but, luckily, one of the employees spoke English. After I explained my difficulty with the website and they said I could print out the application and bring all the papers in but it might take longer to get a visa that way so, I opted for making another attempt at the website to try to save some wait time and went to a nearby restaurant. The wifi was much faster there than it was at the bike shop and the website worked on the first try. The information on the application included just about everything about me, along with my parents birthdays, their nationalities, and several other details about them too. I got my picture, signature, three months of bank statements, and a scan of my passport uploaded, then wrote out an itinerary of my travel plans. Most people weren't familiar with the concept of a bicycle tour so I said I would enter the country by public transportation and depart about 45 days later by cruise ship and included a link to the cruise I planned to book. All together this took a couple of hours. There was a print shop across the street and, after emailing various documents to my email that required a physical copy, I went there to get some passport photos done and printed everything out. Ten minutes later, my pictures were ready and, after gluing my picture to the application, I walked back to the embassy.

They clerk reviewed all my information and said everything was in order except for the itinerary. His boss didn't like the public transportation and ship plan and said I'd have to get a flight reservation instead. He gave me a website called Latam.com where I could get a flight reservation to anywhere in South America without having to actually pay for the flight. Using the wifi at the restaurant across the street, I found a flight from Santiago to Rio de Janeiro for the rough dates I wanted. I booked it at no cost then went back to the print shop to get a paper copy of the reservation. When I finally got back to the embassy, it was approaching noon and they were about to close passport applications for the day. I rushed in and got the okay on the flight reservation and the embassy gave me a voucher to pay the $160 USD fee for the visa at a bank across the street. The clerk at the embassy told a security guard to let me in again when I got back.

At the bank, I got a number and began to wait. Approximately 20 minutes later, it was my turn. I brought the voucher to the clerk and tried to explain my situation in Spanish. He had seen the vouchers before and told me it'd be $160 plus an additional 80 cents for processing, I handed him my card but it said they only accepted cards from their bank and directed me to an ATM around the corner. Getting the cash was easy and I tried to go back to the same clerk after he was done with a customer but, he said I'd have to wait in line again. I retrieved another number and waited half an hour, thanks to a lunch rush, before it was finally my turn again. A different teller was helping me this time and I went through the same process of an attempted explanation in Spanish, then tried to pay the fee. The clerk examined each $20 US bill as if was a precious artifact and deemed four of them as unusable because they all had a 1\10 inch (2.5 mm) long tear along the middle of the bill from age. I was shocked at the idea that the condition of a dollar bill would matter; after I explained that I just got them from their ATM, they shrugged and decided they were okay after all.

Finally done at the bank, I went back to the embassy and turned in the receipt from the bank. They clerk smiled and said my visa should be done within one week. This didn't seem like a big deal; I'd asked earlier about picking up the visa in La Paz, Bolivia and they'd said I could. He began to walk away and I asked for my passport back. '"Oh no" he said. "We have to keep it here so we can put the visa in it." I really didn't want to wait in Lima for another week and tried to explain my situation. He was sympathetic and went to talk to his boss, then came back a couple of minutes later and said it should be done by Friday, I applied on a Monday, and he said he'd email me if he needed anything or if it was done sooner.

Even though I'd successfully navigated the bureaucracy of getting a visa, I felt defeated, another potential week of waiting seemed like too much to bear after I'd already been stuck and wanting to leave for several days. I headed back to John's apartment and broke the news to Jesse; he figured his bike would likely take that long anyways and, in the big picture, it wasn't a big deal. He was right, although I didn't want to admit the possibility of having to wait for several more days, in reality, it wouldn't be a problem long term. We headed out to find something to eat. There was a small restaurant just around the corner that we went to, then we walked in the direction of a grocery store that had ice cream on sale, among other things, and we each bought a tub, then sat outside and ate it all in one sitting. Back at John's apartment that evening, we made dinner for ourselves and our host.

I had to go back for an interview at the Brazilian embassy the day after I applied. In summary, they wanted to know why I was applying in Peru instead of from my home country and what my plans were. I had to give a modified version of my travel plans that fit the fake flights I'd put in my visa application. The next several days were mostly sitting around and waiting. The most exciting thing that happened was that I bought a pair of lightweight hiking pants to replace the heavy canvas ones I'd brought with me and I bought a lighter bike lock too, both of which took a few more pounds (~1.5 kg) off my gear load. Any bike lock can be cut through in less than a minute with the right tools; the lightweight cable lock I bought was just enough that someone would have to premeditate the theft and bring tools with them to steal my bike. I never let it out of my sight for long anyways.

Jesse's bike was supposedly out for delivery and, it being Friday now, the day my visa was supposed to be done, I went to the embassy and it was ready! Next, we went to the bike shop and, by chance, we got there right when Jesse's new bike was being delivered. It took him a couple of hours to get the racks and some other things transferred to the new bike and to get everything ready to ride. Once that was done, it was time for Jesse to pack up his old bike that he'd named the 'Lesbian Seagull' into the box. Instead of being white like his old one, Jesse's new bike was bright red; it was so bright that it was called 'nuclear red' and the brightly colored frame with his neon yellow panniers was difficult on the eyes. My idea for the name of the new bike was the 'Scarlet Explosion' but Jesse didn't want to jinx it and have his bike explode. A few weeks later he named it the 'Psycho Llama.' While I was waiting for Jesse to finish getting his bike assembled, I booked my cruise to Europe. It was only a little more expensive than flying would be but, it put me on a schedule. I wanted to get all the way south to Ushuaia on the southernmost part of the continent and then ride back up to Brazil for my cruise to Europe; by road it'd be almost 10,000 miles (16,000 km) of cycling and I had eight months to do it.

After saying our goodbyes, and giving many thanks, we left our host's apartment the next morning and began working our way out of Lima. Many of the roads were highly trafficked with crazy drivers and it was an exciting experience to say the least, though not in a good way. We finally got to the outskirts of the city and found ourselves on a quieter road, covered with potholes, that had litter scattered along the shoulders. This road took us to the coast and paralleled the highway that also followed the coast for a ways. There was a brisk wind coming off the ocean and we continued working our way south. The scenery was uninspiring; we pedaled by urban sprawl for much of the day and garbage of various sorts lined the highway. Regardless, it was great to be back on the road after the enforced ten day break. We moved along fairly quickly and I had about a 13 mph (21 km/h) average for the day. I think my faster tires helped some. In the smallish city of

Mala, we asked at the fire station if we could stay there for the night and we did.

There was an annoying little kid at the fire station; he questioned us about every aspect of every piece of gear he could see on our bikes and was asking questions nonstop but couldn't grasp the concept that we could not understand his Spanish if he spoke quickly. After a few tries on our part to understand what the kid was saying, several of his questions went unanswered. The kid's name was Cristhian, a Latin American spelling and pronunciation of Christian. Cristhian took a particular liking to Jesse and followed him everywhere, shooting questions at a rapid fire and I was not in the least jealous. I think his attachment came from the fact that he found my name (Jacob) entirely unpronounceable, a common problem for native Spanish speakers; most of the time their attempts sounded similar to 'chicken.' I'd tried in the past to tell people my last name (Ashton) in hopes that it would be easier to say but it was a 50/50 chance on whether they could pronounce it.

CHAPTER 19

Day 207, August 24, 2016

Nazca, Peru

Cycling across the coastal desert of Peru took a couple of days, then we turned inland and cycled across a non-coastal desert for a couple more days. We were still in the desert but this desert had mysterious lines drawn across it called 'the Nazca Lines'. Nobody knows why they were drawn but, supposedly they were made thousands of years ago. The desert surrounding the lines was one of the driest on earth and the lack of wind had helped to preserve them over the eons. In reality, the lines were just trenches that were several inches deep and drawn across the desert. From the hill we climbed to take a look at them, all we could see were curved or straight lines stretching across the desert. From the air geometric shapes or huge drawings of animals like monkeys, fish, or jaguar would be visible but, we didn't shell out a couple hundred dollars each for an hour long tourist flight over the area. After we'd fulfilled our curiosity about the Nazca Lines, we pedaled towards the city of Nazca and went directly to the fire station in town to see if we could stay the night there as we had done almost every night since we left Lima. The fire chief rolled up on a motor scooter just as we arrived; he showed us into the building and where we could pitch our tents for the night before we even had time to ask if we could stay there.

Rolling around nine the following morning, we turned our

wheels inland and back into the mountains. The town of Nazca was at about 2,000 feet (600 meters) above sea level. The climbing began right away, with some small rollers along the foothills instead of a potentially consistent grade if the road had been built about 100 yards (90 meters) to the left. A few miles in, the grade was at about 4-6% and rarely went outside that range. Kudos to the Peruvian road engineers; the climb was constant the entire day once we were a few miles out of Nazca; we didn't descend at all. The tropical sun was horrendously strong and there was a complete lack of shade in the barren landscape. We stopped a couple of times on corners that had a light breeze to try to cool off whenever we felt the need for a rest. As we climbed farther up the mountain; we could see a lone sand dune on the horizon that was supposed to be the biggest sand dune in the world. It was a very large sand dune that resembled a mountain made of yellow sand.

After about four hours of riding, we rode through the first hamlet of the day, Huallhua. We both were in need of water and asked a couple of policemen about water in the area. There was no running water in town and they didn't have potable water but; they gave us about half a gallon (2 liters) that we could filter and directed us to a tienda/restaurant about half a mile (1 km) away. We ate lunch at the restaurant and rested for a couple of hours during which we found out from the owner that there was another town about 5 miles (8 km) away that had running water and we pressed on.

We were in Nuevo Santiago an hour later, the town with running water we'd heard about earlier; we rested by a park with a water tap in the town square while waiting for some water to filter. A man walked up and introduced himself as the teacher at the village school then asked us where we were going to stay for the night. We said we were going to camp in the park; we'd already asked a few people and they said it wouldn't be a problem plus, it seemed pretty safe; the teacher then invited us to camp at the school; they had running water, a bathroom, and he said we could camp in the courtyard/

sports field. Nuevo Santiago was at about 9,000 feet (2,730 meters); we'd gained about 7,000 feet (2,120 meters) in elevation that day.

The climb into the mountains continued the next morning; the grade eased off around 10,500 feet (3,180 meters) and, once we got to almost 12,000 feet (3,630 meters), we had some small rollers but, the road was still trending upwards. We had entered the Pampas Galeras Reserve somewhere along the climb and saw several herds of guanaco, a relative of llamas, which were grazing in the plains surrounding the road. Some of the herds spooked when they saw us and took off running, with their heads bent forward below level with the rest of their bodies, a sight that looked quite ridiculous.

Even with the good weather and a light favoring wind, it was tough going. Grasslands stretched for miles in every direction and created the illusion that we weren't moving at all. Some buildings came into view on the edge of our line of sight and an hour later we were at the buildings. One of them was a restaurant and we stopped for a lunch of soup and a meat stew that might not have been beef but it was served with rice. Once we were done eating, the person running the entire restaurant offered us some coca tea. The tea comes from the leaves of the same plant as the drug cocaine and it was supposed to have a stimulant effect similar to coffee; neither of us had tried it yet and we accepted. It didn't have any notable flavor and the effect wasn't obvious, maybe we mistranslated it. When we got back on our bikes, we were feeling much better than before; it could have been the tea but we did just eat a full meal and sit around for an hour.

Soon after we left the restaurant, the sky darkened as a storm covered the sun; the wind changed to a headwind, then it started to rain. Jesse had put on a jacket after lunch and kept going while I stopped to put mine on. The temperature dropped rapidly and soon we were being pelted with a mixture of rain and hail. When I reached the 13,800 foot (4,180 meters) pass, Jesse was already descending the other side. I stopped to put on my beanie hat and a pair of gloves before I began the freezing descent in the rain. There was oil on the road and when it mixed with water there were small rainbows running across the road in treacherously slick streaks; the oil and water mixture made it so my brakes were barely working. I had several bursts of adrenaline from having to lean hard into a tight corner when my brakes wouldn't slow me down in time. Jesse's bright red bike was parked outside a peaje (toll station) so I pulled over; I found him inside a rest area trying to warm up. He hadn't stopped to put on another layer and was almost hypothermic. The room was heated, we did our best to warm up and dry out our wet clothes; we were there for over an hour before we even considered riding again. It'd stopped raining while we were waiting but, just when we were getting ready to go again, the rain came back; we didn't like the idea of riding in freezing rain with the possibility of having to camp in those conditions and chose to wait it out. The rain stopped an hour before dark. Jesse had bought a tent in Lima and we asked the security guard there if we could camp nearby. He said it wouldn't be a problem and told us we could set up camp across the street.

The next morning was a cold one. For whatever reason, there was a ridiculous amount of condensation covering everything, my sleeping bag included. One of the problems with goose down is that any amount of moisture makes the down lose its insulating properties; my bag was nearly soaked from the condensation and I woke up cold. There wasn't much we could do except wait for everything to dry out. It took a few hours for everything to dry and we finally left the peaje around 10:00. We made it about 200 yards (60 meters); a restaurant/tienda had just opened and we needed food. It was almost half an hour later when we actually started riding. The peaje we had camped at was at about 12,600 feet (3,820) in elevation and we still had some descending left to do. The road snaked its way down the side of a mountain to about 10,500 feet (3,180 meters) over the course of about 10 miles

(16 km). It was an awesome descent; my new tires were much smoother and faster than the old ones and they took some getting used to. Jesse was getting ahead of me on the beginning of the descent but once I got comfortable with my new tires I was catching up and, at the bottom, I wasn't more than 30 seconds behind him; before that, he'd often have to wait several minutes at the bottom of descents. Another climb immediately followed the descent, then the road leveled off and began to contour the mountains after passing through a small town. Yet another descent followed and this one ended in the town of Puquio.

We took a lunch break and considered finding somewhere to stay for the night but, it was still early in the afternoon and I wanted to keep going. After going to a tienda to get some food, we made a stop by a gas station for some water; we didn't expect to reach any services before the end of the day. The climb out of Puqio was gentle, less than 4% in most sections, and we moved along relatively quickly for a couple more hours, then began to look for somewhere to camp. The terrain had opened up and there was a small depression in the earth, off to the right side of the road, with space enough for our tents. We were at about 12,300 feet (3,730 meters) in elevation and wild camping for the first time since before we'd descended to the Peruvian coast.

CHAPTER 20

Day 212, August 29, 2016

Condorcoccha, Peru

The trend of the last couple of days continued; our sleeping bags were soaked from condensation in the morning and we'd wild camped again too. Thanks to the intense sun and low humidity now that we were over 15,000 feet (4,550 meters) in elevation, everything dried out quicker than it had before and we were riding earlier than normal. After several miles of rollers, we had a descent that dropped around 1,000 feet (300 meters) into a narrow valley. On the way down, we saw a cycle tourist heading up, the first in a few weeks, and stopped to talk. His name escapes me but, he was from Germany and was heading north from Ushuaia all the way to Alaska. He had quite a few complaints about having consistent headwinds. I couldn't blame him for complaining as the winds most definitely trended from the north and it made Jesse and I glad that we were going south. After parting ways, we continued down into the hamlet at the bottom of the valley and got some more water before heading up the other side. The 1,100 foot (330 meters) climb to the top of the valley marked the beginning of a 100 mile (160 km) descent that we'd been looking forward to for the last couple of days. It wasn't a consistent descent like the one out of the mountains down to the Peruvian coast had been; there were still some few hundred foot tall rollers scattered throughout the day, but we were heading in the general direction of downhill.

Jesse bought some thick, handmade grey wool socks from a street vendor in small town to solve his problem of cold feet in the evenings. It was around lunch time and we ate at a small restaurant nearby. After the first course of soup, with unidentifiable organs floating in it, we were served a plate of potatoes, rice, and a piece of meat still on the bone that we thought was lamb. Once we were done eating, we asked what kind of meat it was and it turned out to be alpaca. The restaurant was right across from the local bus station. Peruvians didn't travel on the kind of buses you'd see in a western country; they traveled in 18 passenger vans that crammed everyone into the vehicle, seated four per row, with one passenger next to the driver. We happened to bear witness to the unfortunate event of the bus being loaded with everyone's luggage; most of it was bags, but a hogtied goat was going to be strapped on top of everything. Two men at the bottom did a 'heave ho' while the goat was screaming with its tongue lolling, then the men threw the goat into the air where it was caught by another man on top of the bus and strapped down before the bus drove away with the goat still screaming on top. One bus passed by that had two dogs standing on top that didn't appear to be leashed, but they looked like they were enjoying the ride.

After lunch, the rolling descent continued for several miles before coming to the edge of a river canyon and descending steeply for a couple thousand vertical feet. With the help of a tailwind on one of the steepest sections, I reached speeds in excess of 50 mph (80 km/h). The descent leveled out to a river grade in a small town. We'd considered stopping there but, we were through before we realized we'd arrived and chose to keep going. After a few more miles, the wind changed to a headwind and our last 10 miles (16 km) took close to an hour. In the town of Pairaca, we rode to the municipal building to ask about a place to sleep. After a bit of a wait, they had someone lead the way in a truck to a sports field that had some old locker rooms we could stay in. It wasn't very clean but, it was free.

Jesse got up earlier than normal the next morning and he looked like he was in a bad state. He hadn't really slept over the last three days, the first two nights was from the altitude; we'd ascended relatively quickly and he hadn't adapted yet. Last night, he hadn't slept because seemingly every dog in town was barking all night long. The altitude and noise hadn't affected my sleep much. Jesse stood in the sun in a zombie-like state for over an hour. Probably halfway through his standing, he started running his fingers through his hair to remove all the loose ones and soon, a sun bleached blond colored clump that looked like a dead animal was accumulating next to him. Neither of us had gotten a haircut for over a year. I carried a comb for removing my loose hair. It took him even longer to get started packing his gear and it was after 10:00 am when we finally got going.

A headwind picked up a couple of hours later and quickly increased in strength. Jesse was complaining about the wind and I tried not to state the reason why we were fighting the wind too harshly; it hadn't been windy earlier in the morning but, we were still moving pretty quickly. Jesse was feeling weak from lack of sleep and I ended up leading most of the day while Jesse drafted. We were pushing 65 miles (105 km) in a little over 4 hours of riding when we reached the bottom of the 1,800 foot (545 meter) climb to Abancay. Jesse was still fighting fatigue and was having trouble keeping up with me. We were taking a break a couple of miles up the climb when Jesse saw a slow moving truck and decided to grab onto the back to get towed up the mountain. I plugged into some music and started pedaling up the climb alone; grabbing onto a truck would break my rule of traveling only under my own power overland. It took me nearly an hour to get the rest of the way up the climb and I found Jesse sitting on the steps of a building at the top. I joined him for a short break and then we rode to two different fire stations before the second one said they had a place we could sleep for the night. We went out to eat dinner, the restaurant we chose had wifi and that was a major factor in our decision to eat there. I was able to get online for the first time since Nazca about a week earlier and I suspected that a lack of wifi would be a new normal until we got into the more populated areas of Chile and Argentina.

The next day was a lovely day of riding through the Peruvian Andes and we stayed at another fire station that night. The morning started off with a descent. The fire station we spent the night at was at 8,800 feet (2,670 feet) and the descent was broken up by a short climb of a couple hundred vertical feet before continuing the rest of the way down to a river at about 6,000 feet (1,820 meters) in elevation. A few miles after reaching the river and beginning the gradual climb along said river, I hit 10,000 miles (16,000 km) cycled for the trip. It was a momentous occasion and I'd bought a bottle of 'pisco', a Peruvian liquor, a few days ago that I'd been saving to celebrate the occasion. After a toast to many more tens of thousands of miles, and a shot or three each from the bottle, we continued the climb.

It was hot by the river. With my almost empty stomach, and a high metabolism from riding, I quickly felt the effects of the alcohol which seemed to be amplified by the riding conditions. A few miles later, we met a couple of cycle tourists. Alex from France and a woman from Turkey whose name I didn't quite catch; both of them were northbound from Ushuaia with the goal of reaching Alaska. After some introductions, I told them of my recent milestone and offered them some pisco, then we all did shots from the bottle together.

Jesse and I made a stop for lunch a few miles later, after which I was feeling quite sober, having processed the alcohol quicker than normal. It was hot at the bottom of the canyon we were in and, on the climb up, we made a stop in Limatambo for a pint of ice cream each and to refill our water. While we were refilling our water, an entire class of school kids came to watch in fascination as we 'gringos' filled our bottles at a tap. The kids continued to stay and watch us for a couple of hours while we waited for the worst of the heat to pass, then we continued the climb.

The cyclists we did shots with earlier had mentioned a cheap hotel, part of the way up the climb, and that was our goal for the day. After riding about as far as they said it should be, we were in a village on the way up the climb and asked around for the hotel but nobody knew of any hotels other than the ones in Limatambo where we'd eaten lunch; by then, that town was several miles and thousands of feet down the mountain. Backtracking had no appeal in the slightest and we continued riding to find somewhere to wild camp instead. Most of the climb was either lined with houses and fields or too steep to even consider and we were almost at the top when we found a spot that had been used before, based on the small fire ring with ashes in it, and it had a stunning view of a freestanding mountain that was probably a volcano. We set up camp and called it a day at about 12,000 feet (3,640 meters) in elevation.

After less than a mile of climbing the next morning, we were at the top of the climb and, we refilled our water at a toll station near the pass before continuing. A short descent took us to the bottom of a fertile valley that was lined continually with farms and several villages. On the descent, we passed some slow moving trucks carrying sugar cane and, when one of the trucks caught up to us, we made an attempt to catch its draft but, I couldn't accelerate fast enough. There was a weigh station that the truck pulled into not far ahead and it was still there when we passed it. While it was catching up to us again, I drafted behind Jesse up to about 25 mph (40 km/h) then was able to sprint and get into the draft behind the truck. Thanks to the vacuum of air behind the truck we were now flying along at 30 mph (48 km/h). There were some small rollers along the way and I had to pedal as hard as I could to keep up with the truck. Eventually, it was too much and I fell behind. Jesse was able to stay with it and I saw him ride off behind the truck, following it into the distance. Drafting a truck is indirect assistance and as long as I didn't plan ahead or ask for the truck to be there it wouldn't break my rule of traveling under my own power. I liked to think of it as a similar principle as riding with a tailwind.

I made my own way for the next 30 minutes or so and eventually came to a small town where Jesse was waiting for me; the truck had turned off our route and Jesse had been there for over 15 minutes by the time I arrived. Jesse had had to pedal as hard as he could and was just barely able to keep pace with the truck up the hill I got dropped on. The town was at the end of the valley and an inconsistent climb began to work its way up to a pass. As we came closer to the city of Cusco, the traffic increased considerably to the point where we were riding on the shoulder the entire time. Over the top, we began the descent into Cusco. Much of the busy road was under construction and it made for slow going. We took the first possible turnoff to get off the main road and descended into the city on a street made of near identically sized square stones. We found our way to a hostel in the city and booked a few nights there.

The drivetrain on my bike had been skipping in a few of the lower gears; the chain wearing out again. I'd done almost 4,000 miles (6,450 km) on that drivetrain; not near as many as the last but, the boat ride from Panama, coupled with the wet season in Colombia and Ecuador, along with some dirt roads, had caused it to wear faster than it should so, it needed to be replaced. My cassette was worn as well as was my rear derailleur. The cost of replacing everything was going to be significant and, since it was only slightly more expensive to upgrade to a 9 speed drivetrain from the 8 speed that I'd been riding on, that is what I did. Across the street from the hostel, there was a conveniently located bicycle shop that had everything I needed. They'd only sell me the nine speed shifters as a pair at first but, after some discussion, they had a lightly used rear shifter that they were happy to part with for a deeply discounted price. The whole install took a couple of hours and soon my bike was ready to go again.

There were several other guests at the hostel. By chance,

we met a couple from Canada and Australia that we'd previously encountered on the road near Huascaran National Park and they'd just celebrated their one year mark on the road. Another couple was traveling on motorcycles and had ridden from their home in Oregon. One guest was a student from England who'd taken the summer to go hitchhiking all over South America. A German family of three was on a yearlong cycle tour with their four-year-old son and another couple from Germany too. The people traveling by bicycle as a family are the real hardcore travelers; it's enough effort for me to just take care of myself.

Jesse and I took some time to explore the city. Most of the architecture was colonial-era but, it was easy to tell which areas had been built by the Spanish and which had been built by the Inca. The Spanish built the churches of course, but part of an Inca built wall had plainly been integrated into a church too. The Spanish part was all oddly shaped stones held together with mortar while the Inca built section was made of perfectly hewn stones, nearly identical in every way and fit together without any gaps or mortar at all.

CHAPTER 21

Day 225, September 11, 2016

Puno, Peru

Our last significant climb in Peru had been summited a few days ago and it wasn't even that big by Peruvian standards, about 3,000 feet (900 meters) of vertical gain. We were on the edge of the altiplano, which would translate to high plateau; it was pretty high, around 12,500 feet (3,790), and pretty flat too.

Jesse and I had both been laid up with a stomach bug and had to take a sick day in the city of Puno. Coincidentally, some of Jesse's friends from back home were in Puno at the same time and we were able to meet with them the night before. Had it not been for the stomach bug, we wouldn't have gotten to see them.

This was our last full day of cycling in Peru and we were excited about the prospect of crossing into Bolivia after spending more than two months in one country. We made a stop for a late breakfast around 10:00 before heading out of Puno. There was a headwind to contend with for the first few miles out of the city, but, once the road turned to a more easterly direction, we had a crosswind to a tailwind for the rest of the day and spent most of the day riding with a view of Lake Titicaca, considered to be the highest navigable lake in the world, whatever that means.

A few miles after an early afternoon lunch break, we met a northbound cycle tourist, Kamran. He was originally from

Pakistan but had been living in Germany and had started riding north from Ushuaia around March 2016. Kamran was just recently on the road again after an extended break in La Paz. While we were talking, he mentioned another German cyclist who was southbound and only a few miles ahead. After parting ways with Kamran, Jesse and I decided we were going to catch up to the German cyclist; we picked up our pace a bit and, within 20 minutes, saw a slow moving blue dot going up one of the small rollers. We coasted up and talked while we were still riding. I don't recall his name but, unfortunately, he was riding a little less than 2/3 our speed and planned to stop for the day after a few more miles. Jesse and I had plans to get to Pomata, still another 15 miles (24 km) away, and rode ahead after talking for a few minutes.

Another 20 minutes or so of riding brought us to the closest thing we had to a climb that day. It was about 400 feet (120 meters) of elevation gain in 2 miles (3 km). We made short work of the climb and, after a quick break at the top, we coasted down an equally short descent on the other side and then went up again on a short steep climb into the town of Pomata.

In town, we inquired at the police station about somewhere to camp and they recommended one of the beaches a couple of miles up the road. Our plan was to make a stop in town for dinner, then buy some food for the morning before riding out of town to camp on the beach. We saw a tienda in the main square and went in to buy some food and then we got to talking with the shopkeeper. Eventually, she asked us where we were going to stay and we told her of our plan to camp on the beach. Upon hearing this, she insisted that it was far too cold at night to camp so we could stay in one of the spare rooms at her house just up the road. We thanked her for her offer and said we needed to eat beforehand so, she directed us to a restaurant a few doors down and said she'd wait for us.

The sun was setting and the temperature was dropping rapidly by the time we finished eating. We walked back over to the tienda and met the older woman who'd offered us a place to stay earlier. She invited us into her shop and pulled out a few chairs, then began asking the same questions everyone asks about where we're from and what we're doing. She continued to emphasize how cold it gets at night and told us quite a lot about how much better Peru is than Bolivia. It was dark when we walked our bikes over to her house and worked them through the narrow door that led to a small courtyard. While we were getting everything into the room, she continued to tell us how cold it gets at night and just how much more comfortable and warm the spare room she had was. When we had everything unpacked, setup, and she'd shown us where the bathroom was she said it would cost us the equivalent of about $3 US if wanted to stay there. She'd done an excellent job of putting us in a difficult position to say no. It was dark and therefore unsafe or at least difficult to find our way out of a town where none of the roads were marked on our maps and the temperature was already approaching freezing. On top of that, we already had everything unpacked and ready for us to go to bed. It was a difficult choice, but we handed over the money she asked for and, if that wasn't enough, she then said it would be $3 US each. We got hustled by an old lady. For whatever reason this was prominent in my thoughts as I was trying to go to bed and it took me several hours to fall asleep. I didn't mind paying a few dollars for a place to sleep somewhere warm when it really was cold outside but, the idea that it'd happened under the guise of genuine hospitality bugged me.

I was up shortly after dawn the next morning per my usual. The shop owner whose room we were staying in showed up an hour or so later. She was being overly friendly and wouldn't leave me alone; her manner suggested that she really felt like she'd done a good deed by charging us for a place to stay that didn't have power or hot water. To put this in comparison, our hotel in Puno the night before had had hot water, wifi, and working lights, for a bit less than $5 US compared to the $3ish she had charged us. I would have gladly paid an extra couple of dollars for those luxuries had I wanted to pay in the first place. Finally, she left when she realized Jesse was still sleeping but, showed up again 30 minutes later. Jesse was up by then and it was quite obvious that neither of us felt like she'd done us a favor. She asked us to stop by her store on her way out and offered us tea or coffee when we got there for an additional price. I was sick of the whole situation and really just wanted to leave as soon as possible but, Jesse needed some food first and we left as soon as he was done eating.

The Bolivian border was less than 20 miles (32 km) away and we were there within a couple of hours. We stopped just short of the border to try to spend the last of our Peruvian currency at a small roadside shop and tried to buy some wafer cookies. The shopkeeper nervously quoted us triple the price we'd been paying at other shops while covering her mouth to try to hide the lie. She'd probably been told to try to over-charge us by her friends who were sitting outside and we left without buying anything.

The Peruvian side of the border went quickly; we got exit stamps in our passports then exchanged our remaining Peruvian Soles for Bolivian Bolivianos and we were good to go. It was unfortunate to leave Peru on such a negative note after some of the best cycling and most impressive scenery of my life but, it was time to go, nonetheless, and I was excited to be moving on to a new country. The Bolivian side was a hassle; they needed: yellow fever vaccination records, a photo copy of our passports, a hotel reservation that was immediately cancelled after we'd crossed, and a recent passport photo. The border post had some small businesses nearby that were able to handle everything but the actual yellow fever vaccination. I had my vaccination record stored online and was able to print it out there. Jesse didn't have his but, they either forgot about it or let him in anyways. The entire process took an hour and a half and then we went across the street to get lunch after we finished.

In the 13th country of my tour, the road rolled continuously for several miles past the border to the city of Copacabana where our climb of the day began. The climb was around 1,400 vertical feet (424 meters) with the pass being right at 14,000 feet (4,240 meters) in elevation. An inconsistent descent for several miles followed and that took us to a ferry terminal for a short ride from the peninsula we were on to the other side of Lake Titicaca.

The ferry across the lake was a flat bottomed boat, constructed entirely from wood, that would be loaded with a couple of vehicles before being pushed across the lake by a small outboard motor that was tied onto the raft with rope. Our boat had a passenger van and a land cruiser on it. The boat couldn't have been moving more than 3 mph (5 km/h); the deck would flex visibly with every small swell we passed over and the water was only inches below the sides of the boat. The question of the lake-worthiness of this vessel and how often they sink crossed our minds; while Jesse and I were discussing this, we saw an overloaded full size bus that was probably 40 feet (12 meters) long on another boat going the opposite direction and figured that not very often was the answer.

A steep climb, then more rollers, awaited us on the other side. Jankoamaya was our goal for the day and we stopped in to try to find some dinner; it was listed as a town on our electronic maps though, upon asking some of the residents, we found that the closest restaurant was 15 minutes up the road. Giving distances in time was worse than worthless on a bicycle, we figured 15 minutes meant 10 miles (16 km) or more and we got some water, then began looking for a place to camp. There was continuous farmland on both sides of the road and being picky about a spot wasn't an option. A couple of miles up the road was a soccer field, complete with a concrete grandstand. There was a cavernous space below the grandstand that was fenced and gated, but unlocked, so we set up camp inside. We cooked and ate our dinners of pasta and tuna before going to bed.

It was a cold morning on the altiplano up at 13,000 feet (3,940 meters) above sea level. I tried to sleep in but was up around dawn and I read for a while, then ate a pack of cookies, while I waited for Jesse to get up. Both of us were low on food; we'd expected Bolivia to be cheaper than Peru so we'd waited to buy food until we actually needed it. There was a tienda near the soccer stadium where we spent the night and we tried to find something for breakfast there. That tienda made the Peruvian tiendas look like full on grocery stores; they had salt crackers, bulk pasta and rice, condensed milk, and little else. There was another town 5 miles (8 km) up the road and we rode there in hopes of getting a better selection. No such luck, they had a few more brands of crackers and some eggs in addition to whatever the other shop had. Surely, there must be something better further up the road, we thought, so we started riding. The road rolled along the hills near the lake for whatever reason; there would have been plenty of room for the road on the level ground near the lake. After 15 miles (24 km) or so of riding, the road turned inland and flattened out considerably. A multitude of speed bumps were scattered along the road. They weren't normal speed bumps; they were section of road that had been left unpaved about a foot (30 cm) long, stretching all the way across the road in such a manner that made them more dips or washboard than bumps. Usually, there was a smooth section by the edge of the road where we could swerve over to either side in most cases thanks to the low traffic. Other bumps required a drastic cut in speed to maneuver over without risking a crash. The breaks in pavement were spaced at every few hundred yards for miles and miles. When we met up with a more main road, the speed bumps stopped and, because of some road construction going on, we had our own private highway to cycle on for several miles.

There was still nowhere around to buy food besides the tiendas, not even a hole in the wall restaurant or street food stands. I had a pack of four pepperoni sticks that I was rationing to try to make it to the suburbs of La Paz, the capital of Bolivia, where we could hopefully find a restaurant or at least a decent store to get some food. First, 20 miles (32 km) passed, then 30 miles (48 km) and still nothing; we'd been riding for a few hours by then. All I'd eaten was a small pack of cookies and a couple of pepperoni sticks; I had a pounding headache by the time I saw what looked to be a decent sized town up ahead. I asked someone if there was anywhere to get some food and was directed to a tienda that had almost nothing yet again. I'll admit, I was being picky, I obviously wouldn't starve on salt crackers and pasta but I was really hoping for something more substantial. At mile 44 (km 70), we rode into a suburb of La Paz called 'El Alto'. All the buildings were brick and mostly unfinished with neither glass in the windows nor doors and with random bits of electrical wiring going through holes in walls. The constant wind blew sand across the road and the lack of people made it look like we were alone in an abandoned city. The scene continued for a couple of miles but, then we saw some signs advertising lunch and stopped at the first one we came to. A good bowl of chicken stock soup with noodles, complete with organs from said bird, was brought out in quick fashion. I ate everything, including the organs and various unidentifiable parts of chicken that Jesse wouldn't eat. For the main course, they brought us rice served with a meat slop of questionable origin; it didn't look appetizing and it didn't taste much better but, we ate it all just the same. We were feeling much better after lunch and began the gradual climb to the edge of La Paz. The city sat in a large, steeply walled valley with dull brown houses stacked practically on top of each other. I'd never seen anything like it before and we stopped at an overlook to take in the view. Next, we had to descend into the valley. The roads were the steepest I'd ever seen, Jesse had ridden roads pushing a 40% gradient and he said these were even steeper, I agreed. They were steep enough that my back tire would come off the ground while braking. Jesse could barely descend in a straight line because of his higher center of gravity; he had to stand up and get all his weight behind the saddle to be able to brake at all.

I'd arranged us a place to stay at the casa de ciclistas in the city and we found it after a little trouble with the streets being almost stacked on top of each other and not being able to find through roads. The only problem was that no one was there. We rang the bell, knocked, and then settled in to wait in hopes someone would show up. We got there around 5:00 pm and waited over an hour and half until dark, then went to get some food before coming back to try again. While we were eating, we met Denis from Russia. Denis was also a cycle tourist and had been in La Paz for a few days, trying to find someone to ride with through the remote sections south of La Paz; we'd be in the city for a couple of days and exchanged contact information. He had arranged to stay at the casa as well but had been unsuccessful at finding anyone to let him in. We realized at this point that we'd have to find another place to stay and, after trying knocking, ringing, and waiting again, we began exploring our options.

There was supposed to be a fire station nearby and we rode over to ask. Three blocks down the road, left then the next left. We followed our maps to where it was supposed to be, the first left was a bridge, we rode over it, took the next left and... nothing. Our maps and GPS said we missed the turn and we soon realized it was at the bottom of the canyon that the bridge went over. It took a couple of miles of riding and a good bit of searching before we found the road to the bottom of the canyon. When we got to the station, it appeared to have been abandoned for several years. Now it was late, dark, and we were in the bottom of a canyon with nowhere to stay. The fire station was fenced all the way around, no way of using it for urban camping. With heavy hearts, we began climbing slowly out of the canyon and back the way we'd come. There was another fire station only a few miles away but, it was all uphill and steep enough that I had to push my bike on some sections. It took us almost an hour to get up the road to the station and it was easily the biggest fire station I'd ever seen; we were hopeful. We asked. "No, we don't have room." We pleaded our case telling them everything that had happened trying to find a place to stay but they didn't want to help us so we started looking for a hotel.

The fire station was in the most expensive district in town; everything we checked was close to $40 US per night and far outside our budgets. We rode into one of the less nice areas and began looking; we checked a few hotels that were on our maps but they were too expensive; we then came to one that wasn't marked on our maps and checked the price; it was less than $6 US each per night, with hot water and wifi. It sounded too good to be true, but there it was. When we were checked in, it was past 10:30 pm.

CHAPTER 22

Day 229, September 15, 2016

La Paz, Bolivia

After a very lazy first day off in La Paz, we left only left the hotel once to get food, we met up with Denis the following evening at the casa de ciclistas. I'd received a reply to an email that I sent to the owner of the casa the day we arrived and he said one of the guests at the casa should be returning that evening. We weren't feeling very optimistic about getting in to the casa; we hadn't checked out of the hotel and we'd left our bags behind too. Denis recognized the description of the guest and it turned out to be a woman from Japan he had ridden with for a while. Upon contacting her, Denis found that she wouldn't be returning for several days. The casa was a bust so we went to get dinner before returning to our respective hotels.

There were some pretty desolate areas we wanted to cycle south of La Paz, so, we went by one of the grocery stores the next morning and tried to stock up on some things that might be difficult find over the next few weeks. Unfortunately, Bolivia is not the cheapest country in South America as it is often said to be and the prices were the same if not higher when compared to Peru. The selection wasn't the best either; perhaps it was just the store we went to though I figured it would be a trend throughout the country. The best we could find that was worth carrying was some good olive oil and sauce packets for some variety to the pasta dinners that were one of our staple foods plus some cured sausage sticks. The tiendas outside the cities might be poorly stocked, but we wouldn't starve if we could only find salt crackers and bulk pasta.

We met up with Denis, he really does spell his name with one 'n,' around 8:30 am the day we were ready to leave and started riding out of La Paz. The roads going out of the city were the same as the ones going into the city, incredibly steep. Our respective hotels were on opposite sides of the valley from the highway that would take us out of the city and we descended for half a mile (800 meters) then began climbing; Denis and I had to push our bikes most of the way up while Jesse managed to ride the whole way in series of short sprints between waiting for us. This time, I was not the slowest one up the hills; Denis was slower than me so Jesse and I stopped to wait a couple of times.

On our final push out of the city, Jesse and I were waiting for Denis when we saw him coming up the road in the back of a truck wearing his screaming yellow jacket with his bike; Denis had no qualms about taking rides in cars when the going got tough. Jesse and I met him at the top, it'd taken over an hour to get out of the hole the city was in and when it was all said and done we had climbed 1,500 feet (450 meters) in 3 miles (5km) including the downhill part. There was an empanada restaurant on the way out of the city so we stopped for breakfast. Denis was still falling behind on the flat roads across the altiplano and we had to stop on occasion to wait for him.

Patacamaya was our planned stop for the day; when we got there Jesse and I stopped for a late lunch at a place with a good view of the road so we could see Denis approaching. Lunch was dried llama that was shredded and fried in vegetable oil until it resembled a fibrous tangle. Although it was still chewy, the flavor was decent and it was served on top of maize with a few black potatoes and a hardboiled egg. After we were done eating, Denis still wasn't there so we went down the road to a gas station to refill our water. We'd been stocking up on two liter soda bottles over the last couple of weeks and we test rode our bikes loaded down with 16 liters (4.16 gallons) each for the first time. Denis rode up a while later; he was hungry and we referred him to the restaurant we ate at earlier. Jesse and I were about to follow him over when I noticed I had a flat front tire from a piece of wire. There was some shade from some buildings on the other side of the road so I pushed my bike over to them before patching the puncture. Denis came back from his dinner about the time I was done fixing it and we began looking for somewhere to stay. We tried the police station first; they said they didn't have any room but said we could camp in the park. Next we tried a church, it took us a while to find someone to talk to and they almost said no but first asked where we going to stay. When we said we'd probably camp in the park they said we could stay with them. There was a church run school that they were affiliated with and they had a bunk room where we could stay for the night.

After a late breakfast of empanadas we were on the road again. We made a plan with Denis to meet up in the city of Oruro then Jesse and I took off. The ride was more of the flat barren terrain of the altiplano; generally straight roads with gentle rollers. Jesse got a flat from a piece of wire about 12 miles (20 km) in. I waited for him to fix it then we continued riding. He turned off somewhere in search of lunch when he was behind me and I didn't notice for a couple of miles but he had mentioned wanting to stop for lunch so I wasn't concerned with his absence and kept riding alone. The winds varied throughout the day. I passed an electrical storm on my left side: the air pressure from the storm was creating a crosswind, causing some small tornados that were trying to suck me in. The storm was a few miles away and I tried to outrun it, a futile effort in most cases, but this was one of the rare successes of outrunning a storm on a bicycle. I still hadn't stopped since Jesse's flat tire and I kept riding to avoid letting the storm catch up to me. The road leveled out significantly after I outran the storm and I made quick progress. When I realized I'd ridden almost 40 miles (64 km) nonstop I decided to try to make it to 100 kilometers, roughly 62 miles, nonstop since I'd never gone that far nonstop on tour yet.

I reached my goal a few miles outside of Oruro and stopped for a much needed bathroom break. I rode easy into town and met Denis who was waiting on the outskirts. He got caught in the storm I outran which had turned into a dust storm with almost no visibility then he found a car to take him the rest of the way in. Denis and I rode into town in search of some food; there was nothing for a few miles but eventually we came to a group of a few restaurants and street vendors. I hadn't eaten anything since the empanadas for breakfast and was on the verge of passing out from low blood sugar so I bought a drinkable yogurt from one of the vendors and sipped it slowly while sitting on the side of the road. Jesse showed up 15 minutes or so later and met up with us. We stopped by a chicken restaurant for a late lunch. I was beginning to feel nauseous and could hardly eat then went outside and lay down on the sidewalk in front of the restaurant before throwing up a few minutes later. I felt better after vomiting and went back in to try to eat a bit but my appetite hadn't come back and I ended up getting most of food to go.

There was a fire station in town and we rode there slowly. When we asked about staying there for the night, an emergency call came in and we ended up waiting again during which I tried to take a nap on the sidewalk in front of the station and threw up again. When the firemen came back they showed us where we could park our bikes and invited us upstairs for some hot chocolate. The sugar helped and after an hour or so I was feeling almost back to normal; the firemen even shared their dinner with us! After the luxury of a hot shower I felt well enough to eat my leftovers from lunch. There was wifi at the station too and because of it we didn't get to bed till after 11:00 pm.

Before leaving Oruro the next morning, we went looking for one of the several supermarkets marked on our map to stock up for our journey into the desert. We got to the first one which was only a couple of miles away from the fire station and it was closed, apparently it was permanently closed. No matter, the second was only a couple more miles away but it was also permanently closed. The last supermarket marked on our map was someone's name; nine times out ten that meant it would be an open air market. At such markets we, being foreigners, would get overcharged for anything we tried to buy and, since haggling over prices didn't work in Latin America, any attempt at getting a lower price was met with a look of complete confusion on the part of the vendor. We left the city in the most direct route possible; we had already ridden close to 10 miles (16 km) but had progressed barely 2 miles (3 km). We made a plan with Denis to meet up in a town called Challapata then Jesse and I began riding.

After lunch, we had a strong crosswind for several miles that eventually turned into an equally strong tailwind for nearly 20 miles (32 km). The last barren stretch into Challapata was a mix of strong crosswinds to headwinds that would blow giant clouds of sand across the road that coated us in dust. The wind made for slow and difficult riding. We were able to see our destination on the horizon for over an hour of riding before we actually got there. It was mid-afternoon when we arrived in town and we stopped by one of the roadside restaurants to try to find something to eat. The doors were open and people were inside but none of the restaurants were serving anything. When we asked about getting something to eat they looked at us as if we were crazy, apparently no one eats at that hour. This had been a trend throughout Latin America. That, and some places would have huge menus listing all sorts of food but only be serving chicken and rice.

We sat on a curb and ate some snacks while we waited for Denis. Jesse rode through town to look for somewhere free to stay while I waited by the roadside and he returned a while later without any luck. Over an hour passed before we decided it would be prudent to try to fill our water while we were waiting. There was a gas station nearby that had running water and they let us use their tap. Darkness began to fall and we'd been waiting next to the highway for Denis for over 2.5 hours at which time Jesse and I decided we'd waited long enough so we rode into town to look for dinner. We found a rotisserie chicken restaurant and parked our bikes in a very visible spot from the street. Denis showed up right as we were about to finish eating and we waited for him to eat before looking for somewhere to stay. Denis was exhausted from the long day of riding and chose to stay at the first hotel we came to; it seemed overpriced so Jesse and I went in search of something better. One of the hotels advertised hot showers, cable tv, wifi, laundry, and a restaurant on their sign; when we went inside to ask about the price it turned out they had none of those things, not even hot showers. After checking probably every hotel in town, we went back to the one we had left Denis at and ended up staying there. Jesse wanted to get some stuff done online and when we mentioned possibly taking a day off here Denis was more than a little eager to have a day off the bikes.

Since I hadn't been able to buy groceries in Oruro, I walked through the open market in Challapata the next day to see what I could find. I mostly bought food that would keep well: pasta, cheese, cookies, that kind of thing. Some of the items took a few tries, negotiating prices didn't work as usual in South America even though I made multiple attempts. If the price they gave me was higher than I thought was reasonable I went to the next place I found selling the same item then asked again and again at different places until someone gave me a decent price. Although it was a time consuming and tedious process compared to a grocery store it was more interesting; I was able to buy most everything I needed at reasonable prices. I did very little with the remainder of the day which made it a relatively relaxed day for a rest day, it rained a bit in the afternoon.

It was almost lunchtime when we started riding the day after our rest day, Jesse and Denis were moving pretty slowly again. The first 20 miles (32 km) were flat to gentle rollers along the highway with views of recent snow in the mountains a few thousand feet above us. Bright pink flamingoes inhabited some of the roadside ponds and streams; they seemed wildly out of place considering we were at about 13,000 feet (3,940 meters) in elevation. Shortly after we reached our 20 mile (32 km) mark, we were at the turnoff for the road that would eventually take us to Salar de Uyuni, the largest salt flat in the world.

The road was unexpectedly paved and in the distance we could see the first of a few small towns along the route nestled between two hills on the edge of the horizon. We had planned for a lunch stop there but the restaurant that was supposed to be there was no longer open so we made do with a tienda; I bought some eggs and cooked them on my stove outside the store. A storm picked up quite suddenly just as I was finished cooking and we took shelter behind a nearby building but it passed within 30 minutes so we continued out of town. The scenery was breathtaking, the storm created a dark area to the left side of the road and to the right there were still white puffy clouds with the sun's rays filtering through them. The spectacle was accentuated by frequent lightning strikes in the storm that always came in pairs close together. We rode along in awe of the sight of the storm before us. Jesse and I were riding ahead of Denis and we caught up to the storm. It began to rain then it started hailing soon afterwards. The hail was blowing sideways and it stung painfully on all exposed skin; we took shelter under a small bridge to wait out the storm. Denis was riding slow enough that he hadn't caught up to the storm and he showed up shortly after it blew over. Riding again, we were only a few miles away from the village of Bengal Vinto. When we rode into town we saw a large covered area that was the school and government offices of the town; because the weather still looked threatening we asked if we could camp under the covered area. The people in charge were very welcoming and said we could sleep in one the classrooms that weren't being used.

The school we spent the night at was putting on a patriotic play the next morning and it apparently had something to do with Bolivia fighting for independence; one of the kids was dressed a lot like Che Guevara. Around the time we were getting ready to go we were invited to watch once we had everything ready. We waited around till the play ended then had a group photo with us and about 30 school kids.

While we were getting ready to leave Denis was talking with the principal of the school; the principal was saying how the roads were completely flat to our goal town of Sallinas de Garci Mendoza and we should be able to average 30 km/h, about 18.6 mph, the entire 50 some miles (~80 km) there. A quick glance at the principal told me it was highly unlikely he'd done much cycling recently and that even with an excellent tailwind it was equally doubtful that he himself could ride at that speed for almost three hours. Unfortunately, Denis had not experienced the reliability of directions and approximate times from people who don't ride bicycles and he believed the principal despite our attempts to sway him otherwise. The road was paved and most definitely not flat; we pedaled over endless rollers for the vast majority of the day many of them a few hundred feet tall. The eggs I'd eaten the day before gave me some stomach problems overnight and I was feeling weak and riding slow from the resulting dehydration. Apart from me not feeling well, the days' ride was fairly uneventful.

Jesse and I reached Sallinas de Garci Mendoza around 4:00 pm. Our average was barely over 20 km/h, 12.4 mph, and Denis was nowhere to be seen. When we asked about somewhere to camp at the police station and they said we could stay in the empty lot behind the station. It was beginning to get dark after we'd waited for Denis for 2.5 hours; I took a nap on the sidewalk in front of the police station while we were waiting. He still hadn't shown up a couple of hours later so we went looking for somewhere to eat and a more ideal place to camp without him. We found a decent restaurant and had a dinner of llama with rice and potatoes. Denis showed up just as we were finishing our food and I had another plate of fried chicken while Denis was eating. He had several things to say about drivers, their approximate times, and their evaluation of the terrain. There was a hotel in town for a good price, about $4.25 US, but it did not have wifi. Jesse and I chose to camp behind the police station for free while Denis opted for the hotel.

After a breakfast of the cheapest empanadas yet, about $0.35 US each, we left town around ten. The pavement ended abruptly outside of town and today we opted for sticking together at Denis' request. That entailed Jesse and I riding slowly for about 20 minutes then waiting for almost 10. Denis would seem to keep up with us at the slower pace but would inexplicably fall behind at random intervals. The now dirt road rolled through the hills along the base of the volcano Tunupa. The weather had been dry recently and we took the easterly route through what would be mudflats if it was wet. Denis was still going slowly so Jesse and I rode circles and patterns over the dry hard mud while Denis made a more direct path. In the town of Jirira we turned off the road and onto the Salar de Uyuni, the largest salt flat in the world; it stretched out beyond the horizon like an ocean of salt and it sits at almost 12,000 feet (3,640 meters) in elevation. The Salar is so flat and easy to see from space that it's supposedly used to calibrate the elevation of GPS satellites.

The salt crunched beneath our tires as worked our way towards Isla Incahuasi also known as "The Island." Denis was still going quite slowly and we waited quite frequently until The Island appeared over the horizon and it really did look like an actual island in an ocean of salt plains. Once we were confident that Denis could find the way, he could see us from miles away, Jesse and I rode on ahead. It was strange riding in such a large, open area, I lost all sense of depth perception and time seemed to slow to a crawl. The silence on the salt flat was incredible; whenever I stopped riding I could hear my heart beating. I tried to see how long I could ride with my eyes closed and my best was a slow count to 60. The sun was just beginning to set when Jesse and I arrived at The Island and we found the restaurant at the northwest end without any trouble. The prices at the restaurant were close to four times the price of an average restaurant in Bolivia and I cooked my own dinner. Denis showed up an hour or so after and as we did not want to pay to camp at The Island we rode a quarter mile (400 meters) in a clockwise direction around it and set up there. It was a rare windless day on the Salar and we had no trouble setting up camp.

In the morning, we had some fun taking perspective pictures with the endless horizon just like most all the tourists who visit the Salar de Uyuni do. It's harder than it looks; something was always out of focus and messing up the illusion. Denis chose to turn east towards the town of Uyuni while Jesse and I continued south through the Ruta de Lagunas or Lakes Route. After breaking camp and saying our farewells we headed off in our respective directions. It'd been fun hanging out with Denis even though the clash in our riding styles had made it difficult sometimes.

We topped off our water at The Island then began our way south on one of the salt roads; it's called a "salt road" but it's just an area with enough tire tracks that some of the salt has turned black from the rubber off the tires so it was smoother. As with yesterday time seemed to slow to crawl; what could have passed for over an hour of riding was, in reality, only a few minutes. More "islands" crept by over the horizon; the best analogy for the Salar de Uyuni really is an ocean or at least a very large lake.

Eventually, we made it to the south end of the Salar de Uyuni and turned onto a road of broken pavement. The pavement was not in good condition but it was paved nonetheless and, as an unexpected plus, we had a tailwind. The pavement lasted until the short, steep climb up to the town of Colcha K.

There was a restaurant in town and we stopped for a lunch of pan fried chicken and fries. Colcha K was out a dead end road and we had to backtrack slightly to get out of town. A few miles along the dirt road we came to the town of Manica. On the other side of town, there was a steep and sandy climb. I was able to ride up almost all of it except for one exceptionally sandy stretch where I kept losing traction so I felt pretty good about myself for that. We rode over the top and down an equally steep and sandy descent then realized at the bottom that we could have avoided the climb entirely by taking a small track that went around the mountain but it looked pretty sandy anyways.

We chose to take the south road out of the village of Santiago de Chuvica in hopes of avoiding more unnecessary climbing. The road was still sandy and where there wasn't sand there was washboard, although difficult it was rideable. We met up with the 'highway' and turned towards the town of San Juan. The 'highway' was still dirt and one of the main roads in the area and in slightly better condition than the road we had just turned off of, less sand but still washboarded all over.

Looking for a restaurant in the town of San Juan proved unsuccessful. We tried asking someone and they said there weren't any restaurants which seemed odd since there were two hotels in town. One hotel was expensive, at the other we couldn't find anyone to ask about rooms; neither had wifi and this came as no surprise in the remote location. Some people working at the school said we could camp behind their building so we set up there then made dinner, ate, and went to bed shortly after dark.

Jesse was still sleeping when I got up, what else is new. I did an inventory of all my food: three dinners, two of pasta and a bag of quinoa that I'd been carrying as emergency food for far too many miles. Four pepperoni sticks, 900 grams (2 lb) of peanuts, three packs of a four cheese mix for pasta, a pack of crackers, and two granola bars. I checked the PDF information map that I had for the south Bolivia Lagunas route that started in San Juan. It gave the description of the route as being "over 180 miles (290 km) of dirt roads that may or may not be ride-able with little opportunity for restocking food and to plan for eight to ten days." "That's for normal people." I thought to myself, "we'll do it five or six." We went by a tienda in town and bought food. I bought three packs each of sardines and pasta for as many dinners, a sizable chocolate bar, and six packs of cookies. That ought to be plenty.

It was almost 10:30 when we finally left town. We headed south and the road took a turn for the worse right away: wash-board and sand though entirely rideable. We took a turn to the west after a few miles and onto another salt flat that wasn't nearly as big as the Salar de Uyuni but it was still a pretty good size. The surface on the salt flat was smoother than the road had been and we were in Colchani that afternoon. Colchani was a defunct railroad town with an active military base that our PDF map said we could get water at. I had about 9 liters when I left San Juan and took on another 4 there for a total of 13 liters or about 4.5 gallons.

After the salt flats the terrain turned into lava fields. The area here was entirely surrounded by volcanoes but none of them were active as far as I knew. Small and intermittent dried lava flows from ages gone by had left some rough patches that we had to weave around. As we got close to the edge of the salt flat the road turned back into sand and washboard.

The end of the salt flat marked the beginning of our climb of the day, about 1,700 feet (515 meters) up over 8 miles (13 km). I was able to ride the first couple of miles until the wind picked up and started blowing me out of the narrow rideable part of the track and into the soft sand at the edge. This meant I was pushing my bike and I had to push it up the majority of the climb. I'd get tired of pushing every once in a while and try to ride sometimes. I'd make it maybe 100 yards (90 meters) before getting blown off the track and into the sand where I'd fight to keep my balance and usually fall over which resulted in half my panniers falling off and me being covered in dirt.

Eventually I stuck to the continuous forward motion of pushing over the stop and go process of trying to ride. I met Jesse at the top, he'd been able to ride the whole way somehow though granted he did a lot of stop and go. He'd been waiting for almost an hour. I ate a handful of peanuts and drank some water then we started riding again.

Washboard and sand on top of the climb made progress difficult and taxing mentally as well as physically. There were some sheltered areas we could have camped at but I was only a couple of miles away from reaching another milestone so I wanted to keep going. I hit 11,000 miles riding along the base of Cerro Tomasamil, a supposedly inactive volcano but one side of it looked like it was smoking or at least steaming. We rode a couple more miles till we came to a dry river bed that sheltered us from the majority of the wind and made camp. I made a dinner of sardines and pasta spiced with some black pepper steak seasoning for dinner. I'd actually never had sardines before that moment; they turned out to be a decent meal and better than most kinds of canned tuna with pasta especially with some seasoning. Good thing too, I didn't have much else for my next several dinners. I broke off a day's ration of a chocolate bar and checked our progress: we'd done about 1 2/3 days' worth of progress in a day according to the 10 day schedule.

I woke at dawn the next day and crawled out of my tent, excited to start the day. It was too cold for the amount of clothes I was wearing and I went back into my tent to eat then waited until the morning sunlight was hitting my tent before I got out again and started getting ready. Jesse hadn't slept well for whatever reason, probably the elevation; that meant he would take longer to get ready than usual. We started riding around 9:30 and the terrain was much the same as the day before; washboard and sand- ride some then push some.

After a couple of miles we turned onto an international highway. This was still Bolivia however and 'international highway' meant it was a dirt road that might be maintained from time to time that happened to go to a border. It was much better than the road we were on before though and 5 miles (8 km) went by comparatively quickly before it was time to turn onto a smaller road again. We turned onto a dirt double track and began climbing. I was having trouble balancing in the narrow rutted track and my front wheel would catch on the edge of the track which would make me skid to a halt and often end up on the ground. Eventually, I resorted to pushing until the track was wide enough to ride. Over the top of the hill a spider web of different tracks spread out before us. They all went in more or less the same direction but the quality of the surface varied widely. We picked the best ones we could find and made our way forward.

Laguna Canapa appeared after we crested a hill. Its dark blue waters teemed with bright pink flamingoes up where we were at 14,000 feet (4,240 meters) above sea level. Near Laguna Hedionda there was a hotel and an opportunity to fill up on water, we did so and asked about getting lunch at the restaurant. They weren't serving lunch but after a while they came out to where we were filling our water and gave us a small bag of food that they gave to us for free even though we offered to pay for it. The bag contained a few pieces of bread, a can of tuna, and two apples. The apples were bruised in a few places but we hadn't eaten fresh fruit in so long that we were past caring and savored every bite.

We set off again moving slow because of the rough roads but making progress just the same. About an hour before dark we saw a small area were some rocks created a break from the relentless wind. We chose to camp there and set up quickly. The sun soon dipped below the horizon and the temperature began to drop rapidly. Soon I was in my tent and I planned to stay there until the sun came over the horizon in the morning.

CHAPTER 23

Day 242, September 9, 2016

Laguna Hedionda, Bolivia

I struggled to keep my balance while riding in a narrow track then fell over and found myself lying in the dirt. This wasn't the first time this had happened that day. By then, I'd lost track of how many times I'd fallen over while trying to ride on a rough, washboarded, and sandy track through the desert. It didn't really hurt to fall going that slow; normally, I'd get up and get going right away but, this time I laid there for a while seriously questioning my judgment and sanity to take this route through southern Bolivia. "You knew it would be this way!" I told myself as I finally got up and began reattaching the bags that had been knocked off my bike from the fall.

It wasn't an entirely bad day. Jesse hadn't slept well yet again but we'd managed to get started earlier than the last couple of days and much of the morning had been rideable; we climbed through a narrow canyon and descended down the other side. The road deteriorated on the descent and soon we had to pedal to continue moving while riding downhill. At the turnoff for the Hotel Del Desierto, I was at a conundrum. I had 6 liters (1.5 gallons) of water left, enough for the rest of the day and the riding day the next day until about mid-afternoon since it was pretty cold. The hotel had water and potentially food but it was a mile (1.6 km) off route and I didn't want to have to do the out and back; Jesse needed water and was going to the hotel regardless. Eventually, good judgment got the better of me and I rode to the hotel with Jesse. There was a restaurant at the hotel but given its remote location it was expensive. Kindly, they let us fill our water there and then as we were about to leave we were invited in for some bread and a bowl of quinoa soup; we tried to pay after eating but they insisted that it was on the house. After many thanks, we continued into the desert.

Most of the people that came through southern Bolivia were tourists in four wheel drive vehicles on all-inclusive tours. We'd seen several of them each day; driving through the desert or having picnics by the colorful salt lakes that were scattered throughout the area. Some tourists traveled on motorcycles or private cars. One of the vehicles was a giant silver colored diesel powered monstrosity with at least eight wheels that probably cost over a $1,000,000 US.

We were able to ride for about 2 miles (3 km) after leaving the hotel before the road took a turn for the worse; endless miles of pushing our bikes through sand, washboard, and deep gravel. Some sections looked rideable; I'd try to ride and soon find myself lying in the dirt over and over and over again. This process continued for much of the afternoon through a barren landscape of brown gravel with volcanoes on the horizon. With time, we got to the end of what was probably the most difficult section of not quite riding I'd ever done in my life so far and we had a very welcome surprise, a recently graded road. Although it was dirt and graded recently that did not mean it was all rideable; some of the grading had only served to disguise the sandy sections. When we rode into the sand unexpectedly then our tires began to plow through the soft surface which would sometimes cause a crash.

After a few more miles, we saw an abandoned house on the side of the road. The stone walls of the house were falling down in places and it was a lacking a roof, doors, windows, and other things that you'd expect a house to have but it was abandoned and it was also the only place to get out of the incessant winds for miles around. It'd quite obviously been used as a campsite by other cyclists too judging by the footprints and tire tracks in the sand; we stayed there for the night. We only covered 24 miles (38 km) that day.

An hour into our ride the next morning, maybe 5 miles (8 km) tops, we passed the Arbol de Piedra or stone tree that marked the rough halfway point for the Ruta de Lagunas of southern Bolivia. The Arbol de Piedra was a rock that'd taken on the likeness of a tree after being eroded away by the constant wind and blowing sand over the millennia. Since our fourth day had just started, I was still hopeful we'd complete the route by the end of our sixth day.

While we were half riding half pushing down a sandy hill, we met a French cyclist pushing his way north on a couple month long tour through Chile and Bolivia. He asked about the road conditions on the way we had just ridden and we had to tell him the hard truth of the roads he had ahead. According to him, the roads got better in about 20 km (~12 miles). Excited at the prospect of better roads, we pedaled off with renewed motivation.

The bottom of the hill we were on was the entrance to a national park. We paid the extortionate entrance fee of 150 Bolivianos, about $22 US, to get in and the guard claimed he wouldn't let us in if we didn't have the money in cash even though nearest ATM was probably over 200 miles (320 km) away. Soon after the entrance was the Laguna Colorada Refugio. Refugio translates to something like 'refuge' or 'shelter' but in this case it was a collection of buildings where some people happened. We were able to fill our water then I bought beer, potato chips, and cookies for lunch which was very satisfying. I sat in the shade with my lunch and watched some very pink flamingos picking their way through a red colored lake that is the Laguna Colorada with multicolored hills in the background under a blue sky and remembered why I love cycle touring. It's fast enough to get somewhere and slow enough to see things along the way with the freedom to take a break anywhere and enjoy living in the moment.

For the next several miles the roads were mostly rideable, i.e. we didn't have to push our bikes much. About 12 miles (20 km) after we had met the Frenchman we came to the base of a large climb. It was mostly rideable going up but we realized he had mistaken good roads for "it was easy 'cause he was going downhill." We worked our way slowly up the climb while our efforts were hindered by the strong headwind to crosswind that had picked up regularly every day in the late afternoon.

There was a German cyclist on the climb, he was also headed south and we'd been seeing his tracks over the last couple of days. He was going to camp near to where we met him so we chose to keep going. Nearing what looked like the top of the climb there was a dug out area near the road that would serve to shelter our tents from some of the wind. There was little cover elsewhere and when we walked up a small hill we saw that there were no other options for a semi protected campsite. The shelter was not the greatest and, I had to cook in my tent's vestibule to keep my stove from being blown out by the wind.

Jesse took his time getting ready the next morning and we didn't leave camp till after 10:00 am. We hadn't seen the German cyclist pass us so we figured he must ride pretty slowly or be in the habit of starting equally late. The road continued to climb and did not improve contrary to the opinion of the Frenchman we met a day earlier. Our progress was painfully slow, less than 4 mph (6.4 km/h) while bouncing over the huge corrugations left by the tourist jeeps. It wasn't possible to go any faster and I tried a couple of times; my front wheel would begin jumping repeatedly off the washboard and I'd lose control then crash. Some sections were completely un-rideable and our contempt for the Frenchman we met yesterday was growing; the roads had not improved in the slightest.

After 5 miles and almost an hour and half of effort, the climb topped out at over 16,000 feet (4,850 meters) in elevation. By some miracle, the road was actually in decent condition on the other side but perhaps that's because it started going downhill. We descended comparatively quickly for a few miles but the road would turn bad again without warning at random intervals and send our bikes bucking over the washboard if we didn't cut our speed in time. Its condition varied widely throughout the rest of the day.

There was a small shop at the refugio by Laguna Chalviri. We got more water there then had beer and cookies for lunch; they didn't have any affordable potato chips. The road seemed to be in better condition after the refugio, we moved along as quickly as 8 mph (13 km/h) up a gradual incline. Like most days in southern Bolivia, the wind picked up suddenly in the afternoon and it was all we could do to go even 4 mph (6.4 km/h). We decided our energy would be better spent in the morning when there would hopefully be less wind so we camped a little early at a rocky outcropping about 22 miles (35 km) away from the border of Chile.

On our final push for the border of Chile, the road was much more heavily trafficked than our previous days had been and we'd get caught in clouds of choking dust on a regular basis. There were a couple of times where I had to quickly pull over to the side of the road because I was completely blinded by the dust from a passing vehicle. As we got to the edge of the national park the condition of the road began to deteriorate again and we had couple more sections of deep sand to push through. A barrier marked the end of the national park then we began the last few mile long climb to the border. Our raging midday headwind had come early and it hindered our progress; the roads had gone back to sand and washboard which made the last few miles excruciatingly long. A Swiss cycling couple heading north and had just crossed the border; they told us of the wonders of the town San Pedro de Atamcama: pizza, wifi, hotels with hot showers, and many excellent restaurants lay just down the mountain in Chile. Luckily, they'd already heard of the difficulties that lay ahead of them and apart from the desolate but beautiful scenery of the route we didn't have any good news for them. We fought our way up the climb with a renewed strength; motivated by the possibility of pizza and a hot shower that evening.

We rolled up to the border post just past noon, right as they were closing for a two hour lunch break. One of the guards saw us ride up and had enough sympathy to open up again to stamp our passports and send us on our way without making us wait for them to finish lunch. Jesse and I made it through the Ruta de Lagunas in 5.5 days.

Our riding day wasn't over just yet. A Chilean road crew was working on an improved road on the opposite side of the border; it was freshly steamrolled gravel, almost as good as pavement. We rode along in bliss for couple of miles before they said we were damaging the road and told us we had to ride in the sandy washboarded track that paralleled the road. This gesture earned Chilean road crews my instantaneous contempt. In anger, I powered my way through the dirt as fast as I could to get to the paved road sooner. A few miles later we made it to the paved road. Many cyclists take pictures of themselves kissing the paved road at the end of this stretch but we didn't bother. After a quick stop to fill up our tires with air, we began to fight our way into the headwind that had grown even stronger.

There were a few miles of rollers before the steep 6,000 foot (1,820 meter) descent into San Pedro de Atacama. Even with a raging headwind, I hit 45 mph (72 km/h) on the way down. Chilean immigration was located in the town of San Pedro and we stopped to enter the country legally before going into town. The $160 US reciprocity fee for Americans had been recently abolished and we entered the country at no cost. Chilean border guards had a reputation for searching absolutely everything cyclists were carrying across the border and confiscating most, if not all, food. Thankfully, this was not the case; the customs agent asked if we had any food to declare and gave the okay on everything we were carrying. The policy had changed to only fresh fruits and vegetables being a problem with the customs agents and after a more than week of cycling through the desert we didn't have any of those.

Finally in San Pedro, we exchanged our excess Bolivian currency and rode directly to the nearest pizza place. We noticed some price fixing on the hostels on the way to the pizza place and after an exceptionally satisfying large pizza each we checked into the first hostel we saw which happened to be literally next door to the pizza place. A gloriously hot shower awaited us and we rested for the remainder of the afternoon. I had a craving for vegetables and cooked up a pork and vegetable stir-fry for dinner. A group of travelers had seen us riding on their jeep tour through the desert we had just ridden through. One of them was celebrating their birthday and they happened to be staying at the same hostel. They'd bought extra food and invited us to join them for dinner. We accepted their invitation gratefully even though we'd already eaten and shared in a feast of rotisserie chicken, fries, and red wine while sharing some of our stories from the road.

PART THREE

San Pedro de Atacama, Chile to Ushuaia, Argentina to Ecilda Paullier, Uruguay

CHAPTER 24

Day 244, September 30, 2016

San Pedro de Atacama, Chile

I didn't sleep well for a reason unknown to me; perhaps because I wasn't used to sleeping in a bed anymore. I got out of bed around 4:00 am and began catching up on my journal until dawn came a few hours later. The drivetrain on my bicycle had gotten exceptionally dirty riding the Lagunas Route and I took an hour to clean it completely in hopes that I could make it last longer. After a significant amount of effort, I was satisfied with the result; hopefully, doing that more regularly would save me some money on parts in the long run.

Jesse and I went by a supermarket once he was up and ready to go at almost noon. It turned out to be a large and well stocked tienda with marked prices. Food was not cheap and eating out was even more expensive; the town of San Pedro de Atacama is supposedly one of the most expensive places in Chile; we got some snacks for lunch and food for dinner. When we got back, I finished updating my journal then lazed the rest of the afternoon away. Evening came as it tends to do and I made a rice and vegetable stir fry for dinner, I bought some beef for the stir fry also but it ended up being a much higher quality cut than I'd thought and I cooked it as steak instead. It made for another satisfying meal after the serious deficit of fresh food for the last couple of weeks. Despite the challenges of the Ruta de Lagunas, I'd enjoyed the experience but I was happy get to back to a place where I could get decent food again. Before bed, I got most of my gear prepped for an early departure in the morning.

My alarm went off at 6:15 am. I got the rest of my gear packed and affixed to my bike then had some bread with jam and cream cheese and a cup of tea for breakfast. I started riding alone around 7:30 am, my earliest start since the last time I cycled alone a couple of months ago. Jesse could not be convinced to climb Ojos del Salado with me; I chose to get ahead with plans to meet up with him father south. Ojos del Salado is the tallest volcano in the world and the second tallest mountain in South America with a summit at 22,614 feet (6,853 meters); it was only a few hundred feet lower than Aconcagua. I planned for it to be my last big mountain climb before I'd send all my excess gear home to cut weight and make riding more fun. After carrying that excess gear for over 11,000 miles (17,750 km), I was excited about getting rid of it. While I enjoyed climbing mountains, I hadn't been doing anywhere near as much of it as I'd planned to when I left home so it wasn't worth the extra weight.

The climb out of San Pedro started right away, the first one about 600 feet (180 meters) vertical followed by a descent of roughly equal height and then a 3,500 foot (1,060 meter) tall climb to the large plateau that makes up the Atacama Desert which is supposedly one of the driest places on earth; parts of the Atacama Desert hadn't had rain in recorded history. A few hours later I was at the top of the climb. The wind was just beginning to pick up in a crosswind/headwind direction as I'd guessed it would but I'd already gotten a good start to the day. Next, was a long gradual descent into the city of Calama. The wind was increasing in speed gradually; it was getting strong just as I got into the city in the early afternoon. I made a stop by the supermarket first; it was almost definitely the best grocery store I'd seen since Lima, Peru. I didn't need much but it was nice to know I could get just about whatever I wanted again and I wandered the expansive aisles of the supermarket for much longer than usual; I had a new appreciation for being able to find just about any kind of food at any time of year.

I decided to step outside my comfort zone and try asking to stay at a fire station in the city. Jesse had been doing most of the asking during our time cycling together. Asking for a place to stay wasn't something I'd normally do unless I absolutely needed to before that. The fire station wasn't marked on my maps and I asked directions from someone at the grocery store; they gave me a rough location a couple of miles away and I began looking. I got there and rode the entirety of the street they said it was on twice without result before asking someone else; this person pointed me in a direction a few blocks away with no result. I asked a third person and was given very specific directions to the point that I believed they knew where it was and I found it easily. Someone was just leaving who worked there and they said there wouldn't be anyone at the station until 9:00 pm that evening, more than five hours away. I asked if there was another station and they showed me the location on my map but when I rode there I couldn't find it; I tried a clover leaf pattern around the adjacent blocks without any luck and asked yet again. Once more, I tried asking for directions but I still couldn't find it so I began looking for a place to get water with the plan of riding out of the city then camping somewhere in the desert. While I was looking for a water tap I happened upon a fire station. There were two people standing outside and I asked them if they worked there to which they replied that they didn't and said they didn't think anyone was there either. I began looking at my map for a gas station to refill my water at and just as I was about to leave someone opened the door to let the two people waiting outside in; I was able to get their attention before they closed the door and asked if they had somewhere I could camp. They said they'd check with the boss and after some waiting they came back then said they had a place for me; I was welcomed in and shown around then I had a pleasantly cool shower, it was hot in the desert. The station had excellent wifi, a kitchen that I made use of later, and a bed I could sleep in too! I could get used to this.

It didn't look like there was anyone at the fire station when I woke up the next morning; I almost panicked when the thought that I could be locked in crossed my mind but was set at ease when I noticed a key had been left in the lock to the sliding garage door. I had bread and jam for breakfast and the firemen had said I could help myself to tea or coffee so I made some to go with it. I checked the station again as I was about to leave to try to find someone to thank for their hospitality but was unsuccessful and left right at seven.

The winds were favorable for my first few hours of cycling and I nearly flew down the gradual descent towards the coast. Around noon, the wind changed to a headwind but by that time I'd already ridden 80 miles (130 km). An hour and change later I was in the town of Baquedano. There was a fire station there and I went to see if I could stay there for the night but it appeared to be closed, the main gate was locked from the outside. Apparently, small town Chilean firemen had Sundays off. I was running low on water and asked at a shop near a park for some, they gave me as much as I needed and I sat in the park and ate some cookies that I bought from the same shop then read while I waited for the water to run through my filter. I thought I might try to make it a little farther after that and went back to riding. The headwind had increased in strength since I'd stopped and I was only able to ride at half my average speed for the day but that's not saying too much as I'd averaged just over 18 mph (29 km/h) getting to Baquedano. It didn't seem worth the effort to ride into that kind of wind so I stopped in a different park and read some more. Dinner time was approaching and cooking sounded like too much effort so I started riding out of town while keeping my eyes open for an affordable looking restaurant. The one I ended up at was probably the last one in town and I checked about getting something to eat. I got to talking with the owner as I was eating; pretty much the same conversation I have with almost everyone about what I'm doing, where I'm from and where I'm going. When the time came for me to pay for my meal the owner said my food was free; I told him that I had the money and it wouldn't be a problem for me to pay but he insisted on not charging me. I gave my thanks before I left and rode a mile or so out of town before I saw an open area that looked suitable for camping and started pushing my bike across the sand. There was a dry river bed that offered some shelter from the wind and I set up camp there.

My alarm went off at 6:15 am and I wanted to be on the road at 7:00 am. I'd forgotten how long it takes me to get dressed, pack everything, eat and push my bike to the road and I ended up not leaving till 7:30. I had a tailwind again for almost 2 hours of riding before I took the bypass road past the city of Antofagasta and the wind changed to a headwind. Near the turnoff I crossed out of the Tropic of Capricorn, the imaginary line that matches the angle of the tilt of the earth away from the equator. Leaving the tropics made it feel like I was getting somewhere on my southbound journey especially considering that I'd been in the tropics since somewhere in the desert in Mexico.

I rode to a gas station and went to the small market to find lunch. After careful consideration, I got potato chips and ice cream then sat outside in the shade at a table and hoped the wind would change to a tailwind by the time I was done eating. Lo and behold the wind began to change before my eyes as 11:00 am passed by; the wind died slowly till it was almost calm then it began blowing again in a tailwind. I almost couldn't believe it and after collecting another gallon or so (~3.8 liters) of water I started riding again; based on my maps the next opportunity to get water could be 100 miles (160 km) away. The Antofagasta bypass road I was on met up with the road heading south out of the city and marked the start of a gradual 90 mile (144 km) climb.

The road was trending upward but I had a tailwind pushing me along and I maintained a good pace. When I'd cycled almost exactly 80 miles (130 km) that day I arrived at Mano Del Desierto, hand of the desert. Apparently, there wasn't a good enough reason for people to visit the Atacama Desert so Chile had someone craft a giant sculpture of a hand to give tourists something to see. There were a few other people there and a tour bus had just left. With no fences or barrier to keep people from touching the sculpture, it was covered in graffiti on the lower portions. I considered camping near the desert hand but it was barely 3:00 pm. From the desert hand my map said the nearest marked gas station was 100 miles (160 km) away; that would be the first place I'd bet on there being water. Since it would be a shame to waste such an excellent tailwind and I had no guarantee of water being any closer than that gas station I kept riding.

Five pm came and went and I decided I'd ride till I was within a reasonable chance of being able to make it to the gas station where I could get water the next day. A reasonable distance seemed to be about 70 miles (124 km) which would give me 30 miles (48 km) or less of the gradual climb followed by 40 miles (64 km) of an equally gradual descent and therefore a good shot at making it before I ran out of water. I had enough water for an entire day of riding but if I had to go any longer than that I'd be hurting. There was also the possibility of there being water before the gas station too but I didn't know for sure. I reached my goal and it also happened to be my longest one day distance of the trip so far, 110 miles (176 km) and my riding time was just under eight hours. I pushed my bike up the side of a gravelly hill to an area that was relatively flat before cooking a dinner of rice with canned mackerel and seasoned it with a concoction of garlic salt and pepper; that was the cheapest thing they had at the supermarket with a decent amount of protein.

There was a headwind blowing when I woke up, it was bound to happen eventually. My GPS had miscalculated the distance to the gas station and I'd stopped about 75 miles (122 km) away from it. I'd be almost out of water by the time evening came and I likely wouldn't have enough to cook dinner and have any left to drink afterwards. With that in mind, I decided I was going to ride until I got to somewhere I could get water no matter how long it took. The headwind slowed my progress up the gradual climb. I had camped around 5,000 feet (1,520 meters) and the 7,000 foot (2,121 meter) pass was about 35 miles (56 km) away from where I started. It took me about four hours of riding to get to what looked like the top. The descent didn't start right away; the road dipped several hundred feet into a valley then climbed up the other side and continued climbing most of the way up again. A descent into a now raging headwind followed and I had to pedal going downhill to keep my speed above 15 mph (24 km/h) because of how strong the wind was.

When I finally got to where the gas station was marked in the settlement of Agua Verde and stopped at the adjacent restaurant I was at almost seven hours of riding time for the day and I had less than half a gallon (2 liters) of water left. I ate lunch there, bought some food at the tienda inside the restaurant, and filtered enough water to comfortably last me about 48 hours; more than 3 gallons (12 liters) or roughly 26 lb (12 kg) of water. My bike was feeling sluggish with all that water and it did nothing to help my pace. The headwind had not abated in the least; if anything, it seemed to have grown stronger. A couple more miles on a gradual descent brought me to the base of a 500 foot (150 meter) climb. I was going pitifully slow because of the wind and decided I'd push my bike off the road to camp. There was a flattish area up a hill so I began pushing; the hill was covered in loose rock and I was tired from the day's effort but I persevered and made it eventually. Out of breath and exhausted, I laid my bike down on the ground and collapsed next to it. The area I was at had zero shelter from the strong wind and I had to stake my tent out before pitching it to keep it from blowing away. I was still in view of the road but I was tired enough that I didn't care. After I had everything I'd need for the night inside my tent I crawled in and cooked dinner from inside and did my best not to leave my tent until it was time to get up in the morning.

The best way to beat the wind is to avoid fighting it; I got up at 5:00 am and I was riding an hour later. It was still dark when I started. The Milky Way was visible stretching across the sky looking much as its name would suggest, like milk had been splashed across the sky. I had my light on, a super bright taillight that I bought in Lima, but, my headlight had been stolen or fallen off somewhere. I don't recall when I first noticed it was missing. The taillight was bright enough that the passing cars were giving me a wide berth and the illumination from the night sky was enough to see the road. I pedaled over the top of the climb I'd camped on and began descending the other side just as it was getting light enough to see the road in detail and I zipped down the road towards the coast.

There were several sections of road construction along the way. Traffic had been diverted away from the main road and onto dirt for some few mile long stretches. At one of the diversions one of the construction workers said I could ride on a blocked off section of road that was no longer being worked on. By that time, I'd ridden over 50 miles (80 km) and it was barely 10:00 am. I stopped for a break a couple hundred yards before the cars went back from the dirt road to the paved road and tried to decide what to do for the rest of the day. I weighed my options: I could stop early or ride all the way to Chañaral. It'd be another 100+ mile (160+ km) day but if I had good winds it wouldn't be hard; if the winds were favorable, I'd keep going. While I was waiting, a construction worker stopped by to talk to me and gave me a carton of juice which made a wonderful treat way out in the desert.

The winds began to pick up and it was debatable whether they were favorable so I started riding to find out. I had a tailwind/crosswind at first but soon I was going uphill into a headwind. At the top of the climb, I tried to figure out if the road would turn in a direction to where the wind would be in my favor. It didn't look like it would and I rode down the other side to find somewhere to camp. It was barely noon when I saw a shelf on the side of a hill about a quarter mile (400 meters) off the road. It wouldn't be easy to get there but I'd be spending most of the day there so it'd be worth the effort; I'd covered 65 miles (105 km) and that seemed to be enough for the day, all things considered. I set up camp there and lay down in my tent with food and water in easy reach then tried not to get up for the rest of the day. I napped a bit then read for a long while and didn't get up for almost five hours. It was almost 6:00 pm when I got up to make dinner; all I had left was pasta with some olive oil and salt, it would have to do. I read more after dinner then went to bed as it was getting dark.

The next day was supposed to be an easy day into Chañaral, it wasn't. I started riding at dawn, a 1,000 foot (300 meter) climb right off the bat. No big deal, I'd done much harder climbs quite recently; I was over the top and going down the other side in short order. As the road leveled out my drivetrain quit working, it felt like the chain was slipping from being improperly lubricated so I stopped and lubed it. When I tried to start pedaling again, nothing happened; the pedals turned but the wheels did not. I got off my bike and tried to figure out what was happening then cursed under my breath when I saw that the coaster hub was spinning freely in both directions. I didn't have the tools to take apart my hub and dreaded trying to find a replacement. There was still 20 miles (32 km) between me and Chañaral but what to do now? I could hitchhike there but then I'd have to ride back to reconnect my line; I greatly preferred to keep it intact as I'd done so for more than 11,000 miles (17,750 km) so I started walking my bike. I couldn't pedal to turn the wheels anymore but I could coast downhill. It took me about an hour to walk up that hill and then I coasted a mile or so down a hill. Another hour of pushing my bike brought me to the top of a very large hill; the following descent took me most of the way into Chañaral and I couldn't have been happier with my decision not to try to hitchhike.

Once in town, I began asking around about a bike shop. There was one there as far as I could tell; people kept mentioning the same street name in their directions. I found it and walked in with my wheel, it was more of a mechanics shop than a bicycle shop, geared towards keeping bicycles working over selling them. I seriously doubted they'd have a new hub they could sell me but I was hopeful. The mechanic had no idea what was going on with my hub but he let me borrow the tools to take it apart. After taking it apart as much as I could, I couldn't figure out how to get the hub body off and I made a note to look it up online later. When I put everything back together it seemed to be working although I had no idea what the cause was. With my wheel reinstalled, I rode off, it was working again! Problem was, I'd lost all my trust in the hub and decided I'd rebuild or replace it if necessary in Copiapo, the next big city. As I was about to leave someone walked up then handed me a bag of oranges and wished me good luck on my travels; I thanked them as they walked hurriedly away.

I needed more food and went by the grocery store in town. After eating a bag of potato chips I rode by the fire station to ask about somewhere to camp. They recommended a large empty lot that they said would be a quiet place to camp and I rode out of town to try to camp on a beach. I made it about a mile out of town before I came to a small, steep hill. I shifted into a lower gear and, suddenly, I completely lost power; my free hub was spinning in both directions again and on top of that my chain had broken. The quick link of the chain had fallen off and I couldn't find it anywhere on the road so I used my chainbreaker to push out one of the pins enough to break that link then push it back in on the broken end to reconnect it. It was an operation that required three hands, one to de-tension the derailleur, one to line up the chain ends and another to work the chainbreaker. I made do with two hands and used my foot to de-tension the derailleur. Once I had my chain fixed and the link working smoothly I began walking back to the bike shop. It took probably four times as long as it took to ride there but I made it. The shop did not have a new hub or a complete wheel they could sell me. I sat outside the shop completely at a loss of what to do, the only thing I could think of would be to find somewhere to store my bike then take a bus to Copiapo to get a new hub then bus back to ride my bike to Copiapo. It wasn't ideal but it would work. Just as I was getting ready to ask about a place to store my bike and gear the owner of the bike shop came outside and said a very good mechanic had just shown up who might be able to fix my wheel. Alfonso the bike mechanic took it apart (I'd been doing it correctly but hadn't used enough elbow grease to get the cassette body off), filed the worn pawls into a working shape, reassembled the whole thing, and said I'd be good to get to Argentina at least but I wanted to replace it in Copiapo anyways. While Alfonso was looking at my bike he noticed the weld that held the handlebars into my frame was completely broken. This caused my steering to be loose and weakened the structural integrity of the frame but he determined it was not currently in danger of failing. I emailed the manufacturer at the next opportunity. On top of his amazing work he flatly refused any money and asked only that I mention him here. His name is Alfonso, he's a certified bicycle mechanic, sometimes he works at the only bike shop in Chañaral, Chile, and he's an awesome bike mechanic. Thanks Alfonso!

I headed out of town for the second time and when I got to the hill where my hub had failed... nothing went wrong. I resolved to soft pedal the entire 106 miles (170 km) to Copiapo to reduce the stress on the wheel if it meant I could ride the whole way. There was a semi flat area along the shoreline that sat below the road, it was visible from the road at one small spot but it was hidden enough to spend the night at for me. Right away, I decided that I'd forego setting up my tent for the night and just sleep on my tarp so I could hear and see the ocean. I made and ate dinner then went to bed after watching the sunset over the Pacific Ocean.

A fog rolled in from the ocean overnight and completely

soaked my sleeping bag. It was still dark when I started riding and I packed it away with the intention of drying it out later. The road rolled endlessly as I worked my way south along the coast. I was in a ponderous mood; the broken weld on my frame weighed heavily on my mind. I'd experienced so much frustration recently; most of it was caused by the weight of all the gear I'd been carrying. I was committed to climbing Ojos Del Salado and I'd have to carry it at least that much longer. With luck, it'd be less than a week before I could do the climb. I still hadn't been able to email the bike manufacturer about the broken weld. My frame was still under warranty and I hoped it'd be covered.

I rode into a town called Caldera around noon and went to the grocery store; there were actual grocery stores in Chile and I loved it. With the food I bought for dinner and snacks for the next day, I bought a slice of the tres leches cake that I'd grown quite fond of since being in Latin America and sat outside while I ate it. There was a free 30 minute limit per day wifi connection in the town square that I took advantage of; I called home and checked a few things online before it timed out so I rode down to the harbor to take a look around. A seafood lunch sounded great. There was a ritzy little restaurant on the waterfront that was about double the price I was willing to spend. After a quick glance at the menu I knew I wasn't going to eat there. As I was leaving, one of the waiters recommended a cheaper place nearby; I went in that direction and ended up getting some amazing shrimp and oyster empanadas for a few dollars at a small establishment about a block away.

There was a fire station in Caldera and I tried asking there about a place to stay. It was the all too familiar case of the missing commandant who would return late at night and didn't have a cell phone to call and ask either; I'd asked someone who didn't want to say "no" and preferred to place the blame on a different person. It is possible that the commandants in many fire stations are gone all day long making rounds hither and tither and only return late in the evening, I preferred to give them the benefit of the doubt. After all, I was asking for a free patch of ground to sleep on for the night. I rode out of town and found a quiet place where I could camp later. After lying out my damp sleeping bag over my bike to dry out, I began to think on my current plight of carrying too much weight and having a partially broken frame. I was sick and tired of all the extra attention from riding a recumbent bicycle and decided I'd start looking for a normal upright touring bike that I could switch to. It'd take some work; I'd have to begin rehabbing my back and the joints in my arms to go back to the upright position. That was the reason I'd been riding a recumbent in the first place and I'd need some new gear. It would come at a cost but I believed it would be worth it. I'd go entirely to frame bags, and cut roughly in half the amount of gear weight I was carrying with a minimal reduction in practicality. Yes, it is possible to travel the world with less than half the weight I had then and if it wasn't I was about to find out. I wouldn't be able to sleep comfortably in temperatures approaching zero degrees Fahrenheit (-18 C) but they wouldn't kill me either. I'd be better off avoiding such weather in anyways. I'd have the potential to climb much faster and cruise at speed on the flats almost effortlessly compared to my current setup; though I felt I'd likely ride easier and go at least as fast. Enjoying the ride had become my top priority on this trip and the cycling that should have been enjoyable was often frustrating because of the extra weight. I'd still climb Ojos Del Salado but it wasn't far away from where I was and I'd been carrying the gear for it for so long that I felt obligated to use it once more before sending it home along with so many other things. With my problems now settled in my mind and having the plan-ahead mindset that I do, I wrote out a few lists of what I'd need to make everything work. An hour or two later, I was satisfied with my work and started my rehab exercises. If I started right away there was a good chance I'd be ready by the time I got everything I'd need to make the switch. I'd need to do a little every day so I didn't forget or grow lazy, maybe another month of heavily encumbered cycling to go before I could go ultralight. I'd best be prepared.

It was just dark enough to need lights when I started riding in the morning. The road ascended in a gentle rolling climb the entire way to Copiapo. It took me a little more than three hours of riding to get to the city which felt pretty good considering it was 45 miles (72 km) away. Once there I made a bee-line towards the nearest major grocery store to buy 11 days' worth of food for the few days ride up Paso San Francisco and then the mountain climb up Ojos Del Salado plus a little extra just in case. I ended up spending about $75 US on food, the most I'd ever spent on groceries at one time in my entire life. It took close to an hour to pack it all into my bags in a manner that I was satisfied with. I tried to get as much as possible into the front panniers, this ended up being about three cans of sardines in each front bag. Almost all the food made it into my panniers which showed just how ridiculous the amount of excess space I had was but I had an extra plastic bag hanging off the back for a couple pounds (~1 kg) of cookies. Finally set for my upcoming expedition, I began hunting for wifi.

There were several places in the mall that had a signal but the employees had no idea what the passwords were. There was a hardware superstore with a cafe that happened to have a connection so I stayed for about five hours. I spent most of the afternoon looking for a solution to a new bike before coming to the conclusion that purchasing a bike in Mendoza, Argentina then sending my excess gear home would be my best option and I sent out a few emails inquiring about a new bike. There were a few bike shops there and I emailed one about my situation and asked about the possibility of them having a bike ready for me.

I was completely torn as to what to do about my hub going bad; it seemed to be in good condition but it was liable to fail at any time. Spending money on a new hub didn't make sense if I was going to get a new bike in Mendoza but I needed a solution for the possibility of it failing again. Buying the tools to fix it on the road seemed to be a reasonable middle ground to replacing it or doing nothing and I felt confident I'd be able to get it working again after seeing Alfonso do it. I rode to a bike shop but it was closed; I'd have to try again in the morning. I hung around the town square until almost 8:00 pm; I'd arranged a place to stay at a Warmshowers.org host and I wasn't supposed to be at their house until 8:00 pm. I rode over to the address they gave me and eventually found their place after some difficulty. My host Felipe welcomed me into his home and introduced me to his wife and two sons. Felipe had learned about the Warmshowers hospitality site while touring through southern Chile and he hosted cyclists when possible. My hosts were cooking pizza for dinner and after I took a shower I tried to help with the preparation. There wasn't too much to be done and Felipe's youngest son wanted me to watch him and his brother play a video game; I did my best to look attentive while I used the wifi to do more research on a new bike. Dinner was some incredible homemade pizza, likely the best pizza I'd had since leaving home. Felipe spoke English and we stayed up talking well past one in the morning.

My goal for my rest day in Copiapo was to find the tools I'd need to fix my hub if it happened to fail again. I left shortly after noon and walked to the bike shop I'd checked yesterday but it was still closed. It was about lunch time when I went by a grocery store to see what I could find. They had whole rotisserie chicken on sale, I bought one and ate it all sitting outside the grocery store with almost a pound (454 grams) of bread to sop up the grease. Felipe had mentioned there being some bike shops in the mall so I made that my next stop and I checked every shop that sold bicycles there for the tools I needed. There happened to be quite a few shops but none of them had the tools. The same bike shop I'd gone by earlier was still closed, apparently because it was Sunday. No luck finding tools meant I'd just have to be careful not to stress the hub too much and hope that it would hold out. I went to a different grocery store than the one I'd gone to earlier to get a few more cookies for the road on the way back.

Jesse had taken the coastal route as opposed to the desert route that I took. I must have miscalculated something as he was only one day behind me and would arrive in Copiapo that afternoon. Felipe was fine with Jesse staying at his place as well and he showed up an hour or so after I got back. Felipe had invited me to go rock climbing and hiking with him and some of his friends that afternoon. Jesse was invited too but chose to stay behind to rest. Felipe and I met with his friends and drove out of town to do some climbing. The first place we went to was for free climbing. I kind of did my own thing as Felipe and his friends were choosing easier routes. I climbed to the top of a hill and tried to go down a different way that had looked easier from the bottom but ended in a 20 foot (6 meter) overhanging cliff; I didn't want to risk falling and getting injured so I backtracked a long way to meet up with the route I'd climbed up on.

The second place we went to was for top roping. We checked out the area for a bit before getting on harnesses for some more technical climbing. I had T-Rex syndrome from extended cycle touring without really exercising my upper body and I'd worn myself out free climbing; I didn't do well on the more technical climbing. It was dark when we left the climbing area and we didn't get back to Felipe's until after 9:00 pm. Dinner was some more amazing homemade pizza but we didn't start eating until midnight. Conversation and a movie followed, we were up until 3:00 am this time.

I had planned to leave around 8:00-9:00 in the morning but because of the late night the previous evening I didn't even get up till after 8:00 am and didn't leave until a couple of hours later. After many gracious thanks to Felipe, I was on my way. Jesse was staying behind to take a day in Copiapo and we made plans to meet up later. The feeling that I'd forgotten something came soon after I left; at first I couldn't think of what it was but then I realized it was the water bottles that were about 2/3 of my carrying capacity and total supply. Upon checking, I confirmed that I had forgotten them but I was already 5 miles (8 km) away from Felipe's. To ride back and get them then return to where I was could take an hour or more because of the gradual climb I was going up. There happened to be a tienda so I bought a 3 liter of ginger ale as much for the container as the liquid inside that would be enough to get by. A decent bike path lasted for most of the way out of the city. Because I was riding with a strong tailwind, I was soon free of the confines of the city and back on the road again. A sign at the edge of the city that said it was 300 miles (480 km) to the next town with services; it would be by far the longest gap without any populated areas or places to restock I'd ever done.

Immediately after the turnoff for Paso San Francisco and Ojos Del Salado the traffic dropped off to maybe one or two vehicles every hour. In addition to the drop in traffic the road turned to dirt but it was such a well maintained road that I didn't realize it for several miles. After a few hours of riding I saw the wholly unexpected sight of a restaurant. I stopped to try to get more water but the restaurant was devoid of people to the point where it may have been abandoned. There was a barrel of water on the side of the building where I was able to refill my water. I didn't see much else after that. The grade picked up considerably after the restaurant and in order to reduce the torque on my questionable hub I decided that if my speed dropped below 3 mph (5 km/h) I'd start pushing. Sadly, this was very often because of all the extra food I was carrying. An hour or so before dark I saw a large rock near the road that would make a nice windbreak and conceal my tent from the view of passing cars. I stopped with about seven hours of riding time.

The wind was blowing when I woke up; it'd been shaking my tent for half the night. I couldn't tell right away whether it would hurt or help me but there wasn't anything I could do about that. The road climbed fairly consistently with only a few rollers and a couple of flatter sections. Once again I stuck with pushing my bike if my speed dropped below 3 mph (5 km/h) which was pretty often. Approaching noon, I got to Minas De Oro, one of several mines in the area where I'd heard I could get water. It was only midday and I pushed on to try to make it to the border post almost 30 miles (48 km) away. The road deteriorated significantly after I passed the mine and I had to ride all over the road to find a smoother line. Around 10,000 feet (3,000 meters) in elevation the grade picked up again and I was doing more pushing than riding. Several people took pity on my pushing and stopped to give me water or just say hi; by the time I was near the top enough people had given me water that I had enough water to camp and I had a liter of apple juice too.

At just over 13,000 feet (3,940 meters) the damaged weld that held my handlebars onto my frame broke and they fell out of the underside of my bike resulting in me crashing while going about 4 mph from loss of steering; well, this was a fine pickle. The handlebars attached to the underside of the frame on my recumbent bike so I tried tying my handlebars into the frame with some cord. It kept them out of the way but when I tried riding I crashed almost immediately and skinned my knee because of how much play there was in the bars. I really didn't want to push my bike for the next 700 miles (1,120 km) to Mendoza where I hoped to get a new bike so I sat on the side of the road and tried to come up with a solution. I tried tying my ice axe that I used for mountain climbing to the fork and sliding my seat forward so I could reach the axe to steer and still pedal, it kind of worked, I could ride a little but not well at all. Then, when I saw the retaining strap dangling off the edge of my ice axe I had an idea. I slid my seat back again and used one of the straps off my panniers to make 'reins' that I could steer with. I even found that I could hold the handlebars and have use of my braking and shifting while steering with the reins. I was pleased with my work but there was one problem, I'd fall over every time I stopped because I had no way to balance my bike. I hoped it wouldn't break any worse than that. I pushed most of the rest of the way over the 14,000+ foot (4,240 meter) pass then began the slight descent on the other side; I was able to ride though with the increased danger of crashing from the lack of control I kept my speed much lower than normal. Still, it was far quicker than walking. I fell over a few times and had several close calls; mostly whenever I'd try to stop. One such fall had my seat painfully scrape the top couple of layers of skin of my calf, not enough to draw much blood but it exposed the nerves and stung until the wound dried out.

There were a few places to camp that would have been sheltered from the wind but the Chilean border post was just barely in sight and I wanted to accomplish my goal. They were just closing up at 7:00 pm when I got there and said I'd have to wait till the morning to cross. I didn't like the idea of having to wait but they showed me to a bedroom with several bunk beds and said I could sleep there. This was a surprising turn of events and I accepted graciously; I was happy to have a warm place to sleep.

I had to wait for the border post to open in the morning so I could get my exit stamp for Chile. They were supposed to open at 9:00 am at 10 minutes past that hour I went looking for someone and found an official who could help me. Thanks to computer troubles what should have taken a few minutes took more than half an hour, I finally left at 10:00 am. The road had turned to pavement shortly before the border post yesterday and my skill at steering my bike with 'reins' had improved to where I was able to ride pretty well. I avoided stopping as much as possible, not only because I'd left so late but because I had fallen over almost every time I tried to stop because of my handlebars being broken. Since I could no longer ride one handed, I realized just how often I had done so now that I couldn't anymore.

After a gentle rolling incline for about 18 miles (29 km) the road turned skyward. It was steep enough that it took everything I had to stay above 3 mph (5 km/h) in some sections.

It was a frustrating experience working so hard and getting so little in return but I took heart in knowing that I was almost done with the last major pass before I could cut weight and travel lighter. A few miles later the road went back to a gentle rolling incline. The winds were strong, occasionally headwinds or crosswinds but favorable more often than not. Whenever I stopped for a break I'd sit in what little shelter my bike created to keep out of the wind, I couldn't stop for more than 15 minutes without becoming cold enough that I'd have to start riding again to warm up. I could have put more clothes on but then I would have been overheating when I was riding.

About 40 miles (64 km) into my day the pavement ended. The road was in decent condition for the most part though there were a few sandy sections. Eventually, I reached the turnoff for the volcano I'd climb, Ojos del Salado. The road deteriorated immediately after the turnoff to long sections of sand and washboard. Because of my jury rigged steering I had to push more than normal. I crested a small hill and caught sight of the basecamp refugio that was my goal for the day. I pushed my bike the rest of the way there and leaned it against the side of the building before checking out the refugio. It was the run down remnant of what looked much like a house. There was no one else there and it had the look of being ill maintained on the inside; dirty and a few cracked windows. It was a bit drafty but much better shelter than my tent would have been in the powerful winds and I hauled my bike and gear up the short flight of stairs and inside.

It was around 5:00 pm when I got there and I had six hours of riding time for the day. I made and ate dinner: rice, sardines, and a bit of chorizo salami mixed together. There were mattresses inside and I dragged the one that looked in the best condition into an open area on the floor and set up my sleeping stuff. The old foam mattress was much preferable to my leaky air mattress. The sun began to set and the temperature began to drop quickly inside as well as out and I was in bed by eight.

CHAPTER 25

Day 257, October 13, 2016

Ojos Del Salado base camp, Chile

I t was a cold morning; much of my water had frozen, even the bottles I kept right next to my sleeping bag. I waited for the sun's rays to hit the refugio before I went outside and started riding around eight in the direction of Ojos Del Salado's mid camp, the Atacama Refugio. The dirt road was rideable but slow; I made it a little over a mile before I came to a penitente field that stretched completely across the valley I was in with no way to feasibly go around. Penitentes are an ice formation caused by the intense sunlight melting the snow and refreezing from the low air temperature almost instantly that creates a kind of saw tooth surface on ice that sometimes looks like spikes. They usually aren't sharp but they are incredibly difficult or impossible to cross. Some of them can be up to 10 feet (3 meters) tall, but these were 2-3 feet (60-90 cm) tall. I tried taking my bags off and hauling my bike across. After slipping on the ice and almost twisting my knee I realized it wasn't worth the effort and risk to get my bike across. I moved my bike and gear over a small ridge where they would be out of sight from the road and transferred all the gear I'd need for the climb to my backpack; I hadn't seen anyone since I turned off the main road the day before so they'd probably be safe. I walked and crawled carefully across the penitente field and began walking towards the Atacama Refugio 13 miles (21 km) away. My pack was probably around 50 lb (22 kg) loaded with all the gear and food I'd need for up to 4 days. It was already cold enough that I was wearing most of my clothes, hence the lighter pack weight than my climb up Orizaba.

The road could have been rideable for the first mile or two that I walked after the penitentes and I almost regretted leaving my bike behind until I crested a hill and saw another large penitente field that I had to cross. This obstacle was followed by miles of sand and deep gravel that would have been impossible to ride on with my bike. The hike up to the middle camp was the most barren landscape I'd ever seen, grey to brown gravel everywhere with patches of snow surrounded by volcanoes that were covered in scree. The Atacama Refugio was an orange shipping container with a couple of beds inside and a window at about 17,100 feet (5,120 meters) in elevation and I was feeling the effects around four pm. I melted snow from the surrounding snow patches with my stove to get water and make dinner. My pasta dinner turned into mush because of the lower boiling point at the high elevation.

My goal for the next day was acclimatizing; I'd just come out of Bolivia and had spent a couple of weeks there at and above 13,000 feet (3,940 meters) in elevation. I didn't think I'd need to acclimatize too much; after all, I'd climbed Pico de Orizaba just fine and I hadn't really acclimatized at all for that. I took my time getting everything ready and began hiking up the mountain around 9:00 am. The trail felt steep with my heavy pack and I was doing the mountaineers walk of one foot just barely in front of the other; I didn't have far to go so I took breaks whenever I felt like it and maintained an easy pace.

The Tejos Refugio all of 3.5 miles (5.5 km) away from the Atacama Refugio; it was at about 19,200 feet (5,820 meters) and right at the base of the steep push to the summit of Ojos del Salado. This refugio was also made from shipping containers but it was bigger than Refugio Atacama in which I'd slept the previous night. When I walked into the empty refugio before 2:00 pm; I was really feeling the elevation. I laid on one of the old beds all afternoon. I made a much smaller dinner than I'd normally eat and I wasn't able to finish it; I'd barely been able to eat all day; a peanut butter and jelly sandwich when I woke up and a smallish pack of cookies spread out through my day's hike and the afternoon. With dinner, I'd probably eaten less than 2,000 calories; average intake on a riding day for me was 6,000+ calories.

Ojos Del Salado didn't have much of a glacier left; this meant the crazy early starts that are normal for a summit day were largely unnecessary. I was up just as the world was turning grey from the approaching dawn and began my climb shortly after. Because I was surrounded by grey rock with patches of snow the only difference in daylight was the blue sky. There was a trail at first though it soon disappeared in the remnants of last winter's snow and I put my crampons on before working my way across it. What had been a trail was now a scree field, loose rock similar to deep gravel and, one of the most difficult surfaces for climbing. It was three steps forward and two steps sliding back because of the loose surface for the majority of the remaining 3,000 vertical feet (900 meters) to the summit. As I got closer, I switched to climbing up the steep mountainside on my hands and feet in a bear-crawl motion to try to conserve energy. No matter how long I climbed, the summit never seemed to get any closer and it was visible from the refugio; the bottom would get farther away but the illusion remained. The last few hundred vertical feet were a scramble over large rocks; as I was climbing just below the summit, I felt the fingers of my right hand getting cold and saw the middle finger of my glove had ripped open. That was my only chance at the summit and I protected my hand as best I could by shoving it in the pocket of my down jacket then kept climbing. The wind was getting dangerously strong and would come close to knocking me over as I climbed higher; soon, the wind was howling with a fury I'd never felt before and when I worked my way over the crest that marked the summit I was genuinely afraid of being blown off the mountain. I settled for a touch and go of the 22,614 foot (6,853 meter) summit while hugging the mountain to avoid being blown off by the wind. Being blown off the mountain there and getting injured would mean almost certain death. I had a GPS rescue beacon but helicopters wouldn't be able to fly at that elevation with that much wind and I hadn't seen anybody since leaving the main road a few days ago. I was worried that the wind would continue to get stronger as the day progressed and began descending as fast as I felt was safe. Back at the Tejos Refugio a couple of hours later, I assessed the damage. My hands had gotten too cold even though I'd kept them in my pockets as much as possible; I had minor cold damage on the fingertips of both hands and severe frostbite on the middle finger of my right hand. My frostbitten finger was black and blistered from the cold just like it would from heat; it resembled a sausage that had caught on fire then left burning. As the feeling returned the pain came with it; many of the nerves had been so severely damaged that it didn't hurt as much as I expected.

I was experiencing serious symptoms of altitude sickness and made the tough decision to descend to the Atacama Refugio to avoid any more complications. The edges of my vision were closing in; one of the most severe symptoms of cerebral edema, swelling in the brain caused by ascending in elevation too quickly. Excess fluid buildup in my skull was putting pressure on the optic nerve in my eyes and causing the sensation of tunnel vision. That could eventually kill me from the blood vessels in my brain bursting. I was coughing up fluids too, a symptom of pulmonary edema also from the elevation. To die that way would be like drowning in my own bodily fluids. My face was swollen and blistered red from the intense sun and ice was crusted on all the hair on my face. Technically, I could die from that too but the other problems would kill me much faster. Descending in altitude was my only chance at survival and getting to the middle camp had the added benefit of putting me close enough that I could probably make it back to base camp the next day.

The wind was raging up the mountain when I went back outside and it was strong enough that I had to lean into the wind while walking downhill; I got blown backwards up the mountain and knocked off my feet a few times. After talking to people who had experienced such strong winds before, the wind speed was likely above 100 mph (160 km/h). Wind chill at that speed is off the charts. Considering the average summit temperature on Ojos del Salado in October is -10 F (- 25 C). With wind chill the temperature would have been below -60 F (-51 C). At that temperature, frostbite will occur in less than 10 minutes of exposure.

I made it back to the mid-camp Atacama Refugio around 5:00 pm. I collapsed onto the bed and got up only to make a dinner that I wasn't able to eat all of. I took some anti-inflammatories to try to reduce the swelling then went to bed hoping I wouldn't die in my sleep.

I didn't die in my sleep. Coming so close to dying convinced me that I wanted to continue living when I wasn't always so sure before. All of the water that I hadn't placed directly next to my sleeping bag had frozen overnight. I crawled out of my sleeping bag shortly after dawn shivering and sore from yesterday's efforts. After dressed as quickly as possible to try to warm up sooner I tried to eat something even though my appetite still hadn't come back. It was difficult to leave what little comfort the shelter afforded and go out into the wind and below freezing temperatures. It was the only option I had for leaving the mountain and I was almost out of food.

First, I had to get back to my bike where I'd stashed it 13 miles (21 km) away. I was sore from the climb and had to stop frequently to try to regain some strength. After nearly laying on the ground for a few minutes at a time I'd shoulder my heavy pack and get back to walking. I'd been walking for six hours by the time I was crossing the second to last penitente field; on the other side I met some Romanians who were about to head up the volcano I'd just climbed. I wasn't quite in my right mind so I wasn't as helpful as I could have been. I gave them as much information as I could while nearly lying on the ground from exhaustion. Even with all the trouble I'd just had the Romanians didn't seem prepared and they were the first people I'd seen since I turned off the main road five days ago. It was just over 2 more miles (3.5 km) to get to my bike at that point and it took a couple more rest breaks to get there. It would have taken me over an hour to get my bike back into rideable condition, repacking my gear and redoing my steering, so I chose to walk it. Walking is an overstatement; I was balancing my backpack and hobbling. The minutes and distance ticked by mercilessly slow on my cyclocomputer but I progressed as best I could. The crosswinds were incredibly strong and I had to throw my weight to one side or the other to keep from falling. I knew if I did it would take some time before I had the strength to pick my bike up and continue pushing. After more than 30 minutes later of pushing my bike in a special kind of agony I collapsed into the sheltered lower area of the base camp refugio. I lay on my back spread eagled except for my frostbitten hand that was tucked into my jacket and I laid there for several minutes until I was struck by a violent coughing fit. I rolled over into the fetal position and had to cough up more fluid before I could breathe again. A long time passed before I felt I had the strength to start getting my gear back in order and my bike rideable again. I dumped everything out into a pile and began sorting through it. It took a couple of hours because of how slow I was moving but eventually I had everything packed except for what I'd need for the night. I had pasta and chorizo salami for dinner. This time I ate all of it. I was completely stuffed afterwards; my stomach had shrunk over the last few days of barely eating in comparison to how many calories I was burning. I didn't have the energy to read and I laid down on one of the old mattresses in the refugio after I'd eaten and went to bed.

I was understandably quite sore the next morning and started my day with a self-medication of coffee and anti-inflammatories. I was feeling so much better afterwards that

I was actually looking forward to cycling again. I hopped on my bike and started back towards the main road but my happiness was short lived. About 150 yards (135 meters) later I succumbed to the thick gravel and washboard and fell over. My metaphorically full morale spilled into the dirt as I fell and I knew it was going to be a very long day. The washboard and gravel continued on and off until the main road. Steering my bike with reins did not help and I was pushing most of the way while feeling terrible in general. Once I got back to the main road I could ride my bike but I was still going pitifully slow for how hard I felt I was working. The road meandered next to a serene blue lake; as a photograph it would be a stark yet peaceful scene but it was an awful place. Freezing winds blew at almost 15,000 feet (4,540 meters) in elevation while my frostbitten finger pulsed in agony at every heartbeat. I thought I was hallucinating when I saw the pinkest flamingos I'd ever seen fly by. There were flamingos in Bolivia but those ones were a neon pink color that was better suited to a cartoon character.

The road climbed away from the lake and towards Paso San Francisco, I even had a tailwind but still I was feeling awful. Through a turn, what was a tailwind became a crosswind that nearly blew me off the road. I wasn't off the road but I was in a thick gravel patch; with my questionable steering and the gravel the equation ended with me lying in the dirt. My morale reached a record low; I was down in the dumps and feeling sorry for myself, I wondered why I began to put myself through all the pain and suffering of traveling by bicycle. Why hadn't I just given up on mountain climbing and sent my gear home in Peru? There was nothing I could do to improve my situation except start pushing so that's what I did; I walked my bike most of the way up the pass. Occasionally, I'd get tired of pushing and try to ride but it never worked out well. Before long I'd be picking my 120+ pound (55+ kg) bike up off the dirt and have to go back to pushing.

I knew why I was doing this to myself, most of the time

traveling by bicycle was pretty great and overall I enjoyed it. What I was experiencing was type 3 fun. Type 1 fun is fun in the moment, something that's enjoyable as it's happening. Type 2 fun is fun after the fact, like overcoming a challenge. Type 3 fun is never actually fun, it usually comes from a horrendously poor decision though it can make a great story.

I resolved to not only get a new bike as soon as possible but to also get rid of as much gear as reasonable. My gear weight limit dropped steadily in my mind's eye until I was at a reasonable goal of under 10 kilograms, 22 pounds. The prospect of such an improvement boosted my morale significantly and when I saw the pavement over the top of the climb I hopped on my bike, gathered my steering reins, and started pedaling. Nothing could stop me after that and soon I was over the top and going down the other side.

Maybe that did a bit too much for my morale as I hit 45 mph (72 km/h) on the descent and I was down to the border post in an hour. I walked into the border and submitted my passport. It'd been six days since I was stamped out of Chile; the border guards were upset and questioned me. I took off my right glove and showed them my middle finger (not like that, the frostbite part). I'd expected as much and told them the short version of what had happened. After the official picked his jaw up off the floor he told me to wait. Another official came back and said they were going to give me a ride to Fiambala. When I asked why he said it was because the weather was freezing and the winds were strong. I objected vehemently stating that winds and weather were not an issue then told them I could be in the next town Fiambala in a day. Another border official asked me how long it'd taken for me to get there from Copiapo and I told him three days of riding. He figured it'd take me at least that long to get to Fiambala and I reasoned with him that it was mostly downhill and if it took that long it didn't matter to me. He looked at me like I was crazy; he'd seen my frostbitten finger and probably noticed the dark blistered scabs on my face from the second degree sunburn. The wild glint in my eyes from my regained morale likely didn't help but he was probably right in his opinion. He sighed after a moment, then handed me my passport with the Argentina entry stamp and said I was free to go. I was glad and did so.

The road was flat away from the border post and even slightly uphill but soon it turned down the canyon and with a strong wind at my back I flew down the road. The border had taken a while and I stopped at one of the several refugios/shelters lining the road every 15 miles (24 km) or so and called it a day. I looked up how far it would be to get to Mendoza and was pleased to see that it was just over 550 miles (880 km) away. If everything went well that would probably take long enough that I could order my new bike and have it waiting for me when I got there.

The wind was howling when I woke up on the floor of the refugio. Thankfully, it was blowing in a favorable direction. On my bike, I was getting blown down the road so quickly that it was almost unnecessary to pedal at all on flat ground and even on some slightly uphill sections. Early in the day I hit 12,000 miles; I cycled nonstop much of the morning after I hit my milestone. The going was easy and when I did stop I was at almost 60 miles (96 km) for the day in less than three hours of riding down the gentle rolling descent but the road had just turned and the wind was no longer helping me.

I rode another hour or so until I felt my rear tire going soft. It was punctured by an apparent piece of glass, it'd dislodged before I stopped and that conclusion was based on the appearance of the hole in the tube. I patched the tube and then continued on my way. After that I had a headwind and I was going quite slowly. I felt my tire going flat yet again; my initial guess was that the patch had failed. Upon examination the interior of the tire was beginning to come apart and it had caused a patch to come loose. I re-patched the hole and used a piece of cardboard to boot the inside of the tire to hopefully keep it from coming apart.

The last 10 miles (16 km) into Fiambala took over an hour

of riding because of the headwind. Once there I tried to find an ATM, I was low on food to where it was a pressing need. There was an ATM near the main square that I tried but my card wouldn't work. I was growing worried and tried to find a money changer to exchange some of my US dollars that I kept for such a situation, but the one place that could do it was closed. I asked around and finally found another ATM at a bank that happened to work. After buying food I went looking for wifi to figure out what was going on with my bicycle prospects. There was a free connection in the town square and I found to my disappointment that the bike shop in Mendoza could not get me the bike I wanted as it was not available in Argentina. I tried emailing a shop in Santiago, Chile about getting a bike.

I was exhausted after my efforts of the last week or so and decided I'd find somewhere to stay for a rest day or two. There was a municipal hotel but it was much more money than I wanted to spend so they referred me to a hostel a few blocks away. It took some finding but when I did it was half the price of the other hotel. I doubted I was going to find much better and I was the only guest at the hostel so I'd have an entire dorm room to myself. I checked in and took a much needed shower then ate most of my leftover food. The owner noticed my frostbitten finger. He mentioned that Argentina had free healthcare and that there was a clinic a couple of blocks away. This sounded like an excellent idea and I walked over to the clinic. It took some waiting but it was free medical care so I wasn't complaining. They checked out my finger and said they'd need to clean it out to see how bad the damage was. They peeled all the black and blistered skin off with tweezers and a scalpel then scrubbed it out with iodine, but, that small hospital in Argentina didn't have any painkillers and by the time they were finished I was seeing stars and almost fainting from the pain. They told me it wasn't severe enough to need to be amputated but I might not regain full feeling in it. They bandaged it up and shot me up with some antibiotics then gave me some more medication to take over the next few days. They sent me back to the hostel with some supplies in case I was unable to go to a clinic every day to get it cleaned and have the bandage changed.

After I left the clinic it was time to find dinner. While I was on the volcano I'd promised myself that I'd have a steak and wine dinner if I made it out alive; it was time to make good on that promise. I couldn't find any restaurants that served that kind of food so I chose to cook it myself. At the small grocery stores, more like large tiendas, I tried to find out what was cheaper than it should be as there was usually something like that in almost every country; in Argentina one of the comparatively cheaper items was wine. I bought a 1.5 liter bottle of red wine for less than $2. Steak ended up being pretty cheap too. I couldn't identify the cut but I bought over 2 pounds (1 kg). Onions were pretty cheap too and I bought about a pound (500 grams) to sauté with my steak. I went back to the hostel and cooked everything up. It turned out excellently. I had a leftover steak to save for breakfast and 2/3 of my wine left too. I was exhausted after eating so I went to bed and slept well for the first time since before the climb up the volcano.

The wine wore off in the wee hours of the morning and the throbbing pain of my flayed finger woke me up. Wine was the only painkiller I had and I drank more then went back to sleep for a few more hours. I was up early so I started trying to figure out a solution for a new bike. I hadn't heard back from the shop I'd emailed in Santiago; the shop in Mendoza said they could get mountain bikes and after throwing the idea around for a while it sounded like my best option. I tried calling them and found to my great disappointment that they could not get anything bigger than a size large frame. In most cases an XL frame was a little small for me. I was at a loss of what to do next and considered having my road racing bike from home sent out. I was all set with the idea and, out of desperation, I was prepared to pay the high cost of shipping it out. After some deep thought over a couple of hours about getting my bike sent out and after much consideration I remembered how long Jesse's new bike had taken to arrive. There was too much that could go wrong with shipping, customs, and everything else involved with trying to get it to Argentina. Still, I needed a bike and riding to Mendoza to hopefully find something still seemed to be my best option. It would probably end up not being the ideal bike but I reasoned that if I really didn't want to try to finish out my tour on it I could replace it in Europe relatively easily if I wanted. I went by the hospital again that evening to get my frostbitten finger cleaned out and the bandage changed. After that I made some rounds to find something for dinner and ended up making a giant stir fry of rice, peppers, onions and chorizo sausage. I ate it all in an attempt to begin to gain back some of the weight I'd lost on Ojos Del Salado.

Jesse had gotten ahead of me while I was climbing the volcano. When I'd asked him about the road conditions he had mentioned that it was almost impossible to game the wind and he was right. When I left at 7:30 am the morning after my rest day a strong headwind was already blowing. I pedaled slowly out of Fiambala and began counting down the 480 miles (775 km) I had left to get to Mendoza. It was slow going because of the wind but motion in the correct direction is progress and that was the name of the game.

The terrain was rolling desert for my first couple of hours but it soon changed to vineyards all around. I rode through a town called Tinogasta and found myself on a quiet road, with that was a continuous series of small dips so the road could pass over dry river beds. Traffic was down to almost zero and it was quiet riding. The road turned to dirt once I was 15 miles (24 km) past Tinogasta and I would have been somewhat concerned about being on the correct route but Jesse had mentioned that section as well.

A few miles later I rolled through the village of Santa Cruz and got some more water then rode a few miles out of town to camp. It was easy to find a campsite, the fences and property lines disappeared shortly outside every town I passed through and all I was looking for was a spot that would be easy to access. I found a spot quite easily and pushed my bike to the semi secluded area and began making dinner. Just as I was finishing eating I noticed my back tire was flat, the casing was coming apart and I could see the tube popping out of a hole in the tire. The old tire that I'd kept in the anticipation of this exact situation was still in one of my bags so I switched it out. Since I had three spare tubes left I didn't bother with patching the tube and I just put a new tube in; besides, I'd probably switch to the larger 700c size wheels on my new bike in Mendoza or wherever I found one. The bigger wheel is supposed to be faster rolling than a 26 inch too. I cleaned my frostbitten finger with soap and water and replaced the bandage then did some rehab exercises to hopefully smooth the transition to a regular bike before going to bed.

CHAPTER 26

Day 270, October 26, 2016

Mendoza, Argentina

It took me five more days of cycling to get to Mendoza. I'd met up with Denis from Russia whom I'd met in Bolivia randomly on the road and we cycled together a couple of days before I rode ahead. The Argentineans were proving hospitable; I stayed at fire stations for a couple of nights on my way to the city and both of them had checked out my finger to make sure it wasn't getting infected. At the second one, the shower at the fire station had an instant hot water unit and when I brushed one of the exposed wires while washing my hair I got shocked with 220 volts of electricity. It hit me so hard that it made me stamp my foot and gave me a small burn where it exited my body into the floor. As my finger healed more, I began to grow concerned that it would need to be amputated. I wasn't sure how I felt about that; it was one of those it'll-never-happen-to-me situations. I ignored the possibility of needing an amputation, and focused on getting my bike replaced instead.

Once in Mendoza I started checking bike shops. Everything was either excessively overpriced, terrible quality, or didn't fit me, often all three. Denis had mentioned that bicycles, and just about everything else, was expensive in Argentina and, unfortunately, he was right. One pm was approaching so I went by a grocery store to get some food before the entire city shut down for the afternoon siesta. The siesta had been a big part of Argentinean culture; absolutely everything would shut down at 1:00 pm and everyone would go home from work for a few hours before returning and reopening again around 5:00 pm and staying open until around 9:00 pm in the evening, even in the cities. It was bizarre the first time I experienced it. I'd rolled into a town in the midafternoon to try to find food for the night and everything was closed. I'd noticed the business hours outside some of the larger shops and realized what was happening. I'd since adjusted my routine to fit the timing with the opening hours of the shops. I got some stuff for sandwiches then sat in the shade in front of the store and ate. I'd made it just in time; the grocery store was closing right as I was sitting down to eat.

I started looking for somewhere to stay but it turned out that I'd arrived on the weekend of the largest medical conference in Argentina and everything was booked through the weekend. Ten hostels or so later I found one that had a bed available for that night only. I didn't want to have to find somewhere else in the morning but at that point I was running out of options and I took it.

In the afternoon I went looking for a sleeping bag and mat. My zero degree Fahrenheit (-18 C) sleeping bag was far too warm and I'd sweat through it regularly and then get cold from the loss of loft when the down got wet. My air mattress had a leak and was blistering in several places to where I had to sleep in a crescent shape to avoid parts of my body being pushed off the mattress by the bulges. I found a sleeping bag that wasn't exactly what I was looking for but it was close enough and I replaced my air mattress with a cheap foam sleeping mat. I was getting hungry again after all that shopping and bought some pastries for a snack at a bakery.

Back at the hostel, I was still stressing about needing to find a new bike. When I got back I had message from Jesse. I told him about my problems with finding a bike the day I got to Mendoza and he'd gotten in touch with his contacts back home. They'd found a bike shop in Santiago that had a last year model steel framed touring bike, in my size, that they would sell me at a deep discount because of the year. It wasn't perfect but it'd work. I'd send my excess gear home the following day then ride to Santiago to get the new bike the day after that.

It was almost 10:00 pm by then and I hadn't eaten dinner. I rushed out hoping the grocery store would still be open but they were closing right as I arrived. I walked along, dejected and hungry. Nothing that was open looked appetizing. I was kind of just wandering along and hoping I'd happen upon something. It was getting late and I started working my way back to my hostel when I saw a restaurant that looked like a buffet. It seemed too good to be true, happening upon an all you can eat buffet just as I was looking for somewhere to eat. I walked in and tried to ask if it was indeed a buffet, it took the use of an offline translate app but eventually I confirmed that it was, it was even a decent price! They had a paradilla (barbecue) section and I asked for one of everything and was given a heaping plate of various meats hot off the grill. I ate with much gusto then went back for a second giant plate of barbecue with extras of the things I liked best. Most of what they served was pretty normal: beef, chicken, pork, and lamb. The unusual items were goat meat and blood sausage. I tried both, the goat was a little tough and the blood sausage had a slight metallic taste. I wouldn't go out of my way to eat either of them again. I hit up the dessert table next and got a few vegetables from the salad bar too then finished off with an awesome pasta plate. It was glorious. I went back to the hostel and fell asleep almost instantly.

I'd been looking forward to this day for several months now; I would finally be able to send home my unnecessary gear. The hostel I was at had a cancellation and I was going to be able to stay there another night too. Once that was taken care of I began going through my things and packing everything that I'd deemed unnecessary into my backpack. It was a bit of a process to get everything sorted but once I was done

I had my backpack almost completely stuffed with gear. I'd be sending it, and everything inside, home plus my two larger panniers and my cold weather boots. I still needed my ice axe to steer my broken bicycle. I shouldered my pack, took my boots in one hand, and my now empty panniers in the other, and set off towards an international shipping company in Mendoza. It was almost a mile away and when I arrived at the location marked on my map I couldn't find it. I asked in one of the stores nearby and they said it had moved. Luckily they knew where the new location was and pointed it out on my map. Another half mile of walking later and I was there. I walked in and told the man working there that I wished to send everything to the United States. He spoke English well and it made the process fairly straightforward though expensive; however, the gear I was sending home would cost much more to replace than it would to ship. Unfortunately they couldn't send my laptop because of the battery and I couldn't figure out how to remove it. About 3 pounds (1.4 kg) I'd have to continue carrying until I could figure out what to do with it, I figured I could probably try to sell it somewhere later on. All told my package weighed over 28 pounds (13 kg).

Freed of my burden and feeling quite jovial, I began working my way back to the hostel. On the way there was an outdoor store and I stopped in to have a look. I needed a small and somewhat comfortable backpack to carry my hydration pack for when I switched to an upright bike. They had a nice 20 liter backpack for a reasonable price that I bought to serve that purpose. It was a lightweight pack and I filled it with some food I had just bought for lunch before finishing my walk back to the hostel.

I began reorganizing my gear after eating some sandwiches for lunch. I wasn't able to weigh it all to see if I'd met my goal of 10 kilograms (22 pounds) of gear total but I'd just dropped over 20 pounds of gear and that was good enough for the time being. More reductions to follow at the next opportunity! With just about everything done that needed it, I went to bed excited to start my ride to Santiago in the morning.

I'd planned out an easy schedule that would get me to Santiago on November 2nd, the day I was supposed to be able to pick my new bike up. I took my time getting everything ready but when I was bringing my bags down to begin attaching them to my bike my rear tire was flat; one of the patches had failed again. I replaced the patch and then figured out how to get everything to work with my new gear setup. I ate the complimentary breakfast at the hostel then finally got going around 10:30. I was definitely accelerating faster with the reduced weight and it also helped reduce rolling resistance too. I was much faster with less weight and I had a tailwind too, that helped some.

Outside of Mendoza, I followed the signs for Chile and soon turned off the highway and onto a quieter road that would eventually take me over the Andes to Chile. The road climbed gradually and inconsistently for most of the day. I met another cycle tourist, Daniel from Chile, coming down the mountain; he spoke about as much English as I speak Spanish and we conversed back and forth for a while. He spoke mostly in English, while I conversed mostly in Spanish. He started from his home near Santiago and was doing a loop to Brazil and Uruguay before heading south to Ushuaia and back north to where he started, if I understood him correctly. Perhaps our paths will cross again.

It was easily apparent that I was climbing faster now that I had less weight to carry and I was in the town of Portrerillos by three pm with less than four hours of riding time. I needed to get some more food but the small grocery store there was closed for siesta. There was a bus stop across the street that would provide some shade and I waited it out since I didn't have much else to get done. I read and had a few snacks while I waited. It finally opened around 5:30 pm and I bought some bread to go with the salami I had left and some cheap white wine to have with dinner.

The hospital was open by then too and I went by to get my

frostbite injury checked out and cleaned. It'd turned black at the last joint and a half but this had been a similar situation with the frostbite I had on my toes shortly before I started this trip and it hadn't concerned me. The hospital staff said otherwise; the joint and half of my finger was dying and would need to be amputated.

I'd been watching the injury "heal" I'd begun to suspect that it'd need to be amputated so the news didn't come as much of a shock. They couldn't do the operation here but said the hospital in Uspallata might be able to. I'd be there tomorrow and I could stop in then. They cleaned it out and replaced the bandage before sending me on my way.

Now it was time to find somewhere to camp. There were two campgrounds marked on my map, I'd seen free municipal campgrounds before and there was one less than a block away from the hospital. I rode by and it seemed to be open but no one was there. I checked everywhere but couldn't find anyone so I picked a spot that was very visible and started making raviolis for dinner. While I was cooking someone walked up and told me I'd have to pay if I wanted to stay here for the night. It wasn't expensive, a little more than three dollars, but I didn't want to pay to sleep on dirt when the bathrooms were locked and there was a silly sign that said the hot water wouldn't work until the next day or later. I also wasn't keen on taking a cold shower so, I asked if I could finish cooking before I left. He said I could and I thanked him as he left. After I'd finished cooking and eating I left and began looking for somewhere new to camp. It didn't take long, there were no fences and I was at the edge of town already. I saw a shelf up a small hill that would do and carried my bike up to avoid repeating the experience of multiple flats from thorny brush I'd had a few days ago. I had a decent view of the lake and I sat and did some reading while I finished off my wine before going to bed.

I waited till the sun's rays were peeking over the mountains before bothering to get up. I had yet another short day planned and I was in no hurry. I ate some salami sandwiches for breakfast and left around 8:30. The road wound through a canyon next to a river and worked its way higher at a rolling river gradient. Uspallata wasn't far away and it was my planned stop for the day. I stopped every hour or so and had a snack and just took in the scenery.

I was in Uspallata a little after noon and went straight to the hospital to try to get there before they closed. I walked in and after a short wait was called back to see a doctor. They gave me the same diagnosis as the previous hospital and said the amputation needed to be done right away but they couldn't do it there. They said I could get it done in Santiago but it'd reached the point where any delay could cost me more than just part of my finger; if the infection progressed further I could lose the entire hand or even my whole arm. The hospital in Mendoza could do it and they told me I should get the operation done today if possible. I asked almost seriously if they had a big knife that they could just lop it off with real quick so I could get back to riding. They laughed like I was joking; I think I would have preferred that method over having to go back to Mendoza. They bandaged it up and gave me a doctor's note that said I needed emergency surgery.

The potentially infected finger seemed a pretty serious issue now so I asked if I could leave my bicycle at the hospital and take a bus to Mendoza. They said I couldn't park it here but I could see if the bus terminal had a place for it. I made a quick stop by the gas station to get on their wifi and let my family know what was going on then went to the bus terminal to see about getting to Mendoza. They had a bus that left for Mendoza in nine minutes but nowhere to park my bike. I remembered seeing a bike rack at the gas station and decided I'd lock it up there and just hope it wouldn't get stolen. I rode over and quickly stripped my bike of all my bags and anything valuable before locking it to the bike rack and running with all my bags back to the bus terminal. That process was much easier now that I didn't have very many bags. I bought my bus ticket and got on board, the bus started moving before I sat down. I settled in and waited to get to Mendoza. It was odd traveling so fast over roads I'd just ridden and it felt detached sitting in an air conditioned bus while the scenery rushed by. I definitely prefer cycling. I must have been tired because I fell asleep during the ride, when I woke up two hours later I was in Mendoza.

The hospital was a few blocks away from the bus terminal and I walked there carrying my bags with me. I tried the main entrance but was told to go to the emergency room. I checked in and three hours later was called back. A couple of the staff members spoke English and simplified the process immensely. They looked at my finger and then went to get a doctor to check it out. They spoke with the doctor in Spanish for a while then came and said very nervously that my finger needed amputating and were relieved when I said I knew that already. After some more waiting, I was told to go to imaging to get some x-rays. There wasn't a line for the x-rays and I was back and waiting yet again within ten minutes.

It took another hour or so before I was told that the surgery room was ready. I followed the nurse, bags still in hand, to the operation room. They had me place my bags outside then dressed me up in a hospital gown. I went into the operation room and lay down on the table. The staff began laying a bunch of sanitary blankets over me and one of them painted my entire right arm with antiseptic before placing yet another sanitary blanket over my arm. I spoke with the surgeon and tried to ask where they were going to make the cut. With much pointing and gesturing I was told that he would cut it just after the first knuckle going away from my right hand. The English speaking nurse that was present said I'd have to stay in the hospital to recover for two to three days after the surgery. I told her I was concerned about my bike and they said they'd call the gas station I'd left it at and ask them to keep an eye on it. A final blanket was then placed over my face and propped up on the left side to keep it off my face; then they began.

First they gave me several shots of anesthetic into my finger and, by the time they kicked in, I couldn't feel anything in my finger. I was soon very glad of this; they started out by making several cuts in my finger. I could feel torsion and tension and blood running down my hand; as much as I didn't want to know what was happening it gave me a good idea of what was going on.

It would appear finger bones are quite strong; the cut that took most of the finger off was made by an instrument that I imagined looked like tin snips. I could feel the surgeons muscles shaking as he tried to get through the last of the bone. It took a few cuts and rotations but eventually I heard the metallic click of the instrument snapping shut and I knew my finger was off. They cleaned up the cut, folded some of the skin over to cover it, stitched it up, and then bandaged what was left of my finger. The nurse I'd talked to about my bike came back and said she'd been in contact with the gas station and after explaining my situation they said they'd watch my bike until I got back. Hopefully it'd still be there.

I was wheeled on a gurney back to imaging, even though I asked if I could walk there instead, and they took another x-ray to see how the surgery had gone. I was then pushed through the hospital, still on the gurney, to a room that would be my home for the next couple of days. My room was at the end of a hall and a divider separated my room and the adjacent room. There were two other people in my room: an older man probably 75 or older and a younger guy probably in his 30's. In the adjacent room there was another older man of similar age as the first and a middle aged man who happened to speak English fluently. It wasn't clear exactly why all of them were here but they seemed to be an optimistic group.

The anesthetic in my finger began to wear off after another hour or so and my stub of a finger was pulsing with pain at each heartbeat. Another hour or so passed then one of the nurses came in and injected me with antibiotics a few times. Another nurse started an IV in my left arm and I was now almost immobile with my right hand bandaged and hurting and an IV running to my left arm. Eventually some of the painkillers in the IV kicked in and, once I got used to the sensation of having a needle stuck in my arm, I was able to sleep.

Nine months on the road today and there I was stuck in a hospital. I'd anticipated sickness and potential hospitalization at some point during the trip but I never thought it'd be getting half of a finger amputated. Sometimes you just have to take whatever comes your way. I was in the hospital for four days; it was pretty boring, as hospital stays tend to be; not much to do. The staff changed the bandage on my amputated half finger on the second day. I was repulsed when I saw what was left. I'd expected something that looked like a short finger not the gruesome club-like appendage with crude black stitches poking out that I saw.

I was supposed to get out of the hospital around midday and when I asked a nurse what time I'd be allowed to leave they said, "noon". One of the nurses came and took the IV out around 11:30 and I thought it would just be a matter of time before a doctor would show up with my release and prescription papers. Noon came and went. Then one pm. I was served lunch at 1:30 and was almost glad of the delay to be able to have another meal before I left. The doctor showed up just after I had finished eating around two pm. With the help of the English speaking patient in the adjacent room I was told to change the bandage daily and take medication every 12 hours. The doctor gave me the release papers and a prescription to be filled at the pharmacy downstairs. I went to the pharmacy and got my prescription of ten days of antibiotics for free. I showed my papers at the desk as I was leaving and they said I was free to go. I'd had a 30 minute surgery, a four day hospital stay (including painkillers and antibiotics), and all of my meals for the tidy sum of zero dollars! I couldn't believe it at first; the same treatment in the US would have cost tens of thousands of dollars.

Lucky doesn't begin to describe it. I would have had to shorten my trip by years with that kind of bill if I even had any money left at all. I was done and out of the hospital by 2:30 pm and I walked back to the bus station to get to Uspallata as soon as possible. The next bus had less than an hour until departure.

Back in Uspallata, I walked over to the gas station to see if my bike was still there. I went around the corner and there it was, I half expected it to be gone from someone stealing it but it was still there. My previous plan had been to try to part out my bike at one of the small local shops and toss the frame before taking a bus the rest of the way to Santiago to get my new bike then bus back to Mendoza to maintain my line. When I saw my bike still sitting there I couldn't do it. The tires still had air in them and, although it was still worse for wear, it had the possibility of carrying me the rest of the way to Santiago. This was a huge dilemma for me, I'd told the bike shop that I'd be there in a day and I couldn't get a wifi connection to tell them otherwise. I started attaching my bags and after a quick run to the grocery store I rode out of town hoping the shop with my new bike in Santiago would understand.

I started riding up the gentle rolling climb that would eventually take me over the Andes and into Chile. I rode until it was getting too dark to ride without lights before stopping next to a clear mountain stream that ran under the road. I made dinner, then I sat, ate, and watched the stars come out; the Milky Way came into view with the failing light and stretched its way across the sky. Getting the amputation had been devastating and I'd considered ending my tour because of it. I don't think many people would have blamed me considering the circumstances. I'd played out the scenario of quitting my tour in my mind while I was sitting in the hospital trying to figure out what to do: I'd go home and everyone would feel sorry for me for a little while but then I'd have to go back to 'normal' life; a job, school, or whatever. That didn't sound appealing in the slightest and I still had money in savings with no commitments to fulfill anywhere. All things considered I was happier than ever to be back on the road.

CHAPTER 27

Day 279, November 4, 2016

Andes Mountains west of
Uspallata, Argentina

The gradual rolling climb of the previous day continued the next morning though it had to be one of the worst contoured roads I'd ever ridden on. The road would climb a few hundred feet up the side of the canyon then descend almost as far back down to the river that paralleled the road. The huge amount of seemingly unnecessary climbing made progress taxing mentally and the strong headwind I was fighting didn't help either. Just past the lower of the two trailheads to Aconcagua, the most expensive mountain in South America, the wind died very suddenly and the grade became more constant. My original plan had been to climb Aconcagua instead of Ojos del Salado but, as the most expensive mountain in South America, the permit alone would have cost over a thousand dollars. In contrast, Ojos del Salado had been free to climb.

I was concerned about getting over Paso Cristo Redentor. Denis had said the pass over the top of the mountain was closed but I'd have to try it as the only alternative was a tunnel where bicycles weren't allowed. I was at the base of the old road over the pass and began working my way up after a sandwich break. The surface was dirt and complete with sandy patches that I couldn't ride through. Streams of water ran down the road; some sections had enough water that it was like trying to ride up a river. Thick mud kept me from riding as much as I would have liked then, to top it all off, only a third of the way up the road was completely blocked by snow. I tried pushing my bike through it but it was too icy and I slipped then fell right away. I still had thousands of feet to ascend to get to the pass and from what I could see it wasn't about to get any better farther up. It was too dangerous to try to carry my bike and gear across in separate trips because of how icy the snow was. I could very easily slide right off the side of the mountain and be seriously injured from the fall. I sat down on the snow, dejected and heartbroken; my goal of a complete line of cycling seemed to be at an end and there was nothing I could do about it. It was quite obvious that I wouldn't make it over the top so I rode down to the tunnel to try to convince the guards to let me ride through. The mud was bad enough going down that I had to push my bike downhill in a couple of sections.

Eventually I was at the tunnel. There was a toll booth near the entrance, I was told to stop and did so. A very bored looking guard told me I'd have to take a car through. I began playing the 'stupid foreigner.' I didn't actually understand much of what he was saying anyways and he seemed more than happy to ascribe that stereotype to me. I understood enough, there was a car up the road a ways that would take me through the tunnel and I would not be allowed to ride as it was too dangerous with the pollution buildup inside, plus there was no shoulder. He waved me along in a manner that suggested that he didn't really care and I started riding, being very obvious in my efforts to look for the car he had mentioned and doing my best to look lost and confused (I've been told that that look comes naturally to me whether I wanted it to or not).

Incredibly, there was no car and no one was trying to stop me so I started riding into the tunnel, half expecting a police car to blast by me with blaring lights and sirens to make me stop. I'd done some research beforehand and I suspected that the tunnel was downhill in the direction I was traveling. I was correct in my suspicions but the tunnel was also 5 miles (8 km) long. It had lights inside however and all the traffic was coming from the other direction. The pollution buildup was apparent and I was soon feeling a little lightheaded. Soot stains covered the ceiling from years of vehicles passing through the tunnel. The tunnel was downhill at a significant grade and I was moving quickly. A light appeared around one of the bends and I knew I was going to make it through but I was expecting to ride right into a police barricade on the opposite side to be arrested and fined or at least get yelled at once I was on the other side.

As I exited to my impending arrest, no one was there; I'd made it through! I was elated and rode the few miles down to the border post grinning like the Cheshire Cat. I was still concerned the guard might have called to the border post about what I'd done but once again no one said anything.

The border was a madhouse. A couple of buses had just pulled in and it was completely packed. I found what looked like the correct line and waited for about an hour before it was my turn and I was promptly turned away because I didn't have vehicle registration papers. I tried to explain that I was on a bicycle and didn't have registration papers and was referred to a different office. They answered the door and told me to go around the corner to a different desk. Luckily the agent there spoke English and was able to help me. He gave me a paper that he said was for bicycles and told me to wait in the same line I had just waited in. I told him I'd just waited an hour before getting turned away and he escorted me to a side entrance and a clerk that wasn't doing anything. Five minutes later I had my stamps for exiting Argentina and entering Chile, both borders were run from the same building. I had to go back to the agent that'd helped me earlier; he gave me another paper and said I was good to go. Finally, free from the border post and scot-free from my dash through the tunnel, I began working my way down the mountain.

The scenery was incredible. Snowcapped mountains rose high on every side and the road snaked its way down the side of a cliff in a series of hairpin turns that were stacked nearly on top of each other. I had a headwind going down but at that point I didn't care; I'd made it through the tunnel and maintained my line of cycling.

It was mostly downhill all the way to the town of Los Andes. The road leveled out and even went uphill in a few sections but not near as bad as the other side had been. I was in Los Andes with a couple of hours of daylight to spare and tried to decide what to do. I most definitely did not have time to make it all the way to Santiago before dark and opted for trying to find somewhere to stay in town instead. I stopped by the grocery store to get something for dinner. I didn't feel like having to cook so I bought some stuff for sandwiches, a bag of chips, and some orange juice. I ate almost everything sitting on a bench outside the store then rode over to the fire station to ask about somewhere to stay. I had to wait an hour for the commandant to show up but once he did I was welcomed in.

After a hot shower I was invited in for coffee and some sweet rolls with the commandant. He noticed my bandaged finger and had one of the paramedics check it out; everything was fine with no signs of infection. I spoke with the commandant for a while more until he had to get back to work. The fire station had wifi and a room where I could sleep for the night. I got in contact with the bike shop that night and told them that I'd be there by four pm the next day. I didn't want to miss my arrival time again and left the fire station around eight the next morning to give myself plenty of time to get there.

The ride to Santiago was another problem road, bicycles were not supposed to be on the only road going directly to the city. With no other options available I decided to time trial the entire 30 mile (48 km) section, nonstop, and hope I didn't get picked up by the police. A climb of maybe 1,000 feet (300 meters) awaited me about 12 miles (20 km) away from Los Andes. I rode up it without issue, and much faster than I would have before now that I was carrying less weight. At the top was a tunnel, like the Los Libertadores tunnel I'd ridden through less than 24 hours ago, it was entirely downhill; I wouldn't want to try to ride it the other direction. There was a road maintenance station near the beginning of the tunnel and one of the workers started yelling at me when he saw me. I can honestly say that I didn't understand what he was saying and I kept going and blazed through the tunnel pushing 30 mph (48 km/h) most of the time. The road leveled out and came to a toll booth. I've never had to pay at any tolls and sprinted through the gap on the far right side still moving at 25+ mph (40+ km/h). By sprinting up the hills, spinning down the other side, and going hard on the flats I was making great time. A police officer who obviously didn't want me on the highway and couldn't think of an immediate action to stop me blew past me when I was a mile (1.6 km) away from the first side road option. I started sprinting and made it off the highway and on the road where I was allowed to ride before the police could tell me otherwise. I'd averaged almost 16 mph (26 km/h) over the course of the morning, not bad at all considering the climb I had.

I was safely on a side road, and the majority of the way to Santiago, all before 10:00 am so I backed off to an easy pace and just cruised on the byway. Traffic was high as the road was an alternative to the toll highway, but most of the drivers were considerate and passed me safely.

Eventually I was in the city limits and it was still before noon. I saw a grocery store and bought some "on sale" potato chips and peach juice to go with the sandwich stuff I had left. I took my time eating, sitting in the shade outside the grocery store. After eating, I began working my way towards 'Bike Universe Santiago'.

The intercity traffic was awful and I had to keep a watchful eye out for the taxis and buses that were the biggest threat to my safety. There was a decent cycle path that was clogged with pedestrians but it was still safer than riding the road. Although it was slow progress, I was in no hurry to get to the bike shop; it was barely 6 miles (10 km) away and I had nearly four hours to get there on time.

I rolled up to the bike shop around 1:30, I'd made it against all odds with my rear hub beginning to fail again, my handlebars held inside the frame with a pannier strap, my seat mount breaking, and after steering my bike with 'reins' for nearly 1,000 miles (1,600 km), I had made it to Santiago.

My bike had held out far longer than I could have reasonably expected it to with all the problems it and I had. The folks at the shop welcomed me and I immediately began apologizing for my tardiness yesterday but they said they'd heard about all the problems I was having and were more concerned about my safety and not in the least upset about me not making it yesterday.

The new bike was ready and waiting for me right by the entrance. Most of the parts on my recumbent were worn out and what wasn't worn out wasn't valuable enough to try to send home. The parts I did transfer to the new bike were my pedals and front rack. I asked the bike shop to do me a favor and pass on the parts that were still usable to people who needed them and to dispose of the frame.

The excitement of the new bike was bittersweet because with it came the goodbye of the bike that I ridden for the equivalent distance of nearly half the circumference of the earth on this trip but it'd served its purpose and it was time to move on. I bought a set of road tires for my new bike and kept the stock tires for the dirt sections I had planned. Having ridden thus far without a helmet I decided it would be prudent to start wearing one. I bought a helmet along with some new shorts to replace the threadbare and holey ones I had.

The process took a couple of hours and everyone at the shop had a ton of questions and a great enthusiasm for what I was doing. It felt weird being held in such awe, it was something I'd imagine a famous celebrity would have to deal with and I resolved to not let it go to my head; after all, I only go for a bike ride most days anyway. The owner of the shop spoke excellent English and the mechanics insisted on doing most of the work on the bike when they saw the condition of my finger. They had practically rolled out the red carpet for me and bent over backwards to make sure everything was good to go. Thanks, Bike Universe!

With everything fit, mounted, and otherwise attached to the bike, I was ready to go. More pictures, many thanks on my part, and well wishes from Bike Universe, and I was on my way again. It felt like riding a skyscraper compared to how low I sat on the recumbent, and the handling was excellent. It was immediately apparent that vehicles were treating me differently now that I was twice as tall while sitting on the bike. The ride was a bit harsh with the relatively narrow tires but that was to be expected. With the increased height I didn't realize just how fast I was going until I looked at my speedometer. It felt like it had a motor on it with how fast I could accelerate. On top of all that, I had become just another guy on a bike; I wasn't getting yelled at, nobody shouted 'look' as I rode by as had happened incessantly while I was riding the recumbent (regardless of what country I was in) and I was down to few enough bags that I could be mistaken for a commuter, not a cycle tourist. I had the suspicion that other cycle tourists would ignore me now and not stop to say "hello" now that I was carrying so much less. After the constant attention from riding a recumbent bike, I reveled in the anonymity of riding a normal bike.

I'd found a hostel online, before leaving the bike shop, and almost rode past it with how much faster I was moving, I checked in and booked two nights. The hostel staff was friendly and asked about what I was doing. They asked me how much I had paid for the bike and when I told them they said it would have cost twice as much if I bought it in Chile. I didn't bother trying to explain I'd just bought it half an hour ago. The owners were grilling and invited me to join them for dinner, an excellent meal of grilled pork, beef, sausage, and vegetables with some local beer too.

I slept as long as I could the next morning; as usual it wasn't very long. Once I was up, I ate the included breakfast at the hostel: coffee or tea and bread with margarine or other spreads. A light breakfast seems to be common everywhere that's not the US. While I was eating, I started the complete reset on my laptop so I could try to sell it later in the day. It took a long time for it to finish, over four hours to wipe all the data and programs I had on it. Denis, the Russian cyclist I'd met in La Paz, was also in Santiago and staying with a Couchsurfing host. I'd been in contact with him and we met up at the hostel I was at that afternoon. There was a Saturday market a little over a mile away called 'Bio Bio'; supposedly it was possible to buy almost anything there and I brought my laptop with me in hopes that I could sell it since I almost never used it.

Once we were at the market, Denis and I began asking around about somewhere to sell my laptop. We followed directions from several different people and I was beginning to be concerned that we were on a wild goose chase but eventually we were in an area that was all electronics vendors. It took a bit of asking but, eventually, we found someone who was interested in buying it. I started the price out with 30% more than the hundred dollars or so I wanted to get for it to leave room for bargaining. The buyer we found was very firm on his price but I really didn't want to have to carry it anymore and eventually we agreed upon a price that was less than what I wanted. I should have started higher but I really wanted to be freed of the burden of carrying it all the time.

With my total load about three pounds (1.4 kg) lighter now, Denis and I went to find lunch. We chose a restaurant that served fried fish. Santiago was supposed to have excellent seafood, with its large population and close proximity to the coast, and the fish tasted amazing. Denis ate slower than I did and when I was almost done with my plate he spotted what looked like a worm in his fish. He pulled it out with his fork and it looked very much like a worm. He found a few more then called the waitress over. She offered to give him a new plate but Denis was disgusted with the idea. After a quick glance at my plate he spotted some on the remnants of my fish too. We called the waitress yet again and this time she began to tell us that all fish have worms. Denis and I knew very well that fish were not supposed to have worms and waved it off without further inquiry. When it came time to pay we asked for a heavy discount because of the worms. The waitress began going on yet again how all fish have worms and eventually brought another waitress into the discussion. I argued my point as best I could with my limited Spanish and she brought one of the nearby fishmongers into the argument. He proceeded to tell us that all fish have worms and other parasites and went so far as to say that such invertebrates in the fish were good for our health. It was quite obvious that we weren't going to get a discount so we paid and left.

We headed back to the hostel and hung around there for a few hours. The owners were grilling food once again and they offered us some, along with some beer, we accepted graciously. Denis left sometime in the evening.

CHAPTER 28

Day 285, November 11, 2016

Huepil, Chile

My new bike was an improvement in almost every way: it was lighter, faster, and, best of all, people more or less ignored me instead of pointing and shouting all the time like they had on the recumbent. I'd been doing less saddle time and riding easier ever since the switch almost a week ago in order to help smooth the adaptation to the different position. Cycling had been my main hobby growing up and that probably helped make the change to the new bike almost seamless.

I'd tried asking to stay at fire stations for my first few days out of Santiago but, after being turned down repeatedly, I'd become discouraged and just settled on wild camping all the time. The previous night, when I arrived in the town of Huepil, I'd given asking one more try and, after a week of being turned down every time I asked, I was allowed to setup my sleeping mat in the workout room of the fire station and take a hot shower too. There weren't any hotels in town so that probably helped my case.

Since my new bike was much more capable off pavement, I'd rerouted off my previously intended route and onto some dirt roads. As soon as I got to the dirt roads, I switched from the narrow tires I'd been riding on to the wider off road tires that I bought with the bike. Once the switch had been made, I set off. The difference was incredible! Instead of lumbering along on dirt roads like I'd been doing on the old bike, I could almost glide over rough terrain; all of a sudden riding dirt roads was fun! Once I was comfortable with the different feel, I was hammering up the short rollers and flying down the other side.

Once I'd ridden to the town of Ralco, I stocked up on a couple of days' worth of food before riding out of town to camp. There were some dirt roads and trails through the mountains that I wanted to take.

Birds were singing in the trees and the sound of the river woke me near dawn. Still on dirt roads the next morning, I climbed along a rolling river gradient for several miles before the road seemingly dead ended at a small ranch. There were some people working outside and I asked directions. They said I wouldn't be able to make it to Quillaicahue, the town I said I was going to, but there was a dirt track immediately on the right and my maps plainly stated that the roads did go there and I chose not to take their advice. The dirt track quickly degraded into a horse trail, then into something that resembled the rocky bottom of a river bed. Only an exceptionally skilled rider would not have to push up the trail or at least be riding a full on mountain bike and that was a level of skill and type of bike that I did not possess.

I rode where I could and pushed where I couldn't ride. Some of the grades seemed close to 45 degrees. The trails were rough enough that they'd probably be almost impassable if I still had my old bike. The descents were just as steep as the climbs and I had to walk a few of them because of how rough the terrain was. At the bottom of a few such descents was a river crossing. I had to carry my rig through freezing, knee-deep water to get to the trail on the opposite side.

In some sections, the trail turned to flowing single track. Some of this was fun though I soon regretted trying to take a bike with panniers through such terrain. My panniers would snag on strategically placed rocks and plants and jerk my front wheel to one side. I was able to avoid crashing most of the time but it made some of the riding frustrating and I resolved to figure out a different luggage system at the next opportunity.

The track was difficult to follow and I lost it a few times; eventually, I'd have to resort to backtracking to the last place I saw it and look very carefully for a narrow track through the often heavy undergrowth. My GPS was almost useless in the narrow valley I was climbing up; the trail on the GPS went in a completely different direction than it did in real life. Even if it was correct, the trees were blocking the signal and my position on the screen was hopping back and forth. I was still having fun though; it was an adventure! The scenery made up for the hard work too, a nice quiet spot in the mountains of Chile, surrounded by Monkey Puzzle trees. Some of them had branches only near the tops of the tree and all of them were covered in spiny triangular leaves protruding from the bark. The braches were similarly covered in spiny triangular leaves. The tree's name came from a British explorer in the context that it would puzzle a monkey to figure out how to climb that tree!

More river crossings and more pushing my bike brought me to the culmination of the day's ride, a 2 mile (3 km) climb that ascended 3,000 vertical feet (900 meters) in that distance. That meant grades averaging about 28% and parts of it were downhill; I wasn't riding much. Some parts were so steep I had to hold the brakes on my bike while I shuffled forward a few steps then simultaneously release the brakes and shove my bike forward to move up the hill. It took me a couple of hours to get up the pass. I met some motorcyclists near the top and they were able to confirm that I was going the right way and said the track was much better near the top. After another eternity of muscling my bike up the track, I was suddenly on a jeep trail. Oddly enough it was not marked on my map and seemed to be an alternate and infinitely easier way to get to where I now was. The track was almost easy to ride and I was soon over the top and had a great view of the surrounding mountains.

The descent had some dangerous snowy patches that looked like I might be able to walk across, but one slip would mean a steep slide of a hundred feet (30 meters) or more into jagged rocks; I chose to go around and it took a while, but it was the safer option.

The trail I was descending soon deviated from what was on my map but there were no alternative routes that I had seen. The trail emptied out onto a dirt road that was also not marked on my maps and was not signed well either. A sign pointed in the direction of Laguna Las Mulas. That lake was on my map and I chose that direction. Two miles (3 km) later there was a large open area where some campers were spending a couple of days. I asked for directions but they weren't much help. The road I was on seemed to be on my map now but I was going in the wrong direction and decided to turn around and follow my GPS very carefully. My GPS had a narrow hiking trail marked but not the road I was on. I chose the hiking trail as it was on my map and was going in the correct direction. Once again, the trail was steep, overgrown, and difficult to ride. It was downhill, however, and it ended at someone's pasture. A road was visible that seemed to be going in the right direction and I took it. I suspected it was another branch of the road I was on earlier but I wasn't about to ride back to confirm that. I followed it for a few miles until I was at a river with good options for camping and decided to stop for the day. It was 7:30 pm, I'd been going all day with few stops, and I'd only covered 26 miles (43 km), but I'd enjoyed it.

My back tire was flat in the morning. I was near a river and found three holes, by use of the water, that appeared to be pinch flats and I patched them all. I was on roads instead of trails and I was moving right along for my first couple of hours compared to the struggles of the previous day. It promised to be an interesting day; the roads I was supposed to be taking did not connect on my maps but I'd read about other people taking this route who said they did. I asked for directions at an exceptionally remote police station and they were able to point me in the correct direction. The route the police told me to take wound through a scenic valley and involved another river crossing, though this time through frigid mid-thigh deep water, but I made it across without falling in and that was good enough for me.

Eventually the track began to line up with my map and I was glad. It still had some unrideable sections that were literally the bottom of a shallow river, but I was moving in the right direction. Later in the day, my front tire went flat, another pinch flat. I added more air to both my tires after that one. Not only did I have a flat, but my patch glue had exploded from one of the many impacts my panniers had sustained and was unusable. I had to replace the tube with a new one. The condition of the track improved as it neared a lake and turned into an actual dirt road after crossing the small but for some reason named Contraco Bridge.

After many hours of exhausting effort, I was in the village of Troyo around mid-afternoon. There was a small grocery store or a large tienda there and I was just about out of food. I filtered water from a spigot outside and dried my socks and shoes in the sun. They were still saturated from all the river crossings and, of course, I ate a bunch of food too. While I was sitting there, someone came by to talk to me and offered me a place to stay for the night. I accepted eagerly but when I asked where their house was they said to wait and they'd be back in an hour. I found that quite odd but they had also offered dinner and use of their shower so the prospect of somewhere to stay seemed worth the wait. I waited for an hour with no sign of them. Another hour passed and they still hadn't shown up. At 2.5 hours of waiting I'd had enough; I had just enough time left to camp and cook dinner before it got dark. I had apparently become a victim of the offer of hospitality that was no more than an offer. This is unfortunately common in a few different cultures, Latin America being one of them. Was I supposed to refuse the offer? I wasn't sure. To offer help to someone and then not help them but also waste hours of their time was upsetting. I did my best to brush it off, but the incident bugged me.

It rained overnight. I couldn't recall the last time it'd rained so I figured I was about due for some rain only this time I didn't have a tent. All I had was a bivy, basically a sleeping bag cover; it was waterproof but the face was mesh. I ended up working it around so the mesh face was on the bottom and sleeping on my side while breathing through the opening. It was not a very pleasant night but I did get some sleep. Originally, I'd planned to make a tarp tent in Santiago but that didn't happen. It would have to wait until I got back to civilization. I was up at dawn and surprisingly warm and dry for having slept in the rain without a tent. I'd strategically placed my stove within arm's reach the previous evening and made coffee without getting out of bed. It was only instant coffee that I'd bought yesterday and it had a slight taste of last night's canned fish and pasta dinner. My back tire was flat but it was a slow leak, so I pumped it up just before I started riding. I had a beautiful morning of riding; the sun came through the clouds and a light mist hung on the surrounding mountains. The road rolled steeply up and down next to a river: I'd power up the climbs and fly down the descents. A mildly uncomfortable night of camping seemed a good trade for the amount of fun I was having while riding.

It was about 24 miles (38 km) to the town Lonquimay; who really cares how long it took but it was still morning when I got there. I bought some groceries then checked everywhere I could find to try to get some more vulcanizing fluid for my patch kit. I asked at every store I saw and followed recommendations from several people but I was unsuccessful. The library in town advertised wifi, there was indeed a signal but they didn't know the password or wouldn't give it to me. They let me charge some of my electronics before they closed at noon though. It was raining again and there was a headwind too. It was exceptionally difficult to summon the effort to go out into the wind and rain but I didn't want to settle for that short of a distance for the day.

The road was unexpectedly paved outside of Lonquimay, faster riding than gravel but with rain, a headwind, and a slow leak in my back tire that I had to pump up every hour or so, it was tedious progress. In hindsight, I should have just swapped out the tube to one of my spares. Eventually I was at the turn-off for my next stretch of gravel roads. There was a conveniently located bus stop nearby and I took shelter there from the wind and rain for a snack break. I was cold and really didn't want to spend another night in the rain. Looking at my maps I saw there was an alternative route with a small town that had a fire station only 12 miles (19 km) away from where I was. It would be 30+ miles (48 km) on gravel roads to make it to the next town and I decided I'd reroute in hopes of staying at the fire station for the night. I pumped up my back tire again and started pedaling into the headwind.

Only 7 miles (12 km) away from Malacahuello, the town with the fire station, there was a tunnel. It had a sign saying no bicycles but I was going to ride through anyway. There was a stoplight next to the tunnel for whatever reason and while I was waiting for it to turn green a policeman came up to me and said I couldn't ride through the tunnel. I did my best to plead my case, I told him how far I'd ridden completely by bicycle since I'd started but he didn't care and said I couldn't ride through the tunnel. I asked if there was an alternate route to get to Malacahuello and he said that there was not. I checked my maps and confirmed as much. I asked again about an alternate route and was told the only way around was back through the Andes. I hung my head and decided I couldn't let my dream of a complete line of cycling around the world die here at the cost of a single night's comfort and turned my bike around. The policeman yelled after me but I didn't look back. I rode back to the turnoff feeling like I completely deserved what happened for my moment of weakness. I started laughing out loud while I was riding almost to the point of tears at the ridiculousness of what I'd just done. Does knowingly doing something crazy make me insane? Or would I be insane if I didn't think what I'd just done was crazy? Or some other option entirely? I had a tailwind for my 5 miles (8 km) of back-tracking and stopped at the bus stop I had taken a break at earlier to confirm that I was going the right way. I pumped up my back tire yet again and started down a gravel road.

The road began climbing soon after but I was feeling eu-phoric and hammered my way up the entirety of the 1,500+ foot (450 meter) climb in what felt like no time at all. More rollers followed over the top of the climb but now I had a tail-wind and was nearly flying down the road. I felt my back tire going soft yet again and stopped for another snack break then pumped it up again before continuing. I was bombing down the gravel descents, pushing 40 mph (64 km/h) with the tail-wind, and sprinting along the flats, above 25 mph (40 km/h). I hit a section of washboard going over 30 mph (48 km/h) and my front tire abruptly went flat from the inner tube pinch-ing. I stopped to change it and once again had to replace the tube since I didn't have any glue for patches. I pumped both tires up to as high a pressure as I could manage. I only had one tube left and no way of patching them without any glue and I didn't want another pinch flat. Apparently those tires weren't designed for riding washboard at over 30 mph (48 km/h). I'd slow down if it wasn't so much fun. Still going fast downhill thanks to a tailwind I didn't realize just how fast I was going and I passed a turn I was supposed to take by more than 6 miles (10 km) before I realized my mistake during a break at yet another bus stop. I checked my maps while I ate some sandwiches and felt at a complete loss of what to do. It was still raining and the temperature wasn't very far above freez-ing. I didn't want to ride back to the turnoff into a headwind. I was only 12 miles (19 km) away from Icalma, a town near the Chile/Argentina border and after much thought decided I'd make it there before stopping for the day. I pumped my back tire yet again and set off.

I had a tailwind for a few more miles until the road turned and the wind became a crosswind then eventually a head-wind. I rode through the rain being careful not to miss any more turns. I was soaking wet and getting cold when I got to Icalma. I really didn't want to spend another night in the rain and wind and tried to find a cheap hotel for the night. I checked everywhere. There was one place that was a decent price but they didn't have anywhere I could keep my mud covered bike unless I wanted to leave it leaning outside over-night. There were several places offering small cabins but they were well out of my price range. Eventually I resorted to ask-ing at the police station in town. I told the officer there how hard I'd tried to find somewhere to stay and asking if I could sleep on the covered porch area out of the rain. The officer I spoke to seemed like he really wanted to help me but said he wasn't allowed to let anyone stay at the station. I asked if there was anywhere else I could stay that was out of the rain and he pointed out a spot across the street at an under con-struction building where I'd have protection from the rain and said I could use the bathrooms at the nearby border post to wash up. That was more than good enough for me, so I went to the border post first to try to clean up a bit and get out of my wet clothes. I was covered in mud and I washed as much of it off as I could in one of the bathrooms before changing into dry clothes. After washing up and changing into dry clothes, I was somewhat clean and fairly warm. I went over to the building the policeman had pointed out. It looked like what would be-come a tourist information office and there was a small room that would probably be a bathroom later that but didn't have a door yet. It was just big enough to fit my bike into one corner and still have enough room to sleep. I made dinner and tried to decide which way I'd go in the morning. Looking at my maps, I could very easily ride into Argentina and head south there. I seemed to like the Chile side better for whatever reason and found that my wrong turn added a little less than 20 miles (32 km) to the route I'd planned. After much more thought, I decided to stick with my original plan of staying in Chile when I saw that there was a road that would eliminate any backtracking that I could take in the morning.

It was rainy and windy all night long but, thanks to the shelter of the under construction building, I stayed warm and dry. As could have been predicted, the clothes that I had worn the previous day were still wet when I woke up. Changing from warm dry clothes to cold wet clothes outside on a cold and windy morning is among the hardest things I've ever done but it was the only way to keep my dry clothes dry for later. I did it just the same and started riding hard as soon as possible after I had changed clothes to warm up quicker. The road rolled for a few miles outside of Icalma before turning into a couple thousand foot climb. My rear tube still had a slow leak in it and I had to stop every hour or so to pump it up again.

There were beautiful views of tree covered mountains over the top of the climb and a serpentine gravel descent passed by occasional waterfalls as I went down into a valley. I pumped up both my tires as high as I could to prevent them from getting pinch flats then ripped down the road drifting through the washboard gravel corners. It was awesome. The road turned to pavement 2/3 of the way down; I'd expected gravel roads until at least the next town. Pavement made my progress much faster and before too long I was in a town called Melipueco. I went to the first hardware store I saw to see about replacing my patch kit. They didn't have any but directed me to another store a few blocks away that had what I needed and I bought an extra tube of vulcanizing fluid to keep as a spare.

The sun had come out though there was still a headwind so I sat in the park and tried to patch all the pinched tubes I had. It took a while and the one I put back in my rear tire had another slow leak. Unsure of what to do at that point, I looked at my maps to try to figure out what to do. While doing that, I realized I'd been riding for over a week without a rest day. Considering this was on a new bike and an entirely different position than my other bike, I was due for a rest day.

I realized also that I hadn't had any serious issues with the new bike or position even with how hard I'd been riding. It seems the rehab work I'd done beforehand, and several years of road racing in my younger years, had paid off. I'd seen a hostel advertising wifi, among other things, on the way in and back-tracked a bit to check it out. Although advertised as a hostel they actually had private rooms and with only one other guest there, who was gone all day anyways, I pretty much had an entire house to myself for a few dollars more per night than I'd pay for dorm room accommodation at an actual hostel. I booked two nights for much less than the price of one night at the cabins I'd seen the previous night then took a very long and very hot shower. It felt great to be clean and in dry clothes after wearing wet clothes and being covered in mud for a couple of days. I made some coffee and ate the rest of the food I had and rested for a while.

I considered going out to eat for dinner that evening but, when I factored in that my appetite was rarely satisfied with a restaurant meal, I chose to cook dinner myself and buy some wine to go with it. Around midafternoon I went out and bought beef, potatoes, peppers, and onions to make the stew I'd been craving for a while. I bought enough ingredients to have some left over for lunch tomorrow and started cooking right when I got back. I hadn't realized just how hungry I'd been and found myself scraping the bottom of the pot an hour later. With a belly full of good food and good wine, I crawled into bed and soon fell asleep.

After a restful day off the bike, it was time to get going again. I started off my day on paved roads and, after the turnoff for Villarrica, the road turned from flat to rollers. Somewhere along the way it changed to dirt. There was some cleanup work going on along the edges of the road, bushes were being trimmed back in several places. My back tire went flat after hitting a small pile of brush that had been placed in the middle of the road. After 10 more miles (16 km) of dirt roads, I was on pavement again. Freestanding volcanoes seemed to be everywhere in that part of Chile; they were broadly cone shaped and capped with glaciers and made the days ride much more interesting.

The town of Villarrica sat on Lake Villarrica with a view of the volcano Villarrica; somebody wasn't very creative with naming. I went to the grocery store in town and bought stuff to make sandwiches along with some potato chips and a beer then ate most of it sitting outside the store. A good wifi connection from the hardware store nearby extended my stay by an extra hour then I went to the hardware store and bought some things to make a tarp tent. Not a very good tarp tent, all I could find was some plastic sheeting and rope. I hoped I wouldn't have to use it.

CHAPTER 29

Day 293, November 20, 2016

Puerto Montt, Chile

J esse had messaged me his location and it turned out he was only a few days ahead of me. Because of this, and a lack of fairly direct side roads, I stayed on the main road south for a couple of days. Not much happened, I wild camped every night though one night had been in the treed circle of an on ramp to a highway.

Just outside the city of Puerto Montt there was a toll stop for the highway. I'd never had to pay tolls on a bicycle so I rode through and waved as I passed; an attendant waved back and I was good to go. I realized right away that I was in the wrong lane, one that would take me towards the airport instead of the city. I saw a break in the barrier that divides the highway that I could ride through but I forgot about the panniers in my fork. What would have been plenty of room on an unloaded bike wasn't near enough with the low mounted bags on the front of my bike. My right pannier caught on the barrier and threw me off my bike, my highest speed crash of the trip so far at about 10 mph (16 km/h). Skinned knees and a bruised dignity were the worst injuries, my bike was fine. After washing out my scrapes with my water bottle, I got back on and rode into Puerto Montt without issue.

Puerto Montt marked the start of the Carraterra Austral or Austral highway: it was a road I'd been looking forward to for a long time. I'd heard of the magic of the route from several people; a road that wound through the mountains of southern Chile and passed frequent waterfalls, glaciers, and fjords.

The road followed the bay, rolling up and down, occasionally quite steeply. I met a cycle tourist going the opposite direction, Pascal from Switzerland. He was five continents and more than four years into a world tour. He was surprised to hear that I was on a world tour as well when he saw how much gear I was carrying and I told him my story about cutting weight and how much I'd started with. He also had questions about my putting the majority of my gear on the front of the bike. For those unfamiliar with the concept of front loading a touring bicycle the idea is this: the rider's weight is mostly on the rear of the bike and the front wheel is stronger because it is not 'dished.' Front loading gives the bike better balance and makes it easier to stand up and pedal; something that can be very difficult when the weight is on the back of the bike. Even though Pascal was riding north at the time he was going towards Ushuaia too and we exchanged contact info in hopes of meeting again.

The Carraterra Austral was connected by a series of ferries that crossed the various fjords, inlets, and lakes along the route. I made it to the first ferry from La Arena with ten minutes to spare and had a pleasant cruise across a fjord to Peulche with views of glaciers on some of the high mountains. I was making good time while riding on the other side and I pedaled all the way into Hornoprien with a few hours of daylight to spare. I tried to find out when the next ferry was. After asking three people and getting as many answers, I was getting frustrated. A fourth person asked made sense of all three answers. An inbound ferry would arrive around eight pm that evening and depart the next morning at 11:30. I waited around, cooked and ate dinner while I waited until the evening ferry arrived. I was hoping they would make a return trip to Caleta Gonzalo but they confirmed that the ferry didn't run until the next morning. I was stuck for the night and went out to find somewhere to camp. I ended up near a park on the opposite side of the river from the ferry and set up my sleeping mat along a grassy area above the rocks leading down to the fjord.

I was up at dawn as usual. I had nothing to do until the ferry left at 11:30 so I made breakfast and coffee while I watched the sun rise over the mountains above the fjord I'd slept by. I went by a grocery store before heading down to the dock the ferry would leave from. After I bought my ticket at the office, they let me charge my electronics there and I used the government wifi connection while I waited. The ferry left late but, when it finally did, the views were spectacular. I divided my time between watching the mountains and glaciers go by and eating.

The ferry stopped in Leptepu and there was a 6 mile (10 km) gravel road to the next ferry. I wanted to make the first ferry across the short inlet so I powered down the gravel road. I was off the ferry before most of the cars and had quiet riding for a few minutes before an endless stream of traffic began passing me. I was completely covered in dust when I got to the other side, just in time to see the ferry pulling away from the dock. There was nothing I could do about it so I rode down the dock then got off my bike and jumped into the fjord to clean off all the dust. As could have been expected, the water was freezing and I left a patch of muddy water in my wake as I swam a bit then scrubbed off the dirt. I lay down on the dock afterwards and rested in the sun while I waited to dry off. An hour or so later the ferry showed up and I had another, though much shorter, cruise across the next fjord. It was 6:00 pm by the time I was on the other side and I had a couple of hours of daylight left so I tried to get as many hours of riding in before finding somewhere to camp.

The roads were dirt and the scenery was spectacular again. I kept stopping for photos but I didn't need to rush anyways. The setting sun was directly in my face when I pushed my bike off the road and through some brush onto the banks of the Rio Blanco and made camp for the night.

Mosquitoes were abundant in the morning and I was very glad my bivy had a mesh face to keep the bugs away. I could see them try to suck my blood through the mesh but I'd slept with it positioned a few inches away from face to keep them from getting me.

I rode into a town called Chaiten and got on a government wifi connection near the town square and messaged home among other things before riding out of town. The road kept changing surface from pavement to gravel and back again after Chaiten. Some road construction showed that soon most of the Austral Highway would be completely paved. I was soon on a gravel road again and going up a climb of about 1,600 vertical feet (500 meters); a slight tailwind was blowing and happened to be moving at almost the exact same speed I was, effectively riding in still air. On top of that, it was an exceptionally hot day for the area and I was soon drenched in sweat. I remedied the issue by splashing myself with water from a snow fed stream a couple of times on the way up. The other side was gravel for about the first half of the way down then a road construction project was paving there up the mountain I was descending. After a fast 45+ mph (72+ km/h) descent into Villa Santa Lucia I went by a store to get some more food. After a long break outside the store to eat, I decided I'd ride a little more then find somewhere to camp.

I'd been riding for a few miles when I saw an access to the river and stopped for a soak in a glacier fed river that was very aptly named the Rio Frio or Cold River. My knees had been bugging me again over the last couple of days and I hoped the freezing water would help with the mild swelling. I worked my way in, up to my waist, and sat for a while before easing in up to my neck. I couldn't stay in very long at that depth and I was nearly hypothermic when I got out.

I did another 10 miles (16 km) or so, enough to warm up and then began sweating again so I started looking for somewhere to camp. I got some water to filter from a stream then, another hundred yards of soft pedaling later, I found a small clearing through a break in the trees and stayed there for the night.

A headwind was blowing the next morning, slower riding but the secret of riding into headwinds is that if you keep moving you'll still get somewhere. It sounds obvious but many cyclists, especially cycle tourists, seem to forget this and get discouraged. A while after a break, I caught up to a Spaniard on a bikepacking mountain bike setup. I've forgotten his name but we were heading in the same direction and we rode together for a while. He was on a much lighter setup than me but we were riding about the same pace. Our conversation was limited to my knowledge of Spanish, he spoke very little English, and we rode into Puyuhuapi together.

After a stop by a grocery store we sat outside eating for a while before continuing. We barely made it out of town before we were stopped by some construction workers. They were doing demolition projects on the road and it would be closed until five pm. We turned back into town and rode into the park to wait out the three plus hour delay. I took a nap in the sun while I waited.

While we were waiting, Jesse rode up with Jose, a Chilean he'd been riding with for a couple of days. I was as surprised to see Jesse as he was to see me; we both thought that for sure he was still ahead of me. Jesse and Jose had asked to camp on a farmer's land not far north of where we were. The farmer had brought them breakfast and thanks to that, and Jesse's characteristically late starts, they'd only just begun cycling even though it was midafternoon.

The Spaniard I'd been riding with needed to keep going as soon as the road opened as he was on a tight schedule. Jesse, Jose, and I went to get lunch. They had wifi at the restaurant and we were there for a few hours. Jesse started feeling sick an hour or so after eating. Jose and I had eaten fish, it didn't have any worms this time, and Jesse had eaten pork and thus deduced that it was food poisoning. With this development, we decided we weren't riding any farther today and hung around town while Jesse rested; he wasn't doing well and threw up several times then lay down curled up in the fetal position on the grass outside the restaurant.

We setup camp near a river that ran through town. There was a grassy area and the residents of the town were used to seeing cyclists. While we were there, the tide began rising quickly and we moved from the grassy area near the river to the top of a berm that was high enough for foolproof protection from the rising tide. It stayed light out until nearly ten pm and that's how long we were up.

I was up early and made breakfast while I waited for Jesse and Jose to get up. I took my time preparing and eating breakfast and when I was done eating, cleaning up, and all packed up and ready to go both of them were still in their tents. Jose emerged around nine am, Jesse was another 30 minutes or so behind and still feeling sick. The police came by an hour later and told us we couldn't camp there. They weren't rude or pushy about it and said we had to leave that spot by evening that day while suggesting a campground to stay in a block away. Jose didn't like the idea that we couldn't camp on public land because there was a campground nearby and made a comment along the lines of "Chile and capitalism". Since capitalism is a four letter word pretty much everywhere, the policeman was embarrassed that the obvious had been pointed out and left us alone.

Jesse made an emergency run to a gas station bathroom and Jose went to get some more food while I was stuck keeping an eye on our gear so I took a nap in the sun; Chile is pretty safe. We didn't leave camp until midday, Jesse was beginning to feel better but the road had closed again and would be closed until five pm. We waited around town and bought food in preparation for the next day or two of riding. Jesse was still feeling weak and we checked out a couple of hotels but they were all out of our price range. Throughout the day, and while we were checking out some hotels, we got the idea that the people of Puyuhuapi were kind of rude. Even though it appeared to be a tourist town, everyone seemed to hate tourists of all kinds. Using the app iOverlander, an opensource app for travelers sharing tips in certain areas, we saw a wild camping spot marked a few miles out of town and got ready to go.

We were about to leave when a trio of Australians rolled into town. They were northbound out of Ushuaia and we exchanged information about the roads ahead. One of them had an impressive beard that stuck out away from his face almost to his shoulders. They'd been riding in snow and freezing rain for weeks by that time and I was not envious at all.

We were delayed by road construction again on the way out and Jose got a flat tire; eventually we made it to the spot from iOverlander. It was a decent spot, a large pullout after a hot spring resort but only 7 miles (12 km) from where we started that morning. The quality of the spots marked on that particular app varied widely in the practicality and usability. If the spot had been reviewed recently the reviewer was usually correct, though once again the standards varied widely. That particular spot served its purpose and we were left alone.

Jose was out of his tent around nine the next morning, Jesse followed suit soon after. Jesse was still feeling sick that morning too and Jose was ready to go around 10:00 am but Jesse was just over an hour behind. Soon after we started riding, we were at the entrance to a waterfall. Jesse and I had considered hiking to the waterfall with Jose but the entrance price for non-Chileans was over ten times the price. Jose wanted to do the climb so Jesse and I kept riding.

Just before two pm we got to a road block. More construction that would keep the road closed until five pm. We settled in to wait and soon it began to rain. We used my plastic sheeting to make some cover from the rain and I napped for a couple of hours while we waited. They opened up the road on time.

A few more miles of riding brought us to one of the largest climbs on the Carraterra Austral, about 1,600 feet (500 meters) tall. Funny how much standards for a big climb change depending on the location. In Peru such a climb would hardly be worth mentioning.

I was feeling great on the climb and powered my way up the pass. Jesse was still sick and threw up along the way then met me at the top. The sign for the pass was a false summit, a short descent and then another climb took us a couple hundred feet higher. Over the top were some incredible views of glaciers and waterfalls shrouded by mist. A gravel descent that was a few miles long followed the pass.

The road turned into pavement again at the bottom of the descent. We did another hour or so of riding before deciding to camp shortly after riding over a river. I soaked for a while in the frigid water, my knees were feeling better but they were still a little sore.

Jesse still wasn't feeling so great in the morning but we were on the road around nine. A good hour of riding took us to Villa Amengual. It'd been drizzling when we left camp and we dried our gear in the sun. Jesse's stomach trouble had him laid out in the grass for a couple of hours. Once he started feeling better, we began riding again. After another couple of hours of riding later, we caught up with a Polish couple on a cycle tour through South America. They were also heading south but we were still moving faster than them, even though Jesse was feeling sick and we rode on after a few minutes chat.

Once we were in Villa Manihuales, we stopped by a cafe for some empanadas and wifi for a couple hours. We'd heard about a casa de ciclistas in Villa Manihuales. I tried emailing them a week or so ago and never got a reply. We checked the address listed on the website without any luck. The Polish cyclists we met earlier had mentioned people recently having trouble with contacting the casa de ciclistas but had mentioned a free camping area. There was a large park/wooded area in the center of town that was marked as camping on our maps and we headed over. We didn't see the Polish cyclists anywhere in town but found the aforementioned spot was fine for camping.

I made breakfast while I was waiting for Jesse to get ready.

After a stop by the gas station to refill our water on the way out, we left Manihuales and within one mile of riding I hit 14,000 miles. We had a headwind riding out and caught up to the Polish cyclists we had met yesterday quite quickly. We said a quick "hello" then kept going.

A few miles into the day, there was a fork in the road. To the left was a continuation of the Carraterra Austral, on gravel, even though it was marked as a main road. The road marked as a byway was paved and slightly longer. We chose the gravel and within a couple of miles we were cruising along with a tailwind. The gravel road rolled trending upwards for about 3/4 of the day. We passed by more beautiful scenery such as we've almost come to expect on the Carraterra Austral, tall rugged snowcapped mountains and surprisingly frequent waterfalls.

The road turned to pavement about 7 miles (12 km) away from Coyhaique and, after a short climb, we started the last downhill into the city. I was riding ahead of Jesse on the way down. In one particular section the road turned suddenly to gravel; a large pothole in the gravel marked the end of the pavement. I was moving at about 35 mph (56 km/h) and had no way of stopping or going around the pothole; I jerked up on my handlebars and tried to bunny hop my bike over then I was launched skyward by a small lip on the end of the pavement.

Time slowed to a crawl. I was airborne long enough to wonder why I hadn't hit the ground yet, then, with a jolt, my tires hit the gravel. It felt like slow motion, my tires skittered across the gravel in a left turn while I counter steered the slide. The gravel section was only about 30 yards (27 meters) long and I bunny hopped another pothole before my tires hit the pavement and I had traction again. Time went back to a more normal rate; I was breathing hard, my heart pounded in my ears from the adrenaline, and I was smiling ear to ear and almost wishing there'd be another gravel section.

I stopped at the turn for Coyhaique; Jesse was a couple of minutes behind. As soon as he rolled up we had a good laugh, he'd caught air over the same section. We rode into town and began looking for a place to stay. We tried a couple of fire stations without any luck then began checking hostels. After more than five hostels we finally found one that was supposed to be the cheapest hostel in the city that still had hot water and wifi. After checking in we walked by the grocery store to get some food for dinner, which for me ended up being a cake. I'd never eaten an entire cake for dinner before in my life and that day seemed like a great day to do it. I was successful in eating the whole cake in one sitting and, surprisingly, I didn't get sick.

After a semi unproductive morning the next day, I left our hostel shortly after noon to see if I could find fenders for my bike to try to keep some of the mud off from the constant rain. There were a couple of bike shops within walking distance though neither of them had fenders; they'd just add weight anyways.

Next on my agenda was to try to find something to replace my heavy and bulky soft shell fleece. In most cases it was too warm to ride in and it was somewhat redundant because I had a waterproof jacket too. There was an outdoors store that had an on sale thermal pullover that would be about 1/4 the size and weight with almost the same warmth. They had a good pair of gloves on closeout sale that I bought also to replace the very worn, heavy, and bulky ski gloves I was carrying.

Back at the hostel, I did some maintenance on my bike and sorted through my gear. I found a couple of small miscellaneous items that I couldn't recall using for the entire trip or had been rendered unnecessary by my bike switch and escaped a previous gear sweep. A couple of the almost worthless items got thrown away; the rest were added to a giveaway pile with my soft shell fleece and old gloves. This increased my available space by a significant amount. The soft shell fleece had taken up more than 1/3 of a pannier! I'd like to get down to a frame bag eventually and I'd have to replace a few other 'hard to find' items for that but I was getting close. Total weight savings for the day was probably a couple of pounds (~1 kg), which felt pretty good considering where I already was.

It was approaching evening when Jesse and I went out for pizza at a spot we saw earlier. It was very greasy pizza but it hit the spot and it was the first pizza place I've been to in Latin America to have parmesan cheese as a condiment. Other condiments in the pizzerias of various countries have consisted of plain mayonnaise, tasteless paprika, various forms of spicy peppers, garlic sauce, fry sauce, Thousand Island dressing, and sometimes ketchup, which I really hoped wasn't for the pizza.

We had a great tailwind riding out of Coyhaique the following morning. We were going pretty fast and caught up to a group of cycle tourists at a construction stop. Among them was Pascal from Switzerland, the round-the-world cyclist who I'd met south of Puerto Montt. He had taken a ferry from Puerto Montt to a nearby port a day ago. The others were a family from Canada: two parents traveling with three small children, two in a trailer and one on a seat attachment on the back of the bike. They're the real hardcore cyclists; it'd be way more difficult to travel as a family than it is as an individual. We rode with Pascal for a couple of miles until we came to hill, Pascal's heavily loaded bike was holding him back so Jesse and I rode on ahead.

We stopped in a small village for a snack break. The village we stopped in happened to be one quarter of the way around the globe from where I started in Idaho, though it'd taken more than double that distance to get there by the route I took. Pascal rode up shortly before we were getting ready to leave. We stayed to chat for a few minutes before parting company as our paces while riding through the mountains weren't really compatible.

On the way up another climb, we passed the Polish cyclists we'd met a few days ago. Farther up, we caught up to yet another cycle tourist; after exchanging some brief formalities and confirming that he did speak English, he asked if we were both Americans; we confirmed that we were. He then asked if one of us was the guy who had lost half a finger, I showed him my right hand with the amputation and he carried on saying how impressed he was at my story. This was equal parts cool and awkward for me; I think I'd just met my first fan. He was from France and his name was Jean. He had started riding out of Buenos Aires a couple of months ago and was traveling for an indefinite and mostly unplanned amount of time. We rode with Jean the rest of the way up the climb. Meeting Jean also set my record for the most cycle tourists I'd seen in one day, six.

Over the top of the climb was an exciting descent into Villa Cerro Castillo with spectacular views of the surrounding mountains, including the jagged peak of Cerro Castillo. We stopped by a tienda to get some food in town and while we were there, Jean caught up to us; he wanted to do some hiking in the area and was looking for a place to leave his bike so he asked a local about a tourist office; they gave us directions and we found it. On the way there, Jean told us about how he doesn't carry detailed maps or a GPS and always asks directions from locals. Apparently it's been working for him since he started from Buenos Aires though, given my experience with directions from locals, I wouldn't be so trusting. At the tourist office, Jean was informed about a campground that might let him store his bike and the tourist office let us refill our water. Jesse and I weren't interested in hiking so we began looking for somewhere to camp. After searching for a few minutes we happened upon an empty lot in town that had an opening in the fence. The land didn't look like it was being used and we stayed there for the night.

We'd been warned from other cyclists about the difficult terrain south of Villa Cerro Castillo. Apart from the road being dirt again, and some steep hills, we couldn't figure out what the fuss was. There was a headwind but nothing too serious. We'd camped at an iOverlander spot along a river the night after we left Villa Cerro Castillo. It was a nice place really, water access and a protected grove of trees to camp in. It'd rained overnight and it was still raining in the morning. The road rolled along the shores of Lago General Carrera; it was dirt and it was raining on and off but the scenery was gorgeous! The bright blue waters of the lake contrasted nicely with the green of the surrounding trees and the snowcapped mountains in the distance. It was late spring in the south of Chile and wildflowers were blooming everywhere.

A few miles out of Lago Tranquillo, the wind changed to a headwind again. Rain, wind, and steep gravel hills made for slow progress and as soon as we saw a nice shelter along the roadside we stopped for the night. Today was Jesse's one year mark on the road; I had bought some wine and, even though he doesn't like wine most of the time, I convinced him to drink a cup in celebration.

CHAPTER 30

Day 307, December 4. 2016

Rio Barransco, Chile

I t'd been raining every day for the last several days. The night, after our stay in the shelter a couple of nights ago, had been dry, but the night after that, it'd been pouring rain until the early hours before dawn. Our most recent shelter for the night was a construction site. Since it was a weekend and we couldn't find anyone in the vicinity to ask, we'd slept out of the rain on a sheltered porch area of the site and had stayed dry.

The sun was out for a little while in the morning though it was overcast for the rest of the day. After going up a steep climb through the mountains there was an equally steep gravel descent going down the other side into Yungay. On one particularly sharp left turn I was going a little too fast. I braked as hard as I could, without skidding, and rode through the thick gravel lining the edge of the road to try to widen the arc so I could make the turn. My front tire began sliding when it hit the marble like pea gravel on the road; I tried to recover from the slide but it didn't work. I hit the road somewhere between 15-20 mph (24-32 km/h); my head made contact with the road and my helmet did its job. Jesse had seen me slowing down for the turn and had begun braking earlier; he rode through the turn without a problem though not before running over my right leg. Jesse stopped as quickly as he could and began apologizing profusely while asking if I was okay. I sat up and assessed the damage. I had road rash on my knee, hand, and shoulder, all on my left side. My bike had few more scratches and only the clear plastic dust cover for my shifter had broken. My panniers already had small holes in the bottom before the crash and they were made slightly worse but otherwise I was okay. I washed out my scrapes with my water bottle then got back on my bike and we rode the rest of the way to Puerto Yungay without issue.

There was a small tienda in Puerto Yungay. If you're happy eating candy, cookies, salty snack food, and sardines, they had plenty to offer. We bought some cheese crackers for a snack and a few packs of cookies and some peanuts to get us through the 24 hours after which we hoped to get to a town with a decent market. The ferry across the fjord by the village left at three pm. We hung around the tienda and the lady working there gave me some boiled salt water to wash out my road rash; it stung, but it'd prevent the wounds from getting infected.

It started raining while we were on the ferry and it was pouring by the time we got across the lake. As soon as we got off the ferry, we went straight to the shelter near the dock. The shelter offered complete protection from the rain and wind and it even had running water and bathrooms! We'd originally planned to ride for another hour before finding somewhere to camp but chose to stay in the shelter for the night instead of having a miserably cold and wet night elsewhere. We only had enough food to get us comfortably into the town of O'Higgins the next day; it would mean we'd have to do a longer 60+ mile (96+ km) day on gravel roads to keep from going hungry but that was greatly preferable to spending a night in the rain and still having to do a full day of riding the next day anyways.

The rain abated overnight. Once I was up, I sat on the porch of the shelter and made coffee to go with my cookies for breakfast and watched the clouds floating over the fjord and surrounding mountains while I waited for Jesse to get up.

We caught up to a group of five cycle tourists later in the

day. Three cyclists from France plus a German and one Swiss, all southbound; Jesse had met the French trio in Argentina and we talked for a while before Jesse and I continued on. About 10 miles (16 km) later we caught up to another German, also southbound and stopped to talk for a few minutes. A few miles later we met a northbound Englishman; he had just left O'Higgins and recommended a cheaper hostel for us to stay at, among other things.

In O'Higgins, we took the Englishman's advice and checked into a hostel along the main road. After showering, we began asking about a ferry to the other side of the lake. We started at the tourist information office, though they weren't much help. We went to the grocery store and got some potato chips and chocolate milk for a post ride snack then went back to the hostel to see if they had any better information about a ferry. They directed us to building about two blocks away. The ferry would leave in the morning. We'd gotten lucky with the timing; we hadn't been sure which days the ferry ran, but we knew it only went a couple of days a week.

Unsurprisingly, we had some difficulty leaving in time to make the ferry. We planned to leave at 7:15 but didn't actually leave until after 7:30 which was pretty close to a record early start for Jesse. The dock was 5 miles (8 km) away from our hostel and we threw the hammer down to get there. We rolled up to the dock less than 19 minutes later but the people running the ferry were nowhere to be seen. After confirming that the ferry hadn't left without us we posed for some pictures at the sign marking the southern terminus of the Carraterra Austral. The people in charge of the ferry didn't show up until several minutes after eight am, the Latin American concept of time was quite apparent. The boat finally left over ten minutes later, more than 15 minutes behind schedule, but not too bad in all reality.

Argentinean border control was on the other side of the ferry ride and was straightforward. After our passports were stamped, we began riding up the double track trail towards

Lago Desierto. Past the border, the jeep trail we were on turned into single track. Most of it was a fun ride, as long as we kept the possibility of our panniers snagging in mind. Several stream crossings, some with bridges, were interspersed throughout the trail. At the pass in the mountains, a sign marked the border between Chile and Argentina.

On the way down, Jesse's front brake quit working. He tried to repair it but couldn't figure out what the problem was so he opted for walking the steep, downhill sections and riding slowly with just the rear brake.

The trail turned into a mud bog in a few sections and its condition grew progressively worse until it became a deep rut of single track with just barely enough clearance for our panniers while riding at a walking pace. We met some hikers who had walked around Lago Desierto as opposed to taking the ferry. They'd struggled getting across on foot and said that the barely rideable trail we were on was nearly a highway compared to the trail around the lake. We'd considered trying to ride it but their advice swayed us otherwise. We met some cyclists coming up while we were only a mile or so away from the Argentinean border control; all of them had fully loaded touring bikes complete with four panniers and big bag on the rear rack similar to what I'd started my tour with. All of them were getting frustrated with the slow progress. It'd taken them over an hour to cover the mile (1.6 km) from border control to where we met them and they demanded information about the trail they had yet to cover. Having been through many similar experiences myself, I didn't take it personally and told them the truth that the trail opened up at the pass. That was enough for them and they slogged on. Once we made it down to the lake, we went through Argentinian border control. The ferry across Lago Desierto wasn't due until 5:30 pm so we still had a few hours to go and used that time to eat through the rest of our food supplies.

The ferry across the lake was expensive but the scenery remains among the most scenic ferry rides I've ever had in my life. Mountains and glaciers galore; more of what we'd been seeing most every day for the past couple of weeks, but it hadn't gotten repetitive in the slightest.

We landed on the other side with no food left at all and, with only a few hours of daylight remaining, we began powering through the remaining 22 miles (35 km) to El Chalten. Jesse's rear brake failed soon after we started. After walking down a few steep hills, he realized it would be worth the time to try to fix it and we stopped. He switched out the brake pads on both brakes and they started working again. With less than 10 miles (16 km) to go, the screws on the right side of my front rack began to strip and my pannier would bang into my spokes if I hit any bumps on the still gravel road. After tightening them a few times, the screws stripped completely; I emptied my pannier and stuffed as much of its contents as I could into my seat bag. To balance it out, I stuffed most of the things in my right pannier into my backpack. I'd wanted to switch to frame bags and took this as a sign that I should do so at the next opportunity. While I was rearranging my gear, Jesse noticed his frame was cracked. Luckily it was steel and could be repaired. I wish all this trouble we were having when we wanted to get somewhere was a joke but that's really how it happened. Cerro Fitz Roy, one of the most challenging mountains to climb in South America, stood awesomely over the trees as we rode slowly into El Chalten. Its sheer sides, that stretched nearly two vertical miles (3,200 meters) into the sky above us, were nothing less than awe inspiring.

We pedaled slowly into El Chalten and made it just as it was getting dark, nearly 10:00 pm since we were so far south. We'd heard about a casa de ciclistas in El Chalten and after some asking around found it. That casa de ciclistas was different as it was not free for cyclists but was more a hostel/camping area where cyclists tended to gather. It was still relatively cheap and, with everything that had broken over the course of the day; we might need a couple of days in town so we booked a few nights.

We still didn't have any food so, after taking our bags off our bikes, we rode into town to get dinner. It was close to 11 pm and all the grocery stores were closed. We got some empanadas to start and then went for bacon cheeseburgers. It was after midnight by the time we got back.

The hostel/campground we were at was on top of a hill, above the business district of El Chalten. The grocery store was farther away than I wanted to walk so I rode down to get some food for the day. This was the day I would start making a frame bag. Coincidentally, there was a sewing shop in El Chalten that was marked on iOverlander. I hoped they would have the materials but the information on the app said they wouldn't open until 5:00 pm. Once that time finally came around, Jesse and I went to the location where the app said it would be. It was not there and the shop had moved to a new location that was less than two blocks away from where we were staying.

The seamstress spoke English well and that simplified the process immensely. Once I had described what I wanted to make, she was not interested in helping but had the materials in stock: Cordura fabric, Velcro, and a high quality zipper. I bought the materials for less than $20 US. I had to go back into town to find needles, pins, and some good thread. I'd looked up some "do it yourself" bicycle frame bag instructions online and, back at the campground, I began working on my frame bag. I had already made a trace of the frame on cardboard for a pattern earlier in the day and it wasn't too long before I started cutting the fabric. I got all the panels cut before I made and ate dinner. It was getting late by then and I decided I'd start sewing in the morning.

I started working on the frame bag soon after I woke up. I worked on it all morning, probably a good five hours, and had the zipper and most of the panels attached together by noon. It was about that time that I began to admit to myself that I was really terrible at sewing. The panels were the correct size and shape but my stitching was awful. Eventually, I came to the conclusion that I was not going to be able to do this alone. The seamstress opened shop at two pm and I went to ask her for help. She was a little wary of accepting the project at first but, once I showed her exactly what I was doing and completely pinned the bag together, she was much more open to the idea. The design part was done and all she'd have to do was the sewing. She said she had some other projects she needed to finish and to come back at seven pm.

A bunch of other cyclists had shown up at the hostel throughout the day: two more Americans and one Canadian. We all went out for dinner at a burger place on the main road through town. I had to leave at seven to ride back to the seamstress. The bag was sewn together when I got there. I went over it and marked the locations of the velcro straps and some small alterations to get a proper fit. The seamstress said she'd have it done by the time she opened at two pm tomorrow and I went back to having dinner.

After a slow and fairly dull morning the next day, I rode to the seamstresses to pick up my frame bag around two pm. The fit and quality of the bag was better than I could have hoped for. Total cost including the sewing was less than $40 US. I gave the seamstress a large tip as a way of thanks because I really wouldn't have been able to do it without her and went back to the hostel to begin reorganizing my gear.

The process took a couple of hours but, eventually, I had everything packed and test rode it with the bag. It worked great, I had to readjust the load a bit to keep it from bulging, but everything was looking good and I hoped it wouldn't fall apart on me anytime soon. Jesse and I went for a hike to the Cerro Fitz Roy viewpoint that afternoon. It didn't take long to remind me why I don't like walking; it's slow and takes way too much effort compared to cycling. The views were great and there wasn't any other way to see them since bikes weren't allowed. We weren't feeling up to cooking dinner when we got back so, we went out for pizza. My budget seemed to be taking the backseat that month.

Jesse had gotten his frame welded during our stay in El Chalten. With my frame bag done we were ready to get on the road the following morning. I needed to get cash on the way out of town; I tried both of the ATMs in town but neither of them would work and all I had left in Argentinean pesos was the equivalent of about $10 US, but there was nothing I could do about it.

We had a very strong tailwind leaving El Chalten. We were practically flying we were going so fast! A few miles away from town, we caught up to Pascal; he was talking with a couple of northbound cyclists. Pascal rode with Jesse and I for a while before slowing down to his own pace and falling behind. Jesse and I rode 55 miles (88 km) in less than 2.5 hours. Our incredibly fast pace came to a grinding halt when we turned onto the Ruta 40 and into an equally strong headwind. We could only ride at a snail's pace compared to how fast we'd been going earlier but we only had 20 miles (32 km) to go to our goal for the day and we pushed through it. The winds were so strong that we had to be careful which direction we laid our bikes down when we took a break; if we weren't careful the wind would start blowing them away. Even into the wind, it was obvious just how much not having panniers improved the aerodynamics on my bike. Jesse was falling behind on his own and he drafted me most of the way.

Our goal for the day was 'The Pink House', an abandoned restaurant a little over 70 miles (112 km) south of El Chalten. We found it with little difficulty. It was pink after all so it stood out plainly in the relatively featureless pampas now that we were out of the mountains and there were many sets of bicycle tracks leading to it.

Once we were inside, we admired the graffiti left by the hundreds of cyclists who had stayed there. Normally I wouldn't add my name to any random location but, in this case, it added to the atmosphere of the place rather than detracted from it. Pascal rode up a couple of hours later and joined us for the night. He was carrying fishing equipment and went to the nearby river to try his luck then came back an hour later with a massive salmon! It was huge! Close to 8 pounds (3.6 kg) as near as we could guess. Jesse and I gathered wood for a fire while Pascal cleaned his catch. A couple of hours later we were feasting on fresh salmon. It was probably the best meal I'd ever eaten while camping. That day was also my highest average speed of the trip so far 18.6 mph (30 km/h) even with the slow section into the wind.

We got an early start in the morning, by Jesse's standards, around 8:30. We had about an hour of riding before the headwind picked up again. Pascal was riding with us and we formed a pace line to combat the wind. I was feeling tired but I was easily on the lightest and most aerodynamic bike of the group so I had no trouble pulling my share.

After a snack break a couple of hours in, it began to rain on and off. We were still moving slowly because of the headwind and Jesse got a flat tire about the time we got to a small river where we had planned to replenish our water supplies. There was a house nearby and Pascal went to ask for water. He was still gone when Jesse finished fixing his flat and we went to look for him. Pascal was talking with the owner of the house and had learned from him that there wouldn't be any water for close to 50 miles (80 km) from where we were. The owner of the house had invited us to camp on his land and had given Pascal some barbecued guanicoe (similar to llama) meat from an animal he had hunted recently. I was tired and wasn't feeling much like continuing riding into the headwind and didn't have a problem stopping early; Jesse was of a similar mindset, so we made camp.

There was another larger river nearby and Pascal went fishing again. This time he came back with three trout. Supposedly, Patagonia has some of the best fishing in the world. Another fire warmed us that evening and we had another awesome dinner.

The headwind was just getting strong by the time we left the next day. We knew we'd have a 1,200 foot (360 meter) climb a couple of miles in and Pascal started riding as soon as he was ready to get a head start on the climb. He rode a little slower uphill with the extra weight he was carrying. I waited for Jesse and we left about 15 minutes later. I rode with Jesse until I spotted Pascal in the distance and rode ahead to catch up to him. After riding with him for a while, we were near the top and I stopped at an overlook for some pictures of the barren yet colorful landscape below us then caught back up to Pascal. The headwind was even stronger at the top of the climb where Pascal and I waited for Jesse to catch up in the shelter of an abandoned building. Jesse found headwinds demoralizing and his mental state compounded the effect the winds had on him.

We made another pace line once we were back together and worked our way slowly into the wind. Soon, it began to rain and, shortly after that, the rain turned to snow. The snow was blowing sideways and stung at all exposed skin while we pedaled into the teeth of the storm. After an hour of pushing through the storm, we came to some pipes running perpendicular to the road to drain excess water; they were just big enough for us to push our bikes into and we took shelter from the storm.

The temperature was around freezing despite it being almost summertime in the southern hemisphere; our clothes were soaked from the rain and wet snow. The wind was still blowing strongly through the drain and it made for a cold wait. Jesse was not enjoying himself and started stress eating a giant peanut based candy bar that had about 2,000 calories. He ate the whole thing within minutes.

We were mostly dried off and had eaten something that counted as lunch when the sky looked clear enough to go back to riding. After another 10 miles (16 km) was the turnoff for Ruta 7. Jesse and Pascal wanted to take the Atlantic coast to Tierra del Fuego and I wanted to take the Pacific side to avoid some backtracking when I rode north again and see a couple of things. I turned off directly into the headwind and onto the dirt road after saying my farewells. With luck we would meet up again farther south.

Dirt roads and a still raging headwind made for slow progress. After the turnoff, the landscape was some of the emptiest land I'd ever seen. A dirt road stretched over the horizon and not a single hill was visible in the flat landscape. When I spotted a police station marked on my map that was a couple of miles ahead, I thought I'd ask if I could stay there for the night. The station was probably a mile away when I saw it plainly on the horizon and the wind was so strong that I was grinding along in my lowest gear going less than 5 mph (8 km/h). When I finally got to the station, there was no one there. There were no vehicles either and I took temporary residence in an empty and quite clean stable. There was a stream nearby where I got some water to filter and, since my stove was out of fuel, I cooked dinner over a fire that I built in the cut shell of an old oil drum that seemed designed for that purpose. I did some reading and went to bed early with the plan to get an early start in the morning to try to beat the wind. The 47 miles (75 km) I pedaled that day took more than five hours of riding.

I woke up at 1:00 am, I don't know why. I tried to decide what time I should get up and, after some thought, picked 2:45 am. Then the possibility of the wind getting bad just as I got to the pavement crossed my mind. I couldn't fall back asleep and started packing. I was riding by two am. The moon was bright enough I could see without lights. Although the road wasn't in bad condition it was definitely not smooth. By the time the sun was rising my tires had just hit the pavement. I'd been riding for over three hours and covered 30 miles (48 km) by 5:30 am. I pumped my tires back up to a higher pressure to go a little faster on the smooth surface and started off once more. There was a light headwind, maybe 3 mph (5 km/h).

The riding day was relatively uneventful, rolling hills all day and quiet roads thanks to my early start. When I got to the town of Rio Turbio, before noon, I'd just eaten the last of my food and I had almost no water left. I went by a gas station to refill on diesel for my stove then went to the grocery store and bought enough food to carry me through the roughly 100 miles (160 km) to the next known location I could buy food. Shopping was difficult; I was near the border of Chile and I planned to cross the next morning. Chile didn't allow any fruits, vegetables, or meat through customs. That meant I was going to be eating a lot of cookies until I could buy food again. I went by the town square to check for wifi, nothing, but there was a construction crew there that refilled my water. I camped a few miles past town in a vacant field on a hillside. I hadn't really slept in that stable the previous night because of the wind. I'd woken up so early that sleep came easily.

I made coffee in the morning after sleeping in as long as I could. I wasn't in a hurry. I'd have to wait for the border to open and I had no idea what time that would be. A short climb took me to the border. I got there at 7:34 am, I only know it was that time because I checked to see how long I would have to wait until it opened at eight. I made friends with a dog that apparently lived at the border post, while I was waiting.

The Argentina border process went smoothly, a significant line of cars trying to cross the border had built up behind me by the time they opened that would have taken at least as long again as I'd already waited if I'd arrived there any later. After another mile or so of climbing past the border, I'd officially crossed into Chile for the third time and I descended for a couple more miles to the border post. Chile was just as easy as Argentina had been. As with every other border crossing I've had, they did not check my bags. I could have bought other food besides cookies, but chances were that the one time I didn't expect them to check would probably be the time they confiscated my food.

I had a few more miles of descending before I turned south onto Ruta 9 with a light tailwind. I met two northbound cyclists along the way today: a man from Chile and a woman from Australia; both were traveling solo. The Australian recommended a place to camp a ways ahead and I decided I'd make that my destination.

I rode into Villa Tehuelches later in the afternoon. I had some Chilean pesos leftover from the last time I was in Chile and I bought some pasta and wine for dinner and potato chips for right away. After my snack, I went to the library; my device wouldn't connect to the wifi but they had a public computer I was able to use. I hung around for a while then rode to the fairgrounds at the northwest corner of the town. The Australian woman I met earlier mentioned that there were some stable like buildings that offered protection from the wind and rain and people regularly used them for camping. I found one I liked and made myself at home for the night.

The wind was already blowing by the time I left my camp in the fairgrounds stable. Luckily, it was a tailwind and it quickly increased in strength as the morning progressed. I was going exceptionally fast on my way to Punta Arenas and I covered 60 miles (96 km) in slightly over three hours breaking my average speed record yet again at close to 20 mph (32 km/h) this time. The road turned a few miles away from Punta Arenas and my massive tailwind turned into a tailwind/crosswind. It was still slightly faster than no wind but it gusted irregularly and made it difficult to hold a line.

It wasn't even noon when I got to the city. I went to a grocery store and stocked up on a few items that tend to be expensive in small rural stores, primarily olive oil and parmesan cheese to go with my pasta dinners. I bought stuff for a post ride lunch too: a giant bag of potato chips, chocolate milk, and stuff for sandwiches. I ate on a bench outside the store while I tried to figure out what to do next.

After having my old rear hub nearly fail on me in the Atacama Desert a few months ago, I was paranoid about the same thing happening to my current wheels. I rode by the bike shop to see what they had. They had a decent stock of almost everything a cyclist could need. My cheap aluminum bottle cages had broken a couple of days earlier and I replaced them with steel cages and bought some cycling water bottles too to try to make it so I could drink water while riding too. I wasn't quite able to articulate in Spanish what I wanted to do with my wheels, but luckily one of the employees spoke English. They said they could replace my hubs and have them ready the following afternoon. I still wasn't sure I wanted to switch to the new hubs they had and went to switch out my bottle cages while I thought it over. Eventually I came to the conclusion that I'd just have the shop rebuild the hubs I already had. The timeline for the repair was the same and of course they'd need to hold on to my wheels. They recommended a hostel a few blocks away and I rode over and booked a couple of nights. Once I was showered and clean I walked my wheels over to the bike shop so they could rebuild the hubs.

I tried to find a buffet restaurant for dinner but was unsuccessful and ended up at the grocery store again. I ate a whole chicken and a large bag of potato chips for dinner. Wifi and the company of several other cycle tourists kept me up late though it was an enjoyable break from the solitude of the last few nights.

CHAPTER 31

Day 320, December 17, 2016

Punta Arenas, Chile

When I walked down the stairs for breakfast at the hostel that morning, I heard a familiar story being told by one of the cyclists. It was the one about my finger getting frostbitten while I was mountain climbing and needing to be amputated that they'd probably read about in my blog. They didn't recognize me when I walked in so I listened quietly for a while until they messed up one of the details and I corrected them. They didn't believe me so I showed them my amputated finger and the looks on their faces were priceless. One of the cyclists had also attempted to climb Ojos del Salado but they'd climbed from the Argentinean side. There was supposed to be ground water available on that side while on the Chilean side the only water was from snow or ice and that wasn't available year round. This cyclist had found a friend to climb with and when they were one day away from their planned summit day a massive storm blew in and they had to shelter in a cave for a couple of days. The cave had been adequate shelter but there were a couple of dead bodies there that had obviously been there for years that had become mummified by the dry air. They didn't want to share a similar fate as the other unfortunate climbers and they turned around without reaching the summit.

I was up early the following day and began packing my gear and getting ready to get on the road again. I'd rotated my tires during my rest day and my rear tire was flat this morning. It looked like the tube had gotten caught between the tire and the rim and torn a hole in it while I was putting it on. I patched it before going back inside to eat breakfast then started riding at eight. The ferry across the Strait of Magellan to the island of Tierra del Fuego was at nine and I arrived with over 30 minutes to spare. There was one other cyclist on board, a Spaniard who'd stayed at the same hostel I had.

The ride across took about two hours. I bought some more stuff for sandwiches in Porvenir, the town on the other side, before starting off. There were two roads leaving Porvenir and heading east across Tierra Del Fuego, one through the hills and the other along the coast; both are gravel and met up with each other about 30 miles (48 km) away from the town. The route through the hills was a few miles shorter with more climbing but less traffic and that was the route I took.

The road wound through hills before descending to the coast and meeting up with the other road, it was pleasantly quiet riding. Along the way I saw some guanicoe and the famous 'Wind Blown Tree of Tierra del Fuego'. The constant wind that usually blows from the same direction had caused the tree to lean hard to one side in the same way that some bonsai trees have a windswept look. I had a tailwind for most of the day and made it to the bus stop/shelter, at a junction of some roads which was a popular stop for cyclists, in less than four hours. There were a couple of French cyclists there and I talked with them while I took a break in the shelter. Once I was feeling somewhat rested, I started riding towards the penguin reserve about 10 miles (16 km) away. The tailwind I had earlier was now a crosswind and it took about an hour to get there. It was expensive to get in but completely worth it for the experience. I walked over to the viewing point and there they were, penguins.

The penguin experience may not be worth it for some people. There was a wooden barricade that marked the viewing area and ropes everywhere to mark a trail and prevent anyone from getting within roughly 20 yards (18 meters) of the penguins. For me, it was worth it. Seeing penguins in the wild was something I'd wanted to do for years and it was one of the reasons why I wanted to cycle to Ushuaia. Seeing the penguins made me realize just how far I'd come and how much I'd done in nearly 11 months of traveling. I thought about it all for a long while and stood watching them for a couple of hours. They were King Penguins, similar coloring to Emperor Penguins but significantly smaller. They weren't waddling across ice and snow; they were on sand and grass, but it was still pretty awesome.

After the penguins I rode back the bus stop/shelter at the junction. Pascal from Switzerland was there along with two women from France who were northbound. We made and ate dinner and shared some stories from the road.

There was an excellent tailwind blowing when I woke up in the morning. Pascal was going to see the penguin colony so I was riding solo. The roads were still gravel but it was in good condition except for the last 10 miles (16 km) to the border where large exposed rocks made the surface similar to riding on washboard. Nonetheless, I was moving quickly with the tailwind and did the 36 miles (58 km) to the Argentinian border post in little more than two hours of riding. Border formalities were blessedly short and uneventful. At the Argentinian border post in San Sebastian there is a waiting room where they often let cyclists stay the night. I took shelter from the cold wind there and had a snack then refilled my water before continuing.

I had a massive tailwind leaving the border and heading south along Tierra del Fuego, zipping along at close to 30 mph (48 km/h) for much of the day. I hit 15,000 miles while cycling across the barren tundra of Tierra del Fuego. The milestones had become semi routine at that point and I planned to save my celebrating for a couple more days.

I rode into Rio Grande with right at four hours of riding and over 80 miles (130 km) cycled. I found a wifi connection at a park and found out that Jesse was also in Rio Grande. He was staying at a friend of a friend's place and there was room for me too. I rode over and met him there. We had a relaxing afternoon with an excellent wifi connection and our host made dinner for us too!

I still hadn't been able to withdraw any Argentinean pesos since El Chalten. After doing a bit of research as to why my card wouldn't work at the ATMs I discovered that I wasn't the only traveler with this problem. Many of the ATMs in Argentina were not yet equipped to read cards with chips and only larger banks had the more modern machines. There was one in Rio Grande; Jesse and I rode there on our way out of town and I was able to get cash without any problems. When we finally got out of Rio Grande it was close to noon. We had yet another raging tailwind so we had little trouble making our distance for the day.

We met a few interesting people that day. The first was a Chilean couple on bicycles who were northbound from Ushuaia. We saw them from far away on a long and straight road and decided we'd stop to talk to them. We rode up to each other and after a brief greeting they asked, "Is one of you Jacob?" I confirmed my identity and they said that they followed me of on Instagram (@worldbybike_niktia).

The other interesting person we met was while we were stopped for a snack break. We saw something moving in the distance; it was far enough away that we couldn't tell what it was at first but we were able to confirm that it was moving. As it got closer, we recognized it as being someone walking. They had trekking poles and we joked that they were probably walking from Ushuaia to Alaska. They walked up and we got to talking. They had just started walking from Ushuaia a few days ago and were, in fact, walking to Alaska. I didn't catch his name but he planned to thru-hike it in 30 months or about as fast as most people cycle it. On top of that he planned to walk through the Darien Gap between Panama and Colombia, a road-less stretch of swamp frequented by drug dealers that was technically illegal to cross. Jesse and I had gone around it on the sailboat cruise. We were impressed to say the least. This was his second attempt; he had torn his Achilles tendon after walking to Santiago a year ago and decided to restart for another try so he could break the official record by doing the route in half the time of the previous walking record.

We rode into the town of Tolhuin and found the La Union bakery without any trouble. The bakery had a large hospitality area and had hosted the majority of the cyclists passing by in either direction for around 20 years. There were more than ten cyclists there by the time the day ended; one of them was Pascal. He had ridden the tailwind there from the Argentinian border where he had stayed the night and had broken his distance record for his tour at over 200 kilometers or 125 miles.

We left Tolhuin just before noon the next day after a slow morning that included a breakfast of empanadas and pastries at the bakery. We had smooth roads and rolling hills for the first hour or two of riding then a climb about 1,200 feet (360 meters) in elevation. It rained on and off all day long and hailed briefly at one point.

For our last few miles into Ushuaia, the sun broke through the clouds and shined brightly over the bay, illuminating the city that had been both my own and Jesse's goal after nearly a year on the road. It sounds cliché but it actually happened though it began raining again soon afterwards. We stopped for a celebratory lunch of pizza before checking out some hostels. Many were booked completely but we found one that had beds available. Price fixing was in effect; all of them were about $22 US per night or more, easily the most I'd ever spent on a hostel.

It was anticlimactic arriving in Ushuaia but I'd expected as much. It was a strange feeling to make it there. Ushuaia had been my destination and a progress goal for so long that it seemed odd to be done with that leg of my journey. When I first started riding, I often had doubts that I'd make it that far. Ushuaia was also the end of Jesse's tour; he was able to negotiate work at the hostel in exchange for accommodation while he waited for his flight home in a few weeks. Jesse was of a similar opinion: glad to be done, sorry the ride was over for him, but at the same time excited to be moving on to the next thing. I still had no idea what I was going to do when I was done with cycling the world and I was glad that I still had a long way to go.

Dinner was a continued celebration; we went out to dinner with Dante, a cyclist we had met in El Chalten and the only person I've met who has per day mileage average close to mine. He rode from New York to Ushuaia in seven months and covered about 10,000 miles (16,000 km) by bicycle. Dante was also happy about completing his goal and looking forward to his next chapter in life. I wasn't even close to being done with my around-the-world tour yet and that was perfectly fine with me.

CHAPTER 32

Day 326, December 23, 2016

Ushuaia, Argentina

I stayed in Ushuaia for a couple of days. We celebrated the summer solstice on December the 21st (the seasons are reversed south of the equator) by taking a picture with the Fin del Mundo, or End of the World, sign near the end of the road at a bay. At about 55 degrees south of the equator, Ushuaia was the southernmost city in the world and just about as far south as it's possible to go without being in Antarctica.

The day I left Ushuaia was my 25th birthday. A quarter of a century, it seemed like a long time said that way. It was a good feeling though; I was doing exactly what I wanted to be doing with my life. I celebrated the momentous occasion by doing one of my favorite things; I went for a bike ride. I took my time getting ready and, after saying a surprisingly difficult goodbye to Jesse, I started riding north at almost 10:00 am.

On the way out of Ushuaia I passed a kilometer marker that said 3050 km, about 1,900 miles, and the markers counted down to Buenos Aires. Once I got back to mainland South America I could follow the same road the whole way there.

I got stopped at a police checkpoint just outside Ushuaia. They wanted to know where I was from, where I was going, and had me go inside an office so a border guard could write down my passport details. He noticed it was my birthday and wished me a happy birthday as he handed my passport back.

I saw Pascal riding towards Ushuaia a few miles outside the city. He was riding with two Frenchmen and I stopped to talk with them for a bit. Pascal planned to bus north to Buenos Aires after spending a few weeks traveling Patagonia with his family who were flying out to visit him. He had heard the wind was ridiculous the entire way along the Ruta Nacional 3 or RN3, the road that goes from Ushuaia all the way to Buenos Aires. I'd never heard of anyone cycling the complete length of that road without hitchhiking in a car at some point. Perhaps I'd be the first if I made it the whole way.

I had a tailwind and a pleasant ride to Tolhuin. It was strange riding roads that I'd cycled before after being in new places almost every day for so long. I stopped for a snack at the top of Paso Garibaldi, all of 1,400 feet (420 meters) above sea level, and admired the view of Lago Escondido during one of my snack breaks.

While I was eating, a storm began to blow in behind me and it started hailing. I quickly got back on my bike and began the descent to try to outrun the storm. I was successful and, after a few miles, had dry conditions the rest of my ride. I was surprised when I checked my riding time in Tolhuin: 3:45 of riding for the day at about 17 mph (28 km/h). I was really enjoying how much faster my new bike setup was. I stayed at the bakery again; after a shower, I bought some wine from a nearby store, some pastries from the bakery, and then rested for the remainder of the afternoon. If I rode the most direct route to Santos, Brazil I'd need to average less than 45 miles (72 km) per day to make it on time for my cruise to Europe. What was I going to do with all that time?

It was raining when I got up in the morning. I delayed starting as much as I could in hopes it would stop but eventually resigned myself to fate. It rained for my first couple of hours of riding and much to my surprise I had a tailwind again; the prevailing winds were from the north. I expected the wind to change at any moment but my luck held out.

I'd put my camera inside my jacket pocket to protect it

from the rain; when I took it out to take a picture at a snack break it wouldn't turn on. The inside of my jacket had turned into something resembling a sauna and it may have caused my camera's untimely demise.

I stayed the night at Marcelo's house, the same person I'd stayed with less than a week ago while going south and where I met up with Jesse again. He invited me to go fishing with him and a friend of his so I did. We had nice afternoon fishing and caught two fish, neither of them were very large but they were good enough for eating. I don't remember what they called that species of fish but they looked similar to catfish.

Back at Marcelo's, we made dinner of the fish we had caught and some lamb asado he had left over from a barbecue the prior night. It was great being able to spend Christmas Eve with a friend and dinner was awesome.

I was riding by seven that Christmas Day in hopes of beating the wind for a couple of hours. I had no such luck, it was already blowing when I got out the door. As least it was a cross-wind, they're not quite as slow as headwinds. I took it easy, no point in wearing myself out fighting the wind. Eventually I got to San Sebastián and the Argentinian border, and crossed into Chile for the fifth time. There was a small cafe by the border that had wifi; I bought an overpriced beer for the privilege of using the internet connection and called home since it was Christmas. Being so far away from home for the holidays was tough.

It was about 35 miles (56 km) to the bus stop/refugio that I had stayed at going the opposite direction; it was a gravel road still but the wind wasn't all that bad and I pushed on so I could stay there for the night. The gravel was of course slower going than the pavement had been. I passed a couple of walkers pushing heavily laden strollers carrying all their gear into the wind. They didn't look like they were having fun and they didn't say hello back to me. I met a Japanese woman who was cycling in the opposite direction. She was riding solo from Punta Arenas to Ushuaia. That made three solo female cyclists that I'd met in one month, that's got to be a world record. Every single one of them was riding in the opposite direction as me too, just my luck. Maybe if I started riding more miles per day I could catch up to people going the same way as I was. I also caught up to the northbound walker Jesse and I had met north of Tolhuin. I slowed down to talk for a minute and told him about the refugio I would be stopping at.

All told, it took me about 3.5 hours of riding to pedal the 35 miles (56 km) from the border to the refugio. Almost eight hours of riding time for the day. I'd only slept for four hours the previous night so I went to bed almost immediately after dinner. The walker I'd caught up to earlier showed up before dark; I woke up when he came in and talked with him for a few minutes before going back to sleep.

I was up at five; I heard the wind howling outside and it was raining so I went back to sleep. It wasn't getting dark until after midnight and then the sun would begin to rise a few hours later. I got out of bed around seven; the rain had stopped but the wind had not. I got to talking with the walker for a while, his name was Carlo, he was from North Carolina. I don't think he remembered meeting me earlier as he told me again about how he'd injured his Achilles tendon on his last attempt at walking the Pan-American and said he was giving it another shot before he got too old. I asked him how old he was out of curiosity, he was 56. Carlo was in the ultralight realm; he said he carried about 7 pounds (3.2 kg) of gear and he fit most of it into his custom made hollow hiking poles. He had almost no spare clothes except for rain gear and a down jacket and he only carried a bivy with his sleeping bag and air mattress. Carlo started walking towards Provenir after eight. I was northbound shortly after and on new roads again since I'd finished my detour to Ushuaia. The road turned to pavement within a quarter mile (400 meters) and I stopped to pump up my tires. There was a headwind and it began to rain, it was going to be a very long day. The rain didn't last very long but the wind was being redirected by the hills around the road and that made it even stronger.

I stopped at a refugio after doing about 15 miles (24 km) in almost two hours of riding. I had found out what I was going to do with all the time I had to get north to Brazil: I was going to fight for every inch of progress into the wind. After a snack I got going again and made about 14 miles in an hour and half before stopping at another refugio. I had another snack and napped for an hour in the warm dry shelter of the refugio then got back on the road. The terrain began to open up after that and the wind was more of a crosswind than a headwind so I was going a little faster because of it. The road turned east-ward and suddenly I had a tailwind so strong I was going 25 mph (40 km/h) without pedaling. My speed got as high as 32 mph (52 km/h) without pedaling on flat ground and I was able to coast the last 5 miles (8 km) to the town of Cerro Sombrero.

I stopped at the grocery store in town and refilled my water from a hose in front of the gymnasium. I wasn't sure what to do next; there weren't any good options for camping in town and most everything was closed for the holidays. There was a bus stop near the turnoff to Cerro Sombrero and I decided I'd stay there for the night. It wasn't very clean but it was closed on all four sides with an open door and it gave me shelter from the wind. It didn't seem like it got used as a bus stop very often based on its location; the nearest building was over a mile (1.6 km) away. I made dinner and read for a while before going to sleep.

The wind howled all night, I know this because I woke up a few times and heard it. I was riding around 6:30 the next morning and pedaling easy again. The wind was coming strongly out of the west and the road curved repeatedly so the hills were constantly changing the effect the wind had on me.

The 24 miles (38 km) to the ferry took almost three hours. The last 10 miles (16 km) were directly into the wind and my speed hovered around 7 mph (12 km/h). I got to the ferry just as it was boarding and hopped on. The Strait of Magellan had 10 foot (3 meter) plus swells in every direction and the ferry was rolling to the motion of the waves, a few people threw up. One of the crew members gave me some apples.

On the other side was a 10 mile (16 km) section into the wind that took about an hour and a half to cross. The wind began to change from a headwind to a crosswind as I got closer to the hills that were the border of Chile and Argentina. At the base of the hills the road turned east and the wind pushed me up to 20 mph (32 km/h) with no pedaling on my part. A short but slow climb, with a crosswind, brought me to the border and out of Chile. I recharged my electronics at the border post for a while, after finishing the crossing process, and then refilled my water in the bathroom. After that, I sat outside eating some cookies while I tried to decide whether to keep riding. One of the border guards walked up while I was eating and began asking me about my trip. Eventually he asked if I needed somewhere to sleep for the night and showed me a spot on the other side of the border post that was well sheltered from the wind and weather. It had taken almost six hours of riding to get there and I accepted gratefully. He even got me the password to the wifi.

The wind was howling all night long again. I went inside the border office when I woke up to eat more cookies for breakfast, that was all the food I had, and to charge my electronics again. One of the officials there gave me some coffee and even more cookies. I was riding around eight and had mostly crosswinds and tailwinds into the city of Rio Gallegos. I took it easy, I knew I'd be paying for every last inch of progress and there was no need to overexert myself. There was a police checkpoint just outside the city; they had me go inside the office so one of the officers could write down my passport details before sending me on my way.

I took advantage of the post-Christmas sales at one of the grocery stores in the city, lemon pound cakes for less than a dollar each. I ate a significant amount of food sitting outside the store before I got going again. The next section was one I had been dreading for the last couple of days; 20 miles (32 km) directly into the raging wind. I'd planned on it taking three hours or more and considered myself lucky when I was done in about 2:45. There was another police checkpoint outside the city, same routine as the first. One of the officers was kind enough to refill my water.

Once the 20 miles (32 km) of headwinds were done, the road turned north and I had a pleasant surprise, a tailwind. The wind I had been fighting for the last few hours was strong enough that I was going close to 25 mph (40 km/h). Over the last few days of headwinds, I'd decided that if I ever had a tailwind I'd make the most of it and that is what I did.

The wind was almost dead when I stopped riding around eight pm. I'd clocked over nine hours of riding time and shattered my longest one day distance for the trip 142 miles (229 km). Pretty good considering my first 60 miles (96 km) took more than five hours. I found a spot that was free of brush about 20 yards (18 meters) away from the road. I made and ate dinner then fell asleep exhausted.

I hadn't refilled my water since the police checkpoint outside of Rio Gallegos the day before and I was almost out when morning came around. After eating some sandwiches for breakfast, I had only a few sips of water left. I could have refilled later in the day yesterday but I hadn't felt like stopping at the time because of how fast I was going. It took a couple of hours to get to Piedra Buena, the next town, and I ran out of water with less than 10 miles (16 km) to go.

After I crossed the electric blue colored Rio Santa Cruz, I rolled into town and made a grocery run. I ate lunch in a nearby park and refilled all my water while I tried to rehydrate. There was a climb going out of Piedra Buena and the weather was starting to get hot. I was drenched in sweat by the time I got to the top and, consequently, I went through my water much faster than I had before.

I passed a sign marking Laguna del Carbon, the lowest point in the Americas, at 344 feet (104 meters) below sea level. There wasn't much to see nor did I see any roads going into the depression so I kept riding. I had a tailwind right up until mid-afternoon when the wind changed abruptly into a headwind. At about 20 miles (32 km) to go to San Julian, I was running out of water so I kept going even though I would have liked to stop for the day. Just outside the city, I stopped at a religious shrine to rest. There were benches and a water tap with the whole lot surrounded by a concrete wall that made a great windbreak. I didn't have anything I needed to do in San Julian now that I had water so I camped there for the night.

I woke up at 4:30 am and I was riding by 5:00 am to try to beat the wind the next morning. It hadn't stopped completely overnight but it was down to just a few mph and much weaker than it was the previous evening. I went by a gas station on my way through San Julian and filled my water again before leaving the city. I had quiet riding all morning; the reduced traffic from how early it was was nice. A couple of hours in, I realized I was still carrying road tires and not using them so I pulled over and switched out my tires. After I re-calibrated my speedometer and had a snack, I got going again. The road tires were definitely faster, not by a ton but enough that I found myself wishing I'd switched to them at the border from which point the road had been completely paved.

The Patagonian Pampas were definitely not flat as I'd naively expected it to be. Continuous rollers and a few smaller climbs had been the norm of my last few days of riding. Without realizing it, I stopped a few miles short of Tres Cerros at a small cluster of buildings. Tres Cerros didn't look like much on my map and I wasn't expecting much more than the restaurant/tienda/hotel/mechanic shop that was there. I bought a cheap bottle of wine there as a 'thank you' to the storekeeper for refilling my water and rested in the shade for a couple of hours before realizing that the village of Tres Cerros was slightly over a mile farther away. In Tres Cerros there was a gas station/mini-mart that had wifi.

I hung around the gas station and used the wifi. Eventually, I cooked and ate dinner. At about nine pm, a tailwind picked up and I started riding with the plan of continuing to ride until it got dark or the wind stopped. The wind died about 30 minutes later and shortly after I found a culvert under the road and made camp for the night. It was concealed, quiet, and out of the wind, a much nicer place to sleep than behind a bush along the road would have been.

The next morning was mostly crosswinds but nothing too bad. It was easier riding for a few hours compared to the headwinds. Around noon, the wind began to pick up quickly. An hour later, I was fighting just to stay on the road and got blown off a few times.

I stopped to rest about 10 miles (16 km) away from the town of Fitz Roy and tried to figure out what I should do. The road had turned directly into the wind and I was struggling just to keep moving. On top of that, my chain had worn out to the point that it was beginning to skip if I pedaled hard. While I was sitting around, an armadillo came by and inspected my bike while looking for crumbs. Fitz Roy seemed like a good place to call it a day and I got back on my bike. The last 10 miles (16 km) were horrible and took well over an hour because of how strong the wind was; fighting the wind all the time was getting demoralizing. When I finally got into town, I stopped outside a gas station and rested for a while before going to a nearby store to get some food.

On the north end of town there was another gas station that had wifi. I bought some cookies to snack on and ended up staying there most of the afternoon. The wind was so strong it was almost pointless to try to ride into it. Fighting the wind for the last week had taken my mood down a few notches; it's tough working so hard and barely getting any return on the effort. I looked up a wind map online and confirmed that Patagonia is one of the windiest places on earth and probably the windiest place I'd ever be. It was nice to know that I shouldn't have anywhere where the wind was consistently worse than Patagonia. Based on the wind map, I might be out of the worst of it in about 600 miles (970 km), a long way off, but perhaps it could be something to look forward to. Once evening was approaching, I went to find somewhere to camp. I ended up outside a municipal gym, the only place I could find with shelter from the wind.

That day was the last day of 2016. It was odd thinking about it that way. It'd been eleven months since I started riding. The entire time had been a whirlwind of adventure that far exceeded any other year of my life by the sheer volume of experiences I'd had. It was amazing how much had happened. I was excited about the adventures to come and happier than ever that I didn't quit after the frostbite amputation.

CHAPTER 33

Day 336 January 2, 2017

Caleta Olivia, Argentinia

I'd ridden to Caleta Olivia on New Year's Day. All three of the bicycle shops in town were closed for the holiday, no surprise there. I'd had to wait in town overnight for them to open so I could get a new chain for my bike. The old one was so worn it was hardly working now and Caleta Olivia was the only town with bicycle shops for hundreds of miles around. I'd set up my sleeping mat in a vacant lot and tried to sleep in; the grocery store wouldn't open until 8:30. I was successful and got there right at 8:30 but they weren't open. It was still South America so I wasn't very surprised. 15 minutes later they opened their doors even though the sign clearly said 8:30.

The bike shop was supposed to open at 9:30. They weren't open on time either and I waited outside. Ten am came and went but they still weren't open. I saw someone outside a house nearby and they said they wouldn't be open today and maybe not tomorrow either. I was concerned by this but there were a couple other bike shops in town. I had to ask around to find the next closest one and I was very relieved when I saw an open sign in the window and walked up to go inside. The door was locked. I was suddenly crushed by the idea that I might have to wait around for another day. More waiting was something I did not want to do. I was getting sick of Patagonia and its continuous wind and the only way for me to get out of it was to keep riding.

I checked the last bike shop in town. They weren't open yet but shortly after I tried the door someone came and opened it for me. They had the chain I needed. It wasn't cheap but I didn't really have any choice at that point so I bought it. With my bike back in proper working condition I began riding out of the city.

The buildings ended abruptly at the edge of the city but the traffic did not. Cars were speeding by and most of them wouldn't move over much at all to pass me; the road was in terrible condition too, cracks and potholes everywhere that threatened to swallow my wheels and make me crash. On top of all that was the wind, I was barely crawling along into a direct headwind for the first couple of miles then a crosswind later in the day made it impossible to ride in a straight line After over an hour of this, there was an under construction road that was blocked off to cars but still accessible to bicycles. I had to push my bike through some deep gravel and brush to get to it but it took away the most serious of the problems that I was facing on the main road. I was still going slowly because of the crosswind but at least the surface was good and there was no traffic. I reached 16,000 miles cycled that afternoon.

My private highway ended in deep gravel a few miles later and I was forced to go back to the main road. The road was as clogged with traffic as ever and the drivers were just as reckless. It didn't take long for me to get frustrated with the situation and, before long, I was screaming at the top of my lungs in anger at any driver that honked or passed me unsafely.

The road followed the coast, more or less. A few times, I was climbing directly into the wind in my lowest gear and barely able to keep moving. At other times, I was descending into the wind and having to pedal to keep going at only 6 mph (10 km/h). I did have a couple brief tailwind sections but they never lasted long. The crosswind sections were terrible too; it was a struggle just to stay on the road. Eventually I made it to a city called Comodoro Rivadavia. There was a gas station with wifi that I rested at for a while. I was in a better mood after that and went by a grocery store after to stock up on food for the 220 mile (352 km) stretch to the next city. I expected it to take a few days or more. They had just put fresh bread out in the bakery section so I bought a few baguettes and some butter for a post ride snack and to have some left over for breakfast. Eating improved my mood but, I still didn't feel like riding much farther so, I planned to camp at the next opportunity.

The city riding was still busy but there was something of a shoulder and it was not near as upsetting as it was earlier. I found somewhere to camp in a field, just before the last gas station leaving the city and a 12 mile (20 km) westward stretch that would be directly into the wind, and I set an alarm to wake me up so I could try to beat it.

My alarm went off at 4:30 am; the wind was still blowing just as hard as it was when I went to bed, if not harder, and it was still dark, unlike it had been farther south, so I went back to sleep. I was up two hours later and was riding within 30 minutes. I refilled my water at the gas station on the north end of the city and started pedaling. Approximately 5 miles (8 km) of riding later, the road turned west into the wind and began going uphill.

I was climbing up a canyon and the wind was manipulated by the walls of the canyon in such a way that the headwind would stop on occasion but it was still uphill and slow. It took me over two hours to ride my first 17 miles. At the top, I had crosswinds to tailwinds for the rest of the morning. The road would wind around a gully or some other obstacle and I'd have headwinds on occasion. Around the 80 mile (130 km) mark for the day, I had almost a complete tailwind, still enough from the west side that I was getting blown around, but I was moving quickly. It was then that I resolved to ride as long as I possibly could to make the most of the tailwind.

Just past my 100 mile (160 km) mark a freak storm blew up behind me and it started pouring rain. I was only a few miles away from the next gas station and I sprinted to get to its shelter. The wind was strong enough that the rain blew over quickly and I made dinner before heading out. It was more like a late lunch as it was only three pm and I made a strong cup of coffee to go with it and boost my energy. I topped off my water again and rode the next 65 miles (105 km) nonstop. I was hungry again, by then, and stopped for a snack break. At about 185 miles (300 km) I passed kilometer marker 1525 the halfway point between Ushuaia and Buenos Aires. I flew by my 200 mile (320 km) mark at over 25 mph (40 km/h), I couldn't stop in good conscience when I had a tailwind like that and there was still daylight left. 30 minutes later it was starting to get dark and unsafe to ride. I was so tired I was almost falling off my bike, so I found a culvert that passed under the road; it wasn't tall enough for my bike to fit inside but I could crawl in just fine. I rolled out my sleeping mat and ate almost all my food before falling asleep the instant I laid down. I'd cycled for over 11 hours and I'd covered 211 miles (338 km) which broke my one day distance record by nearly 70 miles (112 km).

I was sore in the morning though not as sore as I thought I'd be. I'd only done one double century in my life before that one. Last time I was almost unable to move and had bruises on my hands from leaning on the handlebars for so long and I couldn't sit on a bicycle seat for over a week. I was far more tired and sore than usual and I considered just lying in my culvert for the rest of the day but I didn't have enough water to do that so, I got up and began riding around nine. I had 10 miles (16 km) to go to a town called Trelew; there was a tailwind most of the way and it didn't take too long.

I expected the next 125 mile (200 km) gap to the next town to take at least another day or two and I bought food accordingly. It was beginning to rain and I did a few more miles to a gas station that had wifi and I stayed there until it stopped raining around 1:30 pm. I planned on doing another two hours of riding, maybe three, before stopping for the day. The only problem was that I had a tailwind again. I was almost sad that

I had a tailwind because it meant I couldn't stop early. Instead of stopping early, I continued pedaling easy and set the goal of going as far as I could.

I met a southbound cyclist that afternoon, Michael from France. He was doing a perimeter tour of South America and stopping to work when needed. He'd left Buenos Aires about two months earlier and planned to finish there in a few years. He said I was the first cycle tourist he'd seen on his entire trip. It was painfully obvious that he'd been looking forward to meeting another cycle tourist and I ended up talking with him for close to an hour. He reminded me of myself when I was doing my first couple of months of riding and had gone over a month without seeing another cyclist. He was going to have a hard road south on the RN 3 and I wished him the best of luck.

It rained on and off all afternoon. As soon as I started thinking about taking my rain jacket off, the rain would start again. I was taking it easy but, with the strong tailwind, I did 100 miles (160 km) in under five hours of riding at an average speed of more than 20 mph (32 km/h). I was getting close to Sierra Grande, the town that I had expected to reach in a couple of days, so I rode the rest of the way there to get some wine and better food to reward myself for my second big mileage day in a row and to stock up for the 185 mile (300 km) stretch of almost nothing to the next city. I made it to Sierra Grande and refilled my water at a gas station before leaving town and stopping for the day at the next culvert I saw. I stopped with about 6:30 of riding time and covered 139 miles (223 km), well over a 20 mph (32 km/h) average for the day thanks to yet another strong tailwind.

I woke up briefly to use the bathroom while it was still dark. I'd drank an entire liter (33.8 ounces) of wine with dinner and it hit me harder than usual because of the long riding days and I was hungover. A spectacular array of stars greeted me for a moment outside the culvert but it was difficult to appreciate them with the way I was feeling. I drank as much water as I could before going back to bed.

I still wasn't feeling so great when I got up so, I made coffee and some leftover polenta for breakfast without getting out of bed. I was feeling better after eating but I still didn't get going until nearly nine am.

By some miracle, I had yet another tailwind today, not as strong as the last couple of days had been but it was a good augmentation to my speed nonetheless. Around 75 miles (120 km), there was a gas station where I refilled my water. That point was also significant because it was the spot that I had predicted the wind would begin to die down based on the wind maps that I'd checked farther south. It didn't happen right away but an hour later I stopped and it struck me just how quiet it was. I could hear birds chirping in the bushes and the buzz of insects. The wind had almost died completely. I rode for a couple more hours in sheer bliss. The feeling of just being able to ride again and not having to fight just to stay on the road was wonderful.

I got to about 70 miles (112 km) away from the next city and called it a day in a small grove of trees. I rested in the shade for the remainder of the day and read or just enjoyed the quiet from the lack of wind. It felt great to finally be out of the worst of the wind. The road there from Ushuaia was among the most psychologically difficult riding I had ever done and I counted myself as lucky to have done it as fast as I did.

The wind picked up during the night. I guessed I wasn't out of the wind after all, but it was a crosswind to tailwind once I got riding and only half the speed or less of the winds I had been fighting farther south. I got a flat tire after about 10 miles (16 km); it looked like I'd picked up a thorn from where I'd camped last night. I made a mental note to check my tires for thorns every morning. If I got them out of the tire soon enough there was a chance they wouldn't puncture the tube.

Along the way I passed the 999 kilometer marker on the RN 3, someone had stolen the 1,000 marker, less than 620 miles to go to Buenos Aires. The wind may not have been as strong but, it had suddenly become hot up to 94 F (34 C) later in the day. I wasn't used to the heat anymore; the last time I could remember it being anywhere close to that hot was in the Atacama Desert in northern Chile, more than two months earlier. I took breaks more frequently and only if there was shade. Trees were becoming more common compared to being almost non-existent in the south.

There was a good grocery store in Viedma and I bought food there. Sierra Grande to Viedma should have been the last gap of over 100 miles (160 km) between towns that I'd see for a while. I found a gas station with wifi and I spent most of the afternoon there trying to escape the heat. Approaching evening, I rode down to the Rio Negro and went swimming. I stayed around the river for a couple of hours and cooked and ate dinner there much to the interest of everyone else present. Chile and Argentina were far more westernized than the other countries in South America I'd been to. Blatant staring was rare and I hadn't been called 'gringo' since leaving Bolivia. After dinner, I started riding back towards RN 3 and found a vacant lot, a few hundred yards away from the river, where I could spend the night.

CHAPTER 34

Day 345, January 11, 2017

Tres Arroyos, Argentina

The last several days had been pretty relaxed. I'd found a Warmshowers.org host in Buenos Aires and they wouldn't be available to host me for several more days so that gave me an easy schedule to get there. I was down to the last few hundred miles to Buenos Aires and traffic on the road had increased substantially. I took the opportunity to switch back to my wider tires for the gravel byroads to get off the main road.

I was excited to ride that day, unfortunately, that was the first time in a while. The slog north on RN 3 had been draining with the strong winds and, more recently, with the amount of traffic on the highway. At the same time, I wouldn't have done it any other way. Finally off of busy roads for a while, I made breakfast and coffee before starting around eight am.

The roads were gravel but they were in good condition and I had a crosswind all day, but nothing serious. It was awesome being on a quiet country road after being on busy highways for so long. I didn't have much of a choice farther south. With how remote some of the roads were, there were no other options besides the highway.

I was somewhat surprised when the side roads took me through a few small towns. My maps had some of them marked as hamlets when they were closer to being towns. One place that was marked as a hamlet was a complete ghost town;

old buildings were falling apart and no one lived there as far as I could tell. I saw fewer vehicles on the road in an entire day of riding on side roads than I'd been seeing in a few minutes on the highways.

I rode into Benito Juarez past midday. The heat was becoming oppressive, close to 90 F (32 C), though the humidity was still low. I found a gas station with wifi and bought some chocolate milk and cookies for an afternoon snack then checked my email and found that the Warmshowers host I'd been in contact with for Buenos Aires had something come up and wouldn't be able to host me anymore. I was disappointed, but at least they hadn't waited until the last minute to cancel. I messaged a couple more hosts for that city in hopes of finding a place to stay.

My next stretch of road would be directly into the wind and I planned to wait around for a few hours for the heat and wind to back off before continuing. While I was waiting, someone walked into the gas station and said they worked at the fire station then asked if I needed somewhere to stay for the night. I said "yes please" without much thought and he told me where the fire station was, a couple of blocks away from the town square, before taking off. That was an excellent development, I didn't really feel like riding into a headwind and I no longer had a schedule to get to Buenos Aires either. I got to the fire station in time for something like afternoon tea. I was invited to join everyone there and given maté tea and some cake. Maté tea in Argentina is served out of a communal ceramic cup filled with tea leaves and consumed through a metal straw with a filter on the lower end. The cup is filled with hot water and passed around to everyone present. There was another cyclist there too, Pepé from Spain. He was cycling from Buenos Aires on an open ended tour around South America. I was talking with the commandant later and he asked how long I'd like to stay. Two nights sounded great to me and he asked if I was sure I didn't want to stay longer. Two nights seemed like plenty, a rest day would be nice.

I had a great rest day. I would have had a headwind if I'd been riding and it was hot again outside but the fire station had air conditioning. Apart from going to the grocery store and doing laundry, I spent the day avoiding any physical activity as much as possible. Sometimes it's nice to take a rest day in a place where there's not much to see. If there was nothing to see then I didn't feel obligated to do anything. Benito Juarez was one of those towns; there was some colonial architecture but I'd been seeing a lot of that lately. I got an email today from my Warmshowers.org host in Buenos Aires. The supposed cancellation had been a misunderstanding on my part and he'd be able to host me after all.

A frightening anecdote from the firemen, there was a blood feud going on between two families in the area. It started last year with a murder of one person and a near deadly assault on another. Justice went sour and the victim's families took matters into their own hands and burned their adversary's house down with the aid of some gasoline which resulted in a few more deaths. My rest day there was the one year anniversary of the incident. There were police patrols, a few protests, and the firemen said not to go out at night, though nothing came of it.

I left Benito Juarez the next day. I had a tailwind and rode 120 miles (192 km) on mostly dirt roads and reached 17,000 miles cycled too. I camped on a small by road, just past the town of Cachari. The next day, the side road I was riding degraded quickly from a dirt road into something that resembled a path and I had a headwind. My map still said I was on the correct road so I kept going. The rusted hulk of an old train wreck loomed along the path; for the next couple of hours I saw far more livestock than people.

The narrow grassy trail I was on was blocked by a gate. There was a gaucho, a rancher or cowboy, on the other side of the gate and I asked him if this was the correct road to Las Flores a small town about 20 miles (32 km) away; he said it was and told me I could ride through the gates as long as I made sure to close them behind me.

There were more gates, one every half mile (1 km) or so for a couple of miles. The fences and gates were more for keeping livestock in than for keeping people out. I passed some eucalyptus trees filled with squawking parrots as I pedaled slowly along a rough trail. The path opened back up into a road after a few more miles. I must have looked like I was struggling because a driver pulled up alongside and told me there was a town in ten minutes. I knew enough about people who give distances in time units to ignore what he'd said. I considered asking if it was ten minutes by bicycle but that would have made him feel stupid and me a jerk. Less than 100 yards (90 meters) after the driver said ten minutes the road turned into deep sand. Ten minutes later I hadn't even gone a mile and of course there was no town in sight. About 40 more minutes later I was in Las Flores which was probably the town that was ten minutes away. I refilled my water at a gas station that did not have wifi then made and ate some sandwiches. There was a bakery across the street and I bought a large loaf of bread and some pastries for less than one dollar US. Food prices had been dropping since I passed the city of Bahia Blanca, a couple of days before the wind had begun to slow down. They'd peaked in Ushuaia, everything was expensive there.

I set my sights on a village about 30 miles (48 km) away as my goal for the day. If I rode a little extra I could have an average length riding day the next day and a shorter day into Buenos Aires on the day after that. I still had a headwind after I left and the road turned into sand or washboard on a few occasions but I wasn't in much of a hurry; the roads were quiet and I'd begun to adjust to the higher temperatures. I took breaks in the shade every hour or so and rolled into the village of Gorches after a few hours. I bought some food at a small store and the shopkeeper was kind enough to refill my water. I rode out of town and setup camp in the shade. It was still before four pm, but I'd gone far enough. I read and rested in the shade all afternoon eventually making dinner and going to bed once it got dark.

The humidity was ridiculously high in the morning; everything I had was damp. It wouldn't dry out anytime soon either with the amount of moisture in the air; I packed it up and made a note to air everything out later. The roads turned to sand and, with the high humidity, I was sweating buckets. Both of those things together meant I was soon covered in mud from the dust being kicked up by my tires. It couldn't be helped so I rode on. The road went back to pavement after maybe 25 miles (40 km) in and I had a temporary return to the RN 3. Side roads would have added a several miles to avoid a few miles of highway but that part of the RN 3 had a shoulder.

In the town of San Miguel Del Monte, I rode straight to the nearest lake access and jumped in fully clothed. Everything I was wearing was saturated with sweat and sand and I washed out as much of it as I could then sat in the sun to dry off while I had a snack. I was back to side roads again out of San Miguel. They were dirt roads and a bit sandy, but not near as bad as it was earlier and the road was almost completely devoid of traffic.

During another brief return to the RN 3, I passed through a toll booth. As usual I didn't have to pay to ride on that road. Near the toll booth was a rest area with a bathroom complex, complete with free hot showers. The lake hadn't been all that clean and I was covered in dirt again so I took a shower. The weather was hot enough that I didn't make much use of the 'hot' part of the shower.

A mile or two later was the turnoff for Cañuelas and I was on a cobbled road topped with sand. In town, I found a gas station with wifi and it began to rain shortly after. I was there for a few hours waiting out the worst of the rain. During a dry interlude I made a quick grocery store run then began to look for shelter. While I was still in town, I saw an under construction garage sort of building. A few of the bays were completely open and one of them had a nook I could sleep in. I went across the street, ate dinner, and did some reading while I waited for dark.

There was a huge police presence in Cañuelas for a reason unknown to me. Officers stood at most every intersection and patrol cars went by every few minutes. One of the patrol cars saw me sitting around the bus stop and, after driving by a few times, they stopped to ask me what I was doing. I was reading and resting and told them as much. They asked for my papers and I gave them my passport. They checked it over and called in the number to make sure I wasn't in the country illegally. While we were waiting for the call back, I asked them about somewhere to camp. They said there was a free area in town but there was no protection from the impending rain. One of the two officers talking to me recommended a cheap hotel, I asked the price but it was more than I wanted to spend. Admittedly, it would have had to be around $5 US for me to even consider it and they said it was closer to $20. The call came back that I was in Argentina legally and the officers apologized for disturbing me before continuing on their patrol. They drove by a couple more times. They had the rotating lights atop the car going continuously and they weren't easy to miss. Shortly after one of their passes, I went back to the garage and rolled out my sleeping mat and bag in a nook under some concrete stairs. I was completely concealed from the road though still concerned about being found. By then, it'd started raining again and I opted for warm, dry, and paranoid as an alternative to the possibility of being cold, wet, and miserable but it was still a long night.

I didn't sleep well and I got up at dawn. Good thing too, a construction crew came to work on the garage that I'd slept in while I was making coffee across the street.

I rode one of the secondary highways to get into Buenos Aires. Once I was close enough to the city, I started taking residential roads. I wasn't using my maps to navigate, I just took a rough bearing and kind of guided off the sun, it worked pretty well. I'd ride for 10-20 minutes then check my GPS to make sure I was going in the correct direction. Not using maps took me through a couple of rougher areas. Buenos Aires sprawled significantly, like many capital cities do, and the poorer areas were on the outskirts. It was raining on and off all morning too. Some areas were broken pavement that had fallen into disrepair or just dirt roads that turned into mud bogs by the rain. I slipped and slid my way through the mud but I remained upright and did my best not to think about what was being sprayed onto my legs by my tires. As I got closer to the city, the roads became better and the traffic worse.

Finding a tent was a high priority for my time in Buenos Aires and that's what I began to work on. I'd marked all the outdoor equipment stores on my maps a couple of days ago and started ticking them off my list. It was an incredibly tedious process. I'd ride to store after store after store, asking about tents, only to be shown the same models and brands over and over again. I wasn't supposed to be at the Warmshowers host until eight pm so I didn't have much else to do. I checked more than ten shops and I saw the same two or three brands repeatedly. They were either too short for my 6 foot 6 inch (198 cm) body, too heavy (bordering 8 pounds (3.6 kg) for a two person tent in some cases), or just completely impractical for me for any number of reasons like not having any ventilation. I went by a bike shop too; the first shop I checked had the chain lube and new sunglasses I needed.

Once evening was approaching, I started in the direction of my Warmshowers host. I was making great progress for a while before I got turned around and ended up charging through two miles (3 km) before I realized I was going in the complete opposite direction I was supposed to be. I reoriented myself and arrived at the Warmshowers just after eight pm and was welcomed in by my host Ivan. Despite his name, he was born and raised in Argentina by parents of the same descent. He knew of some good shops I could check for a new tent too.

My attempts at finding a tent were unsuccessful. Everything was either heavy or had zero ventilation and wouldn't be any better than sleeping in my plastic baglike bivy. I explored some other options and eventually bought a hammock. I was inspired by Jesse's use of a hammock and supposedly they worked great for sleeping in hot weather. None of the hammocks I found had an integrated mosquito net so I found some netting and hand sewed one myself. My stitching was about as strong as the netting was so it seemed adequate for the purpose. My other objective was finding a new camera to replace the old one that I'd accidentally sweated to death the day I left Ushuaia. Latin America had a weird thing where shops that sell similar merchandise were often grouped together. I checked about ten camera shops in the space of one block. Cameras were expensive and my attempts to resurrect my old one had failed. I did some more research on a couple of secondhand models I found and bought one the next day. With all my objectives done I was ready to leave Buenos Aires after three days there.

After many thanks to my host, I got out the door at nine and I went directly to the ferry terminal just two miles (3 km) away. I waited in one line so they could check my passport, then another so I could pay for my ticket, and after taking my bike up the escalator to migration. I waited in yet another line for my Argentina exit stamp. When I got to the counter, they asked for my ferry ticket. I thought the papers I'd been handed when I paid were my ticket but no, I had less than 10 minutes until the ferry and I had to run downstairs, again, to wait in another line for my ticket before sprinting back to migration to wait in line again. I had less than five minutes before the 9:45 departure by the time I got my stamp and the guards wouldn't let me go back the way I came to get my bike less than 15 feet (4 meters) away from where they were standing. Instead I had to run to the exit that would take me to the ferry where the elevator wouldn't work. After a minute or so of the elevator not working, I finally found the stairs, ran down the stairs, sprinted back around the building into the ticket office and up the stairs to migration to get my bike. Then, I took off back down the stairs with my bike out of the ticket office and jumped onto my bike without stopping then sprinted to the ferry. When I rode onto the ferry seconds before the scheduled 9:45 departure I was dripping sweat. I parked my bike and went to the passenger area. In accordance with Latin American style the ferry left just over ten minutes behind schedule and I was on my way to Uruguay; it would be country number 16 of my tour and the first 'new' country I'd been to in months.

The ferry ride was pleasant but slow. It arrived in Colonia Sacramento, Uruguay after one pm. I was the first one off the boat and began riding out of town. Just as I got outside Colonia Sacramento, I realized I hadn't gone to an ATM and didn't have any Uruguayan currency. I'd eaten most of my food on the ride over too. Luckily, a few miles away, I found a store that accepted my debit card. I bought food then got to riding on some gravel side roads that paralleled the highway and over some rolling hills, unlike my last few hundred miles in Argentina that had been almost entirely flat. The surface was mostly in good condition. A few sandy sections and some exposed rock but never for very long, a few creeks crossings too, two that were rideable and one that I chose to walk because I couldn't see the bottom; good thing too, it was more than two feet (60 cm) deep.

I refilled my water in a town called Rosario and stopped for a snack break then tried to figure out how much farther I should ride. There weren't any obvious places to stop on my map and I went with the 'how ever far I get' plan. An exciting crossing on an old bridge over the very brown Rio Curfe followed. The wooden surface of the bridge had become warped with age and sections had rotted away entirely but I still rode the whole thing. Once I was down to the last couple of hours of daylight, I saw a good spot to camp near the town of Ecilda Paullier. I wanted some extra time to set up my hammock since I'd never used it before and chose to stop there. It was a wise choice, it took me close to an hour to get my hammock setup correctly and relearn the Marlin Spike hitch that I'd had to look up when watching a video on how to setup a hammock. I made and ate dinner quickly as it was getting dark by the time I was done, and then I closed myself into my hammock before the mosquitos got bad.

PART FOUR

*Ecilda Paullier, Uruguay
to Messina, Italy*

CHAPTER 35

Day 355, January 21, 2017

Ecilda Paullier, Uruguay

Taking side roads would have added about 40% to the distance I had left to get to the capital of Montevideo. I wasn't in any particular hurry, but I felt like getting there, so I took the highway. After a snack break at a gas station, I got back on the highway. A few miles later, I saw another cycle tourist ahead of me. I was catching up to them fairly quickly and picked up my pace a bit out of curiosity. Just as I was about to catch up to them, a police car passed them dangerously close, then pulled off in front of them. The cyclist stopped and a shouting match in Spanish started. I would have been of similar opinion as the cyclist, but my Spanish wasn't good enough for that. The summary of it was that the policeman wanted cyclists to ride on the broken and dirty pavement of the shoulder; the cyclist wasn't having it and argued his point. Eventually, the policeman gave up on arguing and left; then I rolled up and after a bit of venting in English he introduced himself as Mike from Gibraltar. He'd started out of Rio de Janeiro and was halfway into a six month tour of South America. He was heading in the same general direction as me and was glad to have company.

We got to talking about where we were going; Mike said he wanted to try to meet the ex-president of Uruguay Jose Mojica, I'd never heard of him before. Mike said he was a socialist who practiced what he preached. He still lived in the same old house he had lived in before his presidency and he had lived there during his term too. He drove the same old car as he had before he was president and he had given, and still gave, 90% of his income to help the poor. This sounded much more interesting than sitting in a hostel for most of the afternoon and Mike said he wouldn't mind if I joined him. The only trouble was Mike didn't know exactly where he lived so he began asking around. First, he asked a taxi driver who sounded like he knew the approximate area of where to find him. He continued the process of asking people every once in a while as we got closer. Eventually, we knew we were close when someone told us his street was the next one down the road. Mike tried asking at a house in the South American fashion of standing outside the house and clapping. This sounded completely ridiculous to me, I'd never heard of such a thing, but Mike insisted it was the proper way to do it culturally and he asked me to wait down the road a ways to reduce the intimidation factor.

The woman there said Mojica's house was just up the road. We went in that direction and were stopped by a lone and unarmed security guard. Mojica was having a siesta and wouldn't be up for a few hours. Uruguay does siestas too, but they're much more relaxed than Argentina and not all businesses close for the siesta. The guard was friendly and recommended we wait at a nearby beach. On our way to the beach, Mike stopped in at a small roadside store for a soda. While he was there, the woman who sold him the drink mentioned a casa de ciclistas was only a block away; she said the beach would be crowded too since it was a weekend but we went to the beach anyway and chose to look for the casa de ciclistas after trying to meet Mojica. The beach was not crowded after all and was freshwater, part of the giant delta that made up that section of the border between Uruguay and Argentina. If we looked carefully, we could barely spot the line that marked where the freshwater coming from the river met the salt water of the Atlantic Ocean a few miles away.

We waited at the beach until it was getting close to 5 pm, the time the guard had said Mojica would be up, and then rode back to the ex-president's house. Mojica was busy with many of the Uruguayan heads of state and wouldn't be available that evening; though the guard said we could try again in the morning, so Mike and I went to find the casa de ciclistas. It took some asking but we found it eventually and we were welcomed to stay the night by Gabriela, the owner of the casa. There were a few other cyclists there too and we had a wonderful evening together.

Mojica's security guard said the ex-president started accepting visitors at eight and we arrived at his house shortly after eight the next morning. Although there was one other person waiting, we were pushed ahead and shown into Mojica's furnished shipping container of an office. After introductions, we got to talking. Mike's first language was Spanish and he did almost all of the talking. I listened as best I could for the hour we were there. Mike walked me through the conversation as we rode back to the casa de ciclistas after we got some pictures with the ex-president. Mojica and Mike had discussed philosophy, economics, and politics, much of it was lost to me because my Spanish was nowhere close to that level. Although I had little background information as to who Mojica was, he seemed a very down to earth person. His clothes were older and somewhat worn, sweatpants and a button down khaki, and he had a habit of chain smoking hand rolled cigarettes. He smoked at least six while we there. Mojica appeared to be a very humble person overall. Unlike probably every other political leader on earth, he had not profited financially by being president and maintained a modest lifestyle. He had a few philosophies I could get behind too; most notably was not spending your entire life working for things you didn't need and that time really is money in a literal sense because earning money costs time. He was supportive of Mike's and my own journeys and he believed it was important to change the world by first changing oneself for the better.

After collecting our gear, and giving our thanks to Gabriela at the casa de ciclistas, we rode at Mike's pace into Montevideo and stopped frequently for pictures. We checked out the old town; much of the city was fairly lifeless since it was the Sunday afternoon siesta. We found a reasonably priced hostel a few miles away and booked a couple of nights.

We took a day in Montevideo. My hubs were beginning to fail; there was a significant amount of play in the rear wheel and a little in the front too. Mike needed a new rim, his had split down the inner wall after he'd accidentally overfilled the tire with an air compressor, so it needed to be replaced. The first shop we checked, Bici Mundo, or Bike World, was able to rebuild my hubs on the spot and in less than an hour. Then, they wouldn't accept any form of payment despite my offers. We had to check three more shops to get Mike's rim replaced; the first didn't have anything, the second had the rim which Mike bought, and the third was a repair shop only that would have the rim replaced that evening. The shop kept Mike's bicycle and he chose to walk back while I rode. Not too much else happened for the rest of the day.

Mike had some trouble installing a new chain the next morning and had to make a run to the bike shop. I took my time getting ready, I got my journal updated, and called home over the wifi. While I was talking to everyone at home, Mike went by with his bike fully loaded and an exasperated look on his face. Once I got off the phone, I couldn't find him anywhere. It was after noon by that time and I thought he'd gotten tired of waiting and left. I packed up as quickly as I could and raced through the city to try to catch him. I was moving fast enough, and there were a few small hills along the way, that I felt confident I would have caught up to him if he was on the same road.

I was just getting outside the city when I saw a decent beach access. Mike had expressed significant disinterest in trying to ride his heavily loaded bike along the beach. Since I was alone, I walked my bike across the deep sand to the hard packed sand near the waterline. It was good riding, quiet with surprisingly few people in most areas, and I was able to ride on the hard sand near the waterline without any issue.

I had a few stream crossings and chose to walk the deeper one to avoid getting sand and saltwater in my just rebuilt hubs. After about 15 miles (24 km) of riding along the beach, I came to a river. I had no idea how deep it was and tried to walk across. It ended up being neck deep and I swam across without much difficulty, and then got yelled at by a lifeguard. Supposedly, people had drowned trying to swim across the river I'd just swam across. Getting my bike across would be a completely different story though. I swam back to the side my bike was on, but, I skinned my knee on a submerged rock and got stung by a jellyfish, near my right wrist, in the process. I had to backtrack almost a mile (1.6 km) to find a track away from the beach and then I pushed my bike through a few hundred yards of deep sand to get back to a rideable road.

I rode a few more miles until I got to a gas station. They had wifi and Mike had messaged me asking why I'd left without him. He didn't have a cellular plan either but I messaged him back apologizing for the misunderstanding. Based on what time he messaged me, I guessed when he'd arrive and decided I'd wait until then, plus a bit more, and he showed up 15 minutes before I planned on leaving. I apologized again and explained what had happened. He understood the circumstances and we rode off together.

A road cyclist passed us a few miles later; Mike suggested I try to catch him and that he'd catch up later. This sounded like a fine idea to me, so I caught up to the other cyclist. I got to talking with him and he said he wanted to give me some fruit then invited me back to his house a short ways off the road. I accepted and he gave me a couple of bananas and some water, then I went back to the main road to try to find Mike. I couldn't see him and figured he was ahead of me. I took off riding faster than usual to try to catch up to him. I rode for over an hour without seeing him and got to a toll booth. I ate some sandwiches for dinner and waited for about 45 minutes, without seeing him. We'd agreed on a rough location to camp for the night and I had just enough time to get there and setup before it got dark.

Mike wasn't there either and I settled in for the night. Less than an hour later, I woke up to thunder, lightning, strong winds, and rain. I got out of my hammock and dug out the plastic sheeting I had and then draped it over my hammock to keep the rain off. I had to tie off the ends and I was pretty much trying to sleep in a plastic bag. The rain, which ran off the plastic, soaked the underside of my hammock and my sleeping bag. I'd be surprised if I'd slept for more than four hours that night. It was drizzling still when it began to get light; I waited it out in my hammock. I was a bit damp from the storm overnight but I hadn't gotten very cold. There was a strong wind coming off the ocean as I followed the coast. I stopped in Piriapolis, at a gas station with wifi, to try to figure out where Mike was. He hadn't messaged me but I sent him my location and a basic plan for the day.

I took side roads through Punta Negra and tried taking a route marked as a track to avoid some highway riding. It was a bit muddy from the recent rain and dead ended at a gate. It was locked but seemed like it was meant for keeping animals in and I lifted my bike over then continued riding. The area I'd just crossed into seemed to be an exclusive gated community, exceptionally nice houses and land on both sides. I was concerned about getting out but the gate guard saw me coming and he opened the gate for me without any questions.

I was just outside Punta del Este when I went to another gas station with wifi to see if Mike had replied. I still hadn't heard from him and hung around for a while trying to decide what to do. I went by a grocery store across the highway then decided I'd ride into Punta Del Este and see what all the fuss was about since it was supposed to be a huge tourist destination. After a couple of miles, I caught up to Mike. He'd camped a few miles before me and had started an hour later. We rode into Punta Del Este together; it was raining on and off and it'd been stormy for the last few days. Most of the tourists had left and everything was beginning to close for the approaching wet season.

We followed the coast out of the city. The weather was still questionable and we were getting sandblasted from the wind coming off the nearby beach. The road turned to dirt after a very strange roundabout bridge, a literal roundabout on a bridge over a river. We began looking for somewhere to camp but everything was exposed to the wind and rain and would have made for another miserable night.

There were a few groves of trees near some houses and we decided to try asking to see if we could camp on someone's land. The owners of the house we asked responded with an enthusiastic yes and showed us a spot we could setup. They only spoke Spanish and Mike was making the vast majority of the conversation while I listened as best I could. They ended up inviting us in for dinner, though in South America dinner is traditionally at nine pm or later. They followed that tradition; we didn't start eating until after 11. I was struggling to stay awake after sleeping so poorly the previous night. Dinner was great: a pasta and meat dish similar to a goulash with some wine and beer. The family we stayed with ran a cattle ranch and all the beef we had was fresh. It was almost impossible for me to stay awake after eating and I went to bed soon after.

There were several dogs at the ranch we stayed at. I'd slept under a covered area near the barn and, when I woke up, a couple of the dogs were sleeping on or next to me. It was raining again and I waited until I saw Mike getting out of his tent to get up. The ranchers were up and about by then too. We talked more and then they brought their saddled horses out in preparation for the day's work. Some kids helped Mike pack his tent and we both got to ride the horses around the grassy area by the house for a few minutes before we left.

We got going around ten, after many thanks to our hosts. It was raining on and off again, but the wind wasn't as strong. The dirt road rolled away from the coast and back to the highway. I'd stop to wait for Mike after every few rollers. Once we were on the highway, we had about 10 miles (16 km) to go into the town of Rocha and took shelter at a cafe to escape a sudden downpour. Mike got lunch there and I made and ate some sandwiches outside. It was in Rocha we came to the decision to part ways. Mike preferred highways and always riding with music while I liked byways and conversation over music if I'm riding with someone. Our riding styles and paces didn't mesh well even though we got along just fine off the bike. I turned inland on a by road after getting some groceries and Mike continued along the coast on the highway.

I had a tailwind and rode for a couple more hours through the lush rolling hills of inland Uruguay, Then found a grove of trees to camp in then hung up my hammock and read for a few hours, then eventually made and ate dinner before going to bed once it got dark.

CHAPTER 36

Day 364, January 30, 2017

Acegua, Brazil

My last few days through Uruguay had been on dirt roads through rolling hills. Lovely cycling and not much had happened. I crossed the border into Brazil at Acegua late one afternoon. The town was on both sides of the Uruguay/Brazil border. The commercial side was predominantly on the Brazilian side; while most of the residential areas were on the Uruguay side. The border crossing was a bit of a joke. The building for both countries was situated on the main road out of town on the Brazilian side; the middle of the road was the border. The Uruguayan official hardly glanced at my passport before stamping it. The Brazilian official didn't ask about my visa that I'd gotten all the way back in Lima and likely would have let me in without it. I wasn't surprised; it was a smaller border crossing for mostly local traffic. It was nice to know that there were border officials who were somewhat uninformed, but I had too much running on being in Brazil completely legally to take the risk of trying to get in without a visa. Brazil was my 17th country and, for the first time since I got to Mexico, I'd have to learn a new language too; Portuguese instead of Spanish. I'd been studying the new language for the last few weeks; it seemed similar enough that I hoped I could pick it up quickly. I exchanged money at the border town before riding out to camp.

The humidity was high, yet again, in the morning as it had

been the last several days; the sun was getting ever more intense as I slowly worked my way north and towards the tropics. I was on gravel roads for most of the day, low traffic but in poor condition. Washboard and sand frequently had me riding on either side of the road trying to find the best line. That morning, I'd noticed that there was a significant amount of play in my freehub. The stock hub that came with my bike was on its last legs after being rebuilt a few times. I was feeling the need for a couple of rest days anyways; I rode in the direction of the nearest city in hopes I'd be able to get it replaced before I got stranded from a failing hub in the same manner as I did in the Atacama Desert.

I rode into a village called Candiota in the earlier part of the afternoon. The heat was awful, and there was a small grocery store where I bought a liter of ice cream, among other things. There was a gas station on the way out of Candiota; they didn't have wifi but they let me charge my mp3 player. One of the attendants came over to talk to me and asked about what I was doing. I wasn't quite at that level of speaking Portuguese yet, but, with the help of a translate app, I made a few steps of progress. I was finding proper, or at least passable, pronunciation of the language difficult.

There was a gas station that had wifi at the junction of road BR-293. I called home and then tried to find out about some bike shops where I could replace my hub. Pelotas had several and I decided I'd ride another hour or so. A storm blew in while I was riding; once I determined it was blowing towards me, I opted for riding through it then camping on the other side of the storm. I followed a rarely used access to a tree farm then setup among the trees. Another storm blew in just as it got dark; I used the plastic sheeting that I still had to cover my hammock while I was inside and waited for it to blow over. It backed off enough that I could sleep after an hour or so.

It started drizzling, shortly after I got on the road the next morning, which was actually pretty nice; the rain cooled me off enough that I wasn't sweating near as much as I had been the last few days. It was all highways into Pelotas, mostly neutral winds for my first few hours, and then a headwind began blowing around noon. The rain stopped too and then the sun came out in full force; it evaporated the rain water and sent the humidity sky high. Consequently, I was drenched in my own sweat again. I hadn't been able to find an electrolyte replacement at any of the markets; I was getting a headache and feeling weak from how much I was sweating. During one break, I dug out the salt that I used for cooking and ate a pinch with some water to wash it down while I sat in the shade. I was feeling better after ten minutes or so and started riding again.

In Pelotas, I went to one of the few hostels there and booked a couple of nights. I took a long, cool shower, enjoying not feeling like I was about to die from the heat, and stayed inside the air conditioned room for the rest of the day. That was the last day of my first year on the road. I celebrated the occasion and accomplished one of my goals for Brazil, simultaneously, by eating at a Brazilian steakhouse in Brazil. To my surprise and delight, there was an all you can eat steakhouse within a few hundred yards of the hostel I was at. It was expensive, but still much less than a comparable establishment in the US. I was not disappointed; there was an almost endless procession of various meats and I had a Brazilian beer to go with it. It was awesome! I walked back to my hostel almost two hours later well satisfied and very happy. *

*for a summary of Year 1 expenses, refer to the end of the book.

CHAPTER 37

Day 368, February 3, 2017

Pelotas, Brazil

I spent a couple of days in Pelotas. I looked up a bike shop online the first day and found out there was one a few blocks away; so, I walked over with my rear wheel to see if I could get it fixed. The mechanics there were able to check it out right away; they took the freehub completely apart despite the fact that the bike shop in Punta Arenas had said that it was rebuild-able. It was indeed about to fail, and they were surprised that I had caught it. Only one of the employees spoke a few words of English; so, most of our conversing was done through a translate app as my Portuguese wasn't passable yet. They cleaned and rebuilt the freehub in the space of a couple of hours and did it for less than $5.

On my second day in Pelotas, I went to find some ropes for my hammock. The stock ones kept breaking; it's entertaining to think about a hammock rope breaking randomly in the middle of the night, but, it's not fun having to fix them in the dark when they break as I'm getting back into my hammock, after using the bushes. Almost everything was closed and it was barely noon. I couldn't figure out why at first; the siesta didn't usually start until 1 pm; I guessed that it must've been a holiday. Back at the hostel, I confirmed that it was a holiday; an internet search said it was something about an important figure concerning fertility or what not. Everything being closed meant it turned into a planning and resting day.

I didn't leave the glorious comfort of the air conditioning for the rest of the day. People started checking into the hostel in the afternoon but none of them spoke English. It got a little awkward because I knew almost no Portuguese, even though I'd improved over the last few days. The time off was nice, but, I was glad to be heading out in the morning.

Because of the holiday, I went out for groceries that morning and bought some rope, for my hammock, at a small hardware store on the way back. When I finally left around 11 am, I took side roads as much as possible. Most of them were dirt by the time I was outside the city, but, they were in decent condition for the majority of the day. I had one section of highway, about 15 miles (24 km) long, but an incomplete construction project gave me my own private road to ride on for the majority of that stretch. Just before I was about to turn back onto the side roads, a gas station had a small restaurant advertising a 'Buffet Livre' or free/open buffet for less than $4. The price couldn't be beat and I had a couple of plates of food and treated myself to a beer too. The food wasn't quite as good as my one year celebration dinner, but, it was way cheaper.

I had some washboard sections on the next stretch of gravel and my last remaining water bottle cage sheared off. I rode a couple hundred yards back to look for it, once I noticed it was missing, before I gave up and decided I wasn't buying any more cycling water bottles. The roads grew progressively quieter as they got farther and farther away from the main roads, then, the road unexpectedly ended at a river. There was a village on the other side, my maps said there were roads on that side too, but, I hadn't noticed the lack of a bridge crossing the river. I was stuck and wanted more than anything to avoid backtracking more than 10 miles (16 km) to an alternate route. There were people on a beach at the other side and a few boats lined the riverbank. I tried yelling across asking for a ride; but, I was unable to make myself understood. There were some people fishing on the same side as me and I asked one of them to help me communicate that I wanted a ride across. They got the point across and, 10 minutes later, someone came down and motored across in one of the small boats. I tried to negotiate a price beforehand but they waved it off and said it'd just cost the price of the fuel. On the other side they told me it'd cost the equivalent of more than $5. I knew the "price of gas" quote sounded too good to be true. I negotiated it down to less than $3 but, in the end, they got their $5 since I didn't have small bills and they claimed they didn't have any change. They did fill my plastic soda bottles with ice water though.

Out of the village, I rode until the sun was beginning to set. I was a couple of miles away from the town of Santa Rita do Sul when I spotted a grove of trees that would serve as a campsite for the night. It was next to a swampy area and the mosquitos were already coming out as it got close to sunset. I set up as quickly as I could before sealing myself inside the mosquito net of my hammock with some cookies and fruit for dinner. Because of the big lunch, I wasn't particularly hungry.

I watched the sun go down while I waited for it to cool off enough that I could sleep. The mosquitos were out in force; they were of a particularly large and aggressive variety. I had to line my hammock with my sleeping bag to keep them from biting me through both my mosquito net and hammock! As it got dark, I was beginning to get bit all over. I turned on a light then found that there were several mosquitos inside the net and the outside was covered with hundreds of them. There was a hole somewhere; I couldn't figure out where at first. I tried to block off the end of my hammock with the jacket that I used as a pillow, but, they kept coming in. I tried taking off my shirt, and eventually my shorts, to plug up the opposite end, but, they kept getting in. I finally realized that in my hurry to close myself into the net I hadn't closed it properly because of how much I was getting bit through it; it had come open. I closed it as quickly as I could, doing my best ignore the bites I was getting all over my body, to make sure it was sealed and wouldn't come open again. When I finally got it closed, the inside of my net was filled with mosquitoes. I began killing them as fast as I could and it took several hours to get them. I could feel myself getting weaker as I got continually more and more dehydrated and exhausted from sweating while trying to kill them all; it'd barely cooled off and the humidity had skyrocketed with the darkness. I was still lying in my sleeping bag to keep my backside from getting bit. I was soaked in my own sweat and covered in bites, but, I knew I had to keep killing as many of the bugs as possible if was going to get any sleep and fought through it. Eventually, I fell asleep from exhaustion, but, I was still getting bit from the bugs I'd been unable to kill.

I couldn't have slept for more than two hours after the trouble I had with my mosquito net. The world was beginning to turn grey from the approaching dawn; I waited in my hammock until the worst of the mosquitoes had dissipated, then, packed quickly to get away from the place that had been the source of so much misery. I felt awful; dehydrated from how much I'd been sweating, I drank the last of my water when I got my bike back over the fence and onto the road. By then, I was already drenched in sweat.

There was an agricultural business a few hundred yards down the road and I asked somebody outside if I could get some water. They said, "yes", and I was elated when they came back with cold water. I thanked them as best I could. After a few sips of water, I rode into Santa Rita do Sul, and then found a shaded bench in a park where I ate a couple of bananas and some cookies for breakfast. I drank all the water I'd been given earlier and I found a tap on the side of a hospital building; then, I drank as much water as I could before I refilled my bottle and left town. The roads were sandy and washboard was prevalent outside of town. Not bad enough to have to push my bike, but, I was stopped suddenly on several occasions after my front wheel dug into some deep sand. After crossing a bridge, just before Arambaré, the dirt road was freshly graded and I could ride faster. I rode on a bicycle path that paralleled Patos (Ducks) Lagoon through Arambaré. On the very north end of the town, I hit 18,000 miles (29,000 km), the minimum distance for a Guinness World Record for riding a bicycle around the world but I'd only progressed about 65 out of 360 degrees in a west-east direction from where I started in Idaho. No, I wasn't going to try to break the record. I was going fast enough as it was and the world record was well over triple my average daily distance. If I can, I'd like to cycle 100,000 miles all over the world. I was ecstatic that I had so much to look forward to.

The roads were in decent condition most of the way to Tapes; but, many of the corners had washboard on the inside line. It took me a while to figure that out so I could avoid it. It's got something to do with drivers apexing turns and the imperfect differential systems causing the inside wheel to spin from turning at the same rate as the outside from being on a shorter path. In Tapes, I was already tired and feeling beat up; my joints were sore from the pounding I'd taken riding long sections of washboard. I ate some cookies, sitting in the shade, and looked into my options for the rest of the day. I considered stopping in a small town to rest for a day or two but, I really wanted to get to Porto Alegre, a city large enough that I could find decent medical, in case I contracted Zika from all the mosquito bites I'd gotten.

I had a nice ride out of Tapes to the highway; the roads weren't too busy; they rolled past farmlands and forests. The ambient temperature was significantly higher on the blacktop compared to gravel roads and that was my greatest difficulty; but, I was practically gliding along on the pavement compared to how much slower the dirt roads had been and I had a few sections where I was riding on an incomplete highway that was traffic free. I started developing a headache and feeling weak from the electrolyte loss yet I still had at least a couple more hours of riding to go to get to Pelotas. I saw a watermelon truck and went to buy one. When I asked how much it was going to cost, the vendor wouldn't let me pay for it; he insisted that I take it for free. I sat in the shade of an abandoned gas station and ate it all in one sitting. The watermelon was gloriously cold and some of my strength had returned after I rested for a while. I wanted to stop and camp where I was; but, I was concerned that if I contracted a disease from the mosquito bites and developed serious symptoms I might not be able to get help right away if I stayed there. I rode into the city of Guaiba without further issue.

In Guaiba, there was a ferry that would take me to Porto Alegre; in addition to being shorter, I would be able to avoid a long, dangerous, and potentially illegal bridge crossing on the north end of Lake Guaiba. The ferry was completely enclosed and people had taken all the window seats; the crew wouldn't let me go outside during the crossing. On the other side of the lake, and now in Porto Alegre, I went directly to a hostel that I found online while I was waiting for the ferry. I found the hostel and checked in, then, I finally felt like I was able to relax. I took a deep breath to release some of the tension and, when I exhaled, almost lost consciousness from the drop in blood pressure. The stars in my vision went away after I sat down for a minute or two. I took a cool shower, then made and ate a salty dinner of instant noodles with eggs. The salt helped immensely with my energy levels but I was still running on less than two hours of sleep from the previous night. I went to bed and fell asleep almost instantly.

CHAPTER 38

Day 378, February 13, 2017

Rio do Sul, Brazil

Some research showed that the Zika virus could take weeks to germinate before it causes any complications. I spent a couple of days in Porto Alegre and I hadn't experienced any symptoms. Apart from exploring the city on some afternoon walks, I rested most of those days. The exceptionally affordable buffet livres were turning out to be common all over Brazil and I went to one both days I was in the city.

Porto Alegre had been the edge of the mountains of Brazil and, suddenly, the smallest chainring on my bike was getting used constantly for going up steep rolling hills, before that, I'd barely used it. To be fair, it'd been pretty flat for the last 3,000 miles (4,800 km). The heat was as challenging as ever; I took to swimming in rivers or showering in waterfalls, to be comfortably cool, at least once per day. Climbing up to 5,000 feet (1,500 meters) in elevation in the mountains brought some respite from the heat for a couple of days. The jungles and the mountains of the Santa Catarina Province were spectacular.

Over the course of several riding days, I worked my way towards Rio do Sul, Brazil. I'd received an invitation, through my blog, to stay with someone there. Murilo met me on the road on the way into the small city of Rio do Sul; he'd requested that I message him when I was getting close to the city so he could ride out to meet me. We rode into the city and to his house; he'd traveled extensively and we had a lot to talk about. At Murilo's house, I took my first shower in several days; after changing into my cleanest clothes, and eating, I was feeling much better. Murilo even made dinner and, after getting a phone call from a friend, he asked if I would like to attend a birthday party too; I did. Many of his friends there were cyclists and interested in my trip. My Portuguese wasn't close to being at a conversational level yet so Murilo ended up telling several of my stories while some of the kids there practiced their English on me. I had progressed enough that I could make it through some basic shopping transactions without having to revert to a rudimentary sign language though. The party had been a spur of the moment chance and it turned out to be a great experience.

The following day was a rest day and we stayed inside pretty much all day. It rained all day and into the night. During the dry season in Brazil it rains every day; in the wet season, it rains all day. I was there at the beginning of the wet season. Murilo and I went to a bike shop the day after that. All the steep hills that I'd been encountering lately had been bugging my knees. My lowest gear was a 30 tooth ring in the front and a 32 tooth cog in the back; I wanted to try to find a good option for an easier gear. Murilo was able to explain what I wanted and simplified the process of finding parts immensely. The bike shop had an 11-36 cassette that would work and my chain had worn prematurely too; I replaced both and hoped that would be the last time that I had to buy bike parts in South America. Murilo lived on a steep hill and the lower gear made a noticeable difference.

That afternoon, we went for a bike ride to the Magic Waterfall. Riding bicycles was one of Murillo's favorite things, no wonder we got along so well. The road climbed into the mountains before ending at the waterfall and an adventure park owned by a friend of Murillo's. There was a viewing platform from the top of the waterfall; it wasn't looking particularly magical, but, it was a nice view. Supposedly, the real magic was from a different vantage point and we hiked down some slippery rock stairs to get to the bottom. It was cooler because of the spray, but that wasn't unusual; after viewing the falls for a few minutes and getting some pictures, we climbed back up the stairs. The real magic was actually in the pictures, if you looked at them you could see a human shape in the water that made the Magic Man in The Waterfall and that was pretty cool.

After another day at Murillo's place in Rio do Sul, it was time to leave again. Murilo had arranged for me to stay with some friends of his that were a couple of days ride away in Tangara. The first of those days had been some lovely days on dirt roads through the mountains. The heat was still tough but, my new lower gears made the constant steep grades much more manageable. The first night I camped in the shelter of a covered area by a church, there were no houses in the vicinity and it provided shelter from the rain.

I awoke to a different world. A mist had settled over the farmlands around me completely transforming the landscape until it burned off an hour later and changed to blue skies. I had 10 more miles (16 km) of dirt roads to get into Curitibanos. I stopped briefly to refill my water before riding the road out of town. The road was paved and continued the, all too common, trend of rolling steeply through farmlands. It was hot yet again too, thanks to which I drank the last of the two liters of water I had a few miles outside of the town of Frei Rogerio.

I refilled my water at a tap at a gas station; I hadn't been bothering with filtering the municipal water in Brazil unless it specifically said that it was not potable. Outside of Frei Rogeri, the road turned to dirt; I'd naively expected the road to be paved, but the dirt didn't come as too much of a surprise.

The roads were steeper than ever on the dirt. Not for the first time, I was thankful that I'd lowered my gearing only a few days beforehand. I followed dirt roads all the way to the town of Monte Carlo and had to stop at every intersection to make sure on my GPS that I was taking the correct turn. Most of the intersections were not marked on my maps and my actual location on the road was critical to navigating them. I didn't like having to rely on my GPS but, the alternative could've been riding many miles in the wrong direction.

It was early afternoon when I got to the village of Monte Carlo; with the exception of a few minuscule stores similar to the tiendas of the rest of South America, everything was closed. I wasn't feeling too keen on waiting for several hours to buy a couple of packs of cookies and I was already on the edge of town when I realized that nothing was going to be open. I didn't want to backtrack so, I decided I could probably survive the last 24 miles (38 km) of dirt roads to Tangara with nothing more than the one banana that was left in my bags. The rollers weren't near as frequent, or as steep, after Monte Carlo and the roads were in slightly better condition. I got some water from a large enclosed tank by a sports field, roughly halfway between Monte Carlo and Tangara, and ate my last banana. I don't think the water was completely potable but I think I'd built up some immunity to impure water, so, I suffered no more than a barely noticeable stomachache.

I was hot, tired, and hungry when I got to Tangara and I went immediately to the first small grocery store I saw and bought some cookies and a bottle of soda. I sat in a park, in the shade, and consumed a pack of cookies and the entire two liters of guarana flavored soda; guarana is a fruit native to Brazil. I kept the soda bottle to replace my more 'beat up' two liter soda bottle that I'd previously had strapped to the front of my bike to carry water in and rode out of Tangara.

Murilo had gotten me in contact with some friends of his who were also Warmshowers.org hosts, Ana and Andre. He'd met them while on tour near Ushuaia when Ana and Andre were on a two year tour of South America. The couple was back at home in Brazil and hosting cyclists from time to time; I'd asked to stay with them for a few days and they'd said I was welcome to stay as long as I liked. When I arrived on time, they said that I was the first out of about a dozen cyclists to arrive on the day that I said I would, let alone at the time I said. They usually get calls after dark from people delaying their arrival by one or even two days once they realize just how many hills there are around there. They were more surprised when they'd found out where I'd started that morning; it'd taken them three days to get to Tangara from Frei Rogerio because of how steep the hills were.

Ana and Andre lived on a farm a couple of miles, up a hill, outside of Tangara. They kept a fairly laid back schedule of getting most of their work done in the morning, before it gets too hot, then relaxing more in the afternoon. It was a great place to stay, set in a quiet place in the mountains of Brazil and nearly surrounded by jungle on all sides. They had a spring on their property where they collected water that bubbled out of the mountains; I helped where I could on their farm with things like collecting water from the spring every day and harvesting beans.

Ana and Andre had woken up before dawn the next day to drop off one of their other guests/friends off at the bus stop and go for an early morning hike. I wasn't feeling very interested in waking up that early or hiking so, I stayed behind and read a book instead. It was about somebody who'd gotten together with some friends to hunt down sponsors to give them gear for a big bicycle tour then gave up on their goal of riding entirely off road around the world within a couple of days and they were in the habit of staying in cities for a month at a time. Their project completely fell apart when they started fighting amongst themselves a few months later; eventually, they all separated and the author fell in love then quit his tour to be with his new fiancé. It was all horrendously disappointing; I was expecting more of a 'round the world cycle tour' that they said they were going to do, and were given money and sponsorship for, than a love story but whatever.

The town of Tangara was celebrating the 69th anniversary of its founding that afternoon and among the festivities was a bicycle ride. Ana and Andre were going and invited me to join them; I'd been having a lot of days off the bike recently so I accepted. As with many fun rides, it inevitably turned into a friendly competition. I didn't know the route and just hung out in the front with whoever happened to be the fastest rider. On the way back, a local cyclist was leading the way. I rode with him neck and neck up the final short climb before getting back into town and I kept continuously half a wheel in front of him to see how hard I could get him to ride. Eventually, he was sprinting up the hill while I was riding hard just in front of him and I still had a little power to spare. A short descent took us back to the square where we started. We rode easy on the last stretch because of the traffic and he crossed the 'finish line' first. He was riding a high quality mountain bike while I had taken off most of my bags but hadn't bothered with emptying or removing my frame bag. I considered making coffee in the plaza and offering him some as I still had my stove and everything for cooking in my frame bag but I'm not that evil. They had a gear giveaway after the race and Andre won a helmet. Once the festivities were over, we rode back up the mountain to their farm.

CHAPTER 39

Day 387, February 22, 2017

Tres Pinheiros, Brazil

After four days at Andre and Ana's farm, it was time to get back on the road. I was pretty much just waiting for my cruise to Europe that was a few weeks away so, I was trying to do something interesting and fun along the way.

The 22nd of February, 2017, was a rough day for me. The trouble started almost immediately; I missed a turn on the gravel roads I was on and instead of saving 7 miles (12 km) of riding I ended up riding an extra 5 miles (8 km) farther than needed. I was feeling weak and tired all day: the heat was oppressive, the humidity was high, and the roads rolled endlessly and steeply in granny gear climbs that only served to increase exponentially the effects of the heat. I had a headwind too, not particularly strong, but enough to be annoying. By early afternoon, it was all I could do to ride for 15 minutes before collapsing in whatever shade I could find for at least as long before I felt strong enough to turn the pedals over for a few more minutes.

I reached São Lourenço do Oeste in the midafternoon. I was exhausted; I bought food for dinner and chocolate milk at the only grocery store that was open during the siesta. I sprawled out in the shade in front of the grocery and downed half of my 1 liter (~1 quart) chocolate milk in a few gulps before sipping on the rest. I was feeling much better shortly after and decided

I must have bonked (ran out of calories) without realizing it. It didn't make any sense to me as I'd been eating at least as much as I normally would, but, I was feeling stronger afterwards just the same.

Earlier, I had considered stopping in São Lourenço but I was feeling so much stronger that I kept going and rode nearly 20 miles (32 km) nonstop at which point I felt the need for another snack break coming on. On the edge of the town of Renescença, I saw a park; along the lake, there was a shelter so, I asked the caretaker if I could sleep there for the night, he didn't have a problem with it. I set up my hammock inside.

It was getting dark when I was awakened to the flashing lights of a police car and bright flashlights being shined in my face. Two policemen armed with pistols and assault rifles were asking what I was doing in Portuguese. I did my best to explain that I was trying to sleep and didn't speak Portuguese; they asked where I was from and I told them I was American. They asked for my passport and I handed it over. Using an internet translation service they asked my plans for Brazil and I typed in my answer; they saw that I was in the country legally and were satisfied with my answers. The policemen told me, through use of the translate service, that I could sleep there for the night and that I had nothing to worry about so I went back to sleep. Good thing they let me stay too, it started pouring rain not long after they left.

The next day was endless rollers too, though luckily not as steep as the last few days. A couple of hours into my ride, it began to rain. I rode a few more miles before I happened upon a buffet livre, another all you can eat restaurant. The advertised price was less than $5 US so, I stopped for lunch. They even had wifi and, as a result of that, I was there for a few hours while I ate several plates heaped high with food. The rain had stopped by the time I got back to riding. I cruised along admiring the scenery and taking frequent breaks in the shade for a respite from the intense sun and humidity. I stopped at a roadside fruit shop for said wares then decided I'd ride until an hour or so before dark.

I had about 45 minutes of daylight left when I rode through the village of Lindoeste. The skies were threatening rain and I wanted to try to ask about somewhere to stay, but, the municipal building had already closed and there was no one around the churches. I saw a rundown garage next to a gas station; it was very open to the road and its sole occupant was a bus propped up by bricks. I got some water at the gas station then ate some snacks until it got dark. The interior of the bus had been almost entirely gutted and I lifted my bike and gear inside before rolling out my sleeping mat on the floor and calling it a night. There were signs that I was not the first person to sleep in the bus, a few pieces of cardboard on the floor and some trash scattered around, but, there was nothing of value and, based on the amount of accumulated dust, it'd been a while since anyone had slept there. I left my spot in the abandoned bus at dawn the next morning to avoid any confrontations from someone seeing me taking my bike out of it.

Just as I was leaving the small town of Santa Teresa do Oeste, I heard the metallic ping of a spoke breaking. It was the rear wheel and a drive side spoke too. I had some spare spokes but I didn't carry the tools that I'd need to remove the cassette so I could replace the spoke, but, this was the first time I'd broken a spoke in the entire trip. I couldn't fix it so I checked the tension on the other spokes and opted for riding carefully then getting it fixed at the first bike shop I saw. Some 40 miles (64 km) later in the town of Medianeira, I saw a bicycle/motorcycle repair shop just off the highway and stopped in. My Portuguese wasn't at a good enough level to say exactly what the problem was but showing them the wheel made it obvious enough. The mechanic there was able to look at it right away and replaced the spoke with one of my spares then trued the wheel, all in less than 20 minutes. I got to talking with the owner of the shop in Portuguese with the usual discussion of where I was from and what I was doing, that just about exhausted my knowledge of the language. Once they were done, the shop wouldn't accept any form of payment for their work even though I tried to offer them money for their efforts, several times.

Right when I got to the edge of the town with the bike shop, I started getting hungry and realized I hadn't bought any food; I was completely out of food with the exception of my emergency dinner which would have needed water and cooking. The next town was less than 10 miles (16 km) away and I kept my eyes open for a store, but, everything was closed for siesta. I bought some cookies at a gas station that happened to be the only place that was open and ate all of them while sitting outside the convenience store. Only 30 miles (48 km) remained between me and the city of Foz do Iguaçu where I'd arranged to stay at the casa de ciclistas. In the town of Santa Terezhina de Itaipu, I reached 19,000 miles cycled.

Finding the casa de ciclistas took a bit of looking but, eventually, I found it and was shown around then given a key. There was one other cyclist there, a Brazilian, who was a few months into an approximately four year tour of South America. He wasn't riding fast but, when he told me about his route, it sounded like he planned to go just about everywhere. He didn't speak English so our conversation was in Spanish and Portuguese.

After a quiet rest day in Foz do Iguaçu, I wanted to try to get into Paraguay. The information I'd been able to find on entering Paraguay as an American was limited to saying that US citizens could get a visa on arrival at the airport in Asunción, but, I couldn't figure out if the same was true at a land border. I left the casa de ciclistas around midday and rode the 6 miles (10 km) to the border. That particular border of Brazil has a 'friendship bridge' that makes it easy for people to cross back and forth between Foz Do Iguaçu in Brazil and Ciudad del Este in Paraguay, much like the border where I crossed into Mexico from the US and accidentally rode across the entire country without an entry stamp. Getting into Paraguay was even easier; I rode slowly right past the border post and across the pedestrian area of the bridge with the trickle of people that were walking across without stopping at the border post either.

On the other side, I did same thing; I just cruised right past the border post into Ciudad del Este and my 18th country for the trip, Paraguay. After changing some of my Brazilian Reals to Paraguayan Guarani at the highest exchange rate yet, 5,680.60 Guarani to $1 US, I rode around the city looking for somewhere to get lunch. Almost everything was closed for siesta, even the major fast food chain restaurants. I ended up riding through a shady part of the city, only a few blocks away from the main road. A couple of the people I passed shouted something in Spanish that I didn't understand while I rode by. There were all the signs of the area being poverty stricken: broken pavement, trash everywhere, rundown buildings covered in graffiti, broken glass was mortared into the tops of the walls to prevent thieves from breaking in, and the stench of open sewers was common. I didn't stop until I was back in a better part of the city.

Near the main road, I saw a street vendor grilling various meats and stopped for lunch. I still had a significant amount of Paraguayan Guarani left so I rode around and stopped at the next place I saw that looked open for business; they sold a kind of pizza that I think was actually the Turkish version of the dish. I talked with the owner in Spanish for a while and remembered how much easier it is to get things done with a basic understanding of the language. My Portuguese still had a ways to go to catch up with my Spanish. I didn't have anything else to do so I rode back to the Brazilian border. I repeated the same process of riding very slowly past both border posts, and the bridge inbetween, and nobody said anything. Once I was back in Brazil, I rode back to the casa de ciclistas, then had a rather dull remainder of the day compared to the earlier events. I tried to surf the web for a while in the evening, but, the internet cut out. The casa de ciclistas in Foz didn't have its own wifi; the signal, that someone acquired the password for, came from a business across the street. The internet was usually only turned on in the evenings and the running theory was that the business with the wifi signal was a front for some drug dealers.

The next day was also a rest day for me, though, I'd arranged an important event that evening, a meeting with fellow round the world cyclist, William Bennett. He'd been cycling the world for the last couple of years and had started from his home in Ireland. His cycling resume included having to get rabies shots while riding across the Middle East after getting attacked by wild dogs in Turkey and crossing China in the winter, among other exciting events. William was of a similar mindset as me in that he rides absolutely everything and has an unbroken line of cycling from Ireland across Europe, Asia, Australia, and South America to where I met him with the exception of a few airplane flights in between. His blog was one of the inspirations for starting a journey of my own too. William and I had shared a bottle of wine after getting dinner at a nearby restaurant and spent the evening swapping stories from various adventures around the globe.

William had been riding on a broken rear shifter, and effectively a three speed bicycle, for his last 1,500 miles (2,400 km) of cycling since he'd been unable to find a replacement. Someone had left behind an old shifter at the casa de ciclistas and I helped him install it. After that, we rode to Iguazu falls, the waterfall with the highest volume flow in the world. It was easily one of the most amazing sights I'd ever seen and it was topped off by a visit to the infamous horseshoe shaped section of the falls that's been featured in several movies. A wooden walking platform went right to the middle of the horseshoe; the reverberations and sight of the massive amount of water pounding into the river with the accompanying spray was almost a sensory overload.

We went by a buffet livre on the way back for a late lunch and, on our arrival back at the casa, we began preparations for getting on the road the next day. You may remember that I met a Brazilian cyclist while I was riding through Colombia; his name was Jose and we exchanged contact info before departing in our respective directions. Jose had heard that I was in Brazil and said that if I ever planned to pass through Curitiba to let him know. I messaged him saying that William and I would be there on March 6th, an easier schedule of about 60 miles (96 km) per day. He messaged back saying his brother wanted us to come to a barbecue on March 4th. After discussing it briefly with William, we decided it would be worth the effort and committed to making it on the 4th. This would be an outrageously tight schedule of having to average close to 90 miles (144 km) per day, for 4 consecutive days of riding, to make it by midafternoon when the barbecue would start but, the thought of an authentic Brazilian barbecue made it sound worth the effort, the Brazilian Barbecue Brevet* had begun. We'd both been drinking cheap Brazilian liquor made from sugar cane called 'Canchaça', mixed with soda, while we made that decision. The taste reminded William of a similar drink that he'd consumed in Peru and he wasn't much help with finishing off the bottle that neither of us wanted to carry or waste. I was hungover less than an hour after I finished drinking and was puking behind a tree in short order. What other way is there to start some of the longest consecutive riding days of the trip?

*Brevet is a randonneuring term for a very long bicycle race, sometimes in excess of 300 miles (480 km).

CHAPTER 40

Day 394, March 1, 2017

Foz do Iguacu, Brazil

We started bright and early and by that I mean 7:15; surprisingly, I didn't have a hangover. William's bike and gear weighed much more than mine did, so, he was a little slower than me. We set off on the principle that it's possible to get anywhere as long you keep moving; I got a flat tire from a nail within a few miles and William agreed with me when I suggested that he ride ahead while I fixed it. I caught up not too long after I'd patched my flat and we rode along together then, eventually, stopped at a buffet livre for lunch. They had wifi and William got going a little before me while I made a call home and afterwards, I caught up to him on a smaller climb. The heat, while cycling on the exposed climb, was intense and we had to refill our water barely an hour later. After that, I rode ahead for 90 minutes or so, then waited under a bridge for William.

It started raining while I waited, the hardest it had ever rained on my trip so far. Water was coming from the sky in torrents and creating small rivers along the highway in the process. When William rode up, he was soaked to the bone; he was one of the only people who I wouldn't be surprised to find riding in such a deluge. He said it was the second hardest rain of his trip. The first was when he'd ridden through a monsoon in Thailand where the rain had been falling so hard that he'd worn swimming goggles to keep from being blinded by the rain.

After taking a couple of minutes to get our rain jackets on and to make sure everything was protected from the rain, we set out and rode through the city of Cascavel, a few miles later. It was a very busy, though small, city that had a highway built over the rolling hills that wound around its outskirts. We had to stop at one point to try to eat what little food we had left, during which, I came to the conclusion that I wasn't finding cycling in the pouring rain over rollers while traffic roared by and sprayed us with water from the road, very enjoyable. We stopped at a gas station and bought some more cookies before continuing out of the city. Darkness fell as we passed the edge of the city; we got our lights out and kept going. We had to pass through a toll booth on the way out. As cyclists, we've always been allowed to just ride through and that's what we did; but, an alarm began blaring as we rode around the lowered gate and William heard someone yelling at us. Hoping we wouldn't be chased down by the police, we continued on slowly. Shortly after that, William's front tire went flat from a piece of wire and we stopped in the still pouring rain to fix it. Not long after, a van with emergency lights flashing drove up and stopped by us in the darkness. We both held our breaths expecting to be forced to put our bikes in the van. They said something to me in rapid fire Portuguese that I couldn't understand. 'No?' I said quizzically and they drove off. After a brief moment of eye contact wondering what had just happened, we relaxed into laughing about the situation and feeling like we'd dodged a proverbial bullet. Not two minutes later, several police vehicles rolled up; I gave the thumbs up with one hand to let them know we were okay and waved them by with the other. None of them stopped. We both laughed out loud at the ridiculousness of the situation. There we were, changing a flat tire in the driving rain and hoping upon hope that we wouldn't get forced to take a ride that would break our respective lines of having cycled every inch since we started. With William's bike once again in mostly operable condition, we continued riding in the darkness and rain.

We were surrounded by dense jungle and insects buzzed loudly in the foliage surrounding the road. William's headlight created a small cone of light in the vast darkness while my taillight helped avert disaster from the occasional passing car; the rain fell steadily. Another hour later, when we were a good 10 miles (16 km) past our target distance, a police checkpoint came into view. We weren't too excited about camping in the rain; neither of our setups would offer adequate protection from the deluge, so we asked if we could sleep at the checkpoint. An officer walked out as I approached; I tried asking in my broken Portuguese if we could camp there. When the officer asked what we wanted in English, we were both relieved and began explaining that we were looking for somewhere to sleep with protection from the rain. He showed us around and said we could setup just about anywhere; we chose the sheltered area in front of the checkpoint. It was close to the road, we'd hear traffic and get flashes from headlights all night, but, it was shelter from the rain. Very kindly, the officer moved one of the cars to block some of the lights from passing traffic and also to protect us from any cars that might try to pull in as the night progressed. The policeman offered us use of the small kitchen so we made dinner there, after changing out of our wet clothes, and there was even a decent wifi connection. It was 9:00 pm when we stopped. I'd clocked over 10 hours of riding and William was pushing 12 hours of pedaling. We fell asleep, exhausted, after eating; William in his tent and me in my bivy. A successful day one of the Brazilian Barbecue Brevet was in the bag.

William checked the weather forecast in the morning and stated with much enthusiasm that it was not going to rain. The road rolled endlessly in accordance with the Brazilian standard for road building. My back tire went flat at one point and, after we had decided to regroup at the grocery store on the horizon, William pressed on; I fixed my flat and met William just up the road. After I bought some food, William got going minutes later while I had a snack. I hadn't been able to find the hole from the flat while on the roadside and found it using a bathroom sink, then patched my tube before riding off and catching up to William again.

We rode together for a couple of hours before it began to rain. It was later in the day by then and William didn't seem to be enjoying himself very much. Since it was William's birthday, I tried to bolster his motivation by singing him an edited version of happy birthday:

Happy Birthday to Will
Happy Birthday to Will
It's raining really hard
Happy Birthday to Will

I couldn't decide whether it helped but, he did smile and say thanks or 'cheers' rather because he's Irish and apparently that means the same thing as 'thanks' in Ireland. Just as it was getting dark, the rain redoubled its effort to crush our spirits. It was pouring rain harder than yesterday and it was on par with the hardest rain I'd ever seen in my life.

We were cycling up our zillionth roller of a long riding day that had now stretched into the dark when William had to use the bushes. We'd gotten some questionable water at the grocery store earlier and it was giving William some stomach troubles; I was lucky enough to remain unscathed, even though I drank from the same source. I held William's bicycle while he made a dash off the road. He didn't make it very far before he had to drop his pants. At that exact moment, a long line of vehicles drove by and included a crowded and a well-lit tour bus, filled with people who were gawking at the driving rain. William mooned them all unintentionally as he squatted on the edge of a field; his pale backside was gleaming like a beacon in the darkness.

We got to riding again and, as luck would have it, my back

tire began to go flat, yet another puncture. The amount of wire spread all over the highway from shredded car tires was exceptional and this was already turning into one of the worst places for flat tires I'd ever seen. It was a slow leak, however, so we rode to a gas station just over a mile away. It was still pouring rain, so we tried asking for a sheltered area to sleep at an adjacent restaurant. It was a touristy sort of place and we weren't surprised when they said 'no' in a manner that suggested they were surprised that we'd even tried asking. We went back to the gas station and tried asking if they had somewhere sheltered from the rain where we could pass the night. It took a few minutes to get the point across and a few more for brainstorming but eventually we had permission to sleep under the covered area of an inactive mechanics shop. The metal roof there was protection from the rain and that was good enough for us. We bought some beer at the gas station as a way of thanks to our hosts and to toast to William's birthday. After changing into dry clothes we toasted to William's health and success over our dinners of instant noodles.

William took off about 30 minutes ahead me on the morning of day three of the Brazilian Barbecue Brevet and I caught up to him soon after as he'd gotten yet another puncture. My back tire felt soft too and I found a piece of wire stuck in my tire. I pulled it out and air began rushing out of the tube. While I was pumping up my tire, I saw a nail stuck in it; I pulled it out and the tire deflated within seconds; two flats for me and one for William before we'd covered 20 miles (32 km) for the day.

The endless rollers continued; they turned what could have been fairly relaxed days into an almost insurmountable task. I'll try to give you an idea of just how much climbing we had to do; there was more vertical feet of climbing between Foz do Iguaçu and Curitiba than there is going from sea level to the top of Mount Everest. If we weren't struggling enough already to make our minimum distance for the last couple of days, William's rear hub began clunking. He'd had the same problem a few months before and it had transitioned from clunking along to grinding to a halt within 25 miles (40 km). We were 15 miles (24 km) away from a small city and we hoped it would last long enough to find a bike shop and get it repaired. Our luck held out; William limped his bike into the city of Guarapuava while his wheel clunked horrendously with every rotation. There were a couple of bike shops marked on our maps; all of them were over 2 miles (3 km) away from the highway. It'd eat up some of the precious time we had to make it to Curitiba but we had no other choice. The first shop we checked wouldn't be able to have it ready for over six hours; such a loss of time would cost us dearly in sweat and sleep deprivation to try to make up so we moved on to the next shop. That one didn't have the bearings to repair it but they had a new hub at a reasonable price and said it'd be done in two hours. William knew just how difficult it would be to recoup this loss and valiantly offered to stay behind and get his bike fixed while I rode on to the barbecue and met up with him there a couple of days later; riding by myself I'd have an excellent chance of arriving on time for the barbecue. I didn't like the idea of leaving him behind and we decided that we'd stick it out together even if it meant missing the barbecue.

We went to get lunch at a nearby buffet livre and discussed our options; we came to the conclusion that the only way to make it would be to ride as late as we could then sleep for a couple of hours and get up at dawn the next day to power through the remaining distance to Curitiba. The bike shop had wifi and I'd received a message from our hosts in Curitiba asking how we were progressing. I told them of our problem with William's hub and they said that they were postponing the barbecue a day to Sunday because of the rain. That'd give us an entire extra day to get there and we wouldn't arrive completely exhausted from only sleeping for a few hours. That sounded immeasurably better as we probably wouldn't have been able to enjoy the barbecue because of how tired we'd be so, we told them we'd arrive Sunday.

Once William's bike was working again, we rode out of

Guarapuava in the rain. The incredible amount of rolling hills continued to impede our progress though we did have a 1,000 foot (300 meter) descent towards the end of the day. Even with the extra day to get there, the huge amount of saddle time we'd been putting in over the last few days was taking its toll on me. My hands were bruising from the amount of time on the bike and I was getting joint pain everywhere. I could manage the distance at my own pace but the saddle time at a slower pace was killing me.

Daylight was waning and the consistent traffic we'd had all day was dying down when we found ourselves on a road winding through the jungle. What cars there were wouldn't expect to see anyone on bicycles in the dark so we setup camp on one side of the road in a recently tilled field with a flat area for William's tent and a couple of trees to hang my hammock. Lightning was visible on the horizon and we hoped it wouldn't rain overnight. I had limited protection from rain with my hammock and William's tent wasn't waterproof anymore. To top it off, the field we were in would probably turn into deep muck if it rained and that would make it incredibly difficult to get our bikes back to the road in the morning.

While I was setting up my hammock, one of the trees I was using broke with a tremendous crack; I fell about 6 inches (15 cm) down to the ground. It'd likely been weakened by disease and my weight was enough to take it down but now I was stuck with nowhere to put my hammock. It wasn't cooling down very much as it got dark; my only option would be to zip myself into my bivy for protection from the bugs. In this situation, sleeping in a bivy would be akin to sleeping in a plastic bag when the temperature was 80 F (27 C) and humid; rain would increase the misery exponentially. William offered to share his tent, it was big enough for both of us and moderately ventilated. I didn't want to but, I was getting eaten by bugs while I ate dinner and when I changed out of my shorts I found a fresh crop of saddle sores had sprung up on my nether regions. That was enough to crack my resolve and I accepted his offer. William took one side, I took the other; there was some ventilation, but we were still sweating.

We were fortunate enough that it did not rain overnight though, neither of us had slept well. While big enough for two people, William's tent was still cramped for space and we'd sweated most of the night away. Even without the rain, it took a significant amount of effort to push our bikes up the rough incline of the field and back to the road. We got a good hour of riding done before stopping at a restaurant/gas station for some empanadas. Both of us were tired; the saddle time wasn't taking quite as much of a toll on William so he got going before me. The rollers weren't quite as bad as the last few days, still frequent, but not as steep or as long. We did a leapfrog sort of progression. William would ride ahead then I'd catch up and ride with him for a while before taking off and waiting somewhere for him to catch up. William was plagued by flats all day; he had three that day while I had one if I remember correctly. His final flat pushed him over the edge; he made an attempt to contain his anger but it was apparent that the continuing stress was getting to him.

Our goal for the day was Palmeira, a town that was less than 50 miles (80 km) away from our goal in Curitiba. We agreed to get a hotel after all we'd been through the last few days; it took a few tries, but eventually we found one. The southern countries of South America are more expensive than the northern ones and that was the closest I'd had to having a private room since the Carraterra Austral; Brazil is no exception, though still not unreasonable at $18 US each for the night. For the first time in several days, we stopped riding before dark; we went out for dinner too. William had a higher budget for his tour than I but I'd planned for it by avoiding paying for a place to stay for the last couple of weeks before I met him; the luxury certainly was nice. The streets of Palmeira were almost deserted even though it was a Saturday evening; almost everything was closed and our options were limited to the only restaurant that we found open, a pizzeria.

The prices were average based on a world standard and while we were waiting for our food, William told tales of a magical place called Europe where, according to him, 'everything just works' - shops had actual opening hours, grocery stores were numerous, most of the drivers weren't homicidal maniacs, and you don't have to go searching through town to find the owner of a small store to buy food. We enjoyed our pizzas, thoroughly, and had a couple of beers to go with it. I'd intended to get caught up on my journal that evening but I was too tired and fell asleep right away.

We shoveled ourselves full of as much of the hotel breakfast as we could manage before getting on the road. Both of us had slow leaks in our back tires; mine, once filled, would be good for most of a day of riding. I pumped it up to a rideable pressure then stopped at the first gas station I saw and used their compressor to get it to a higher operating pressure while William rode ahead. We'd agreed to meet at a gas station about 25 miles (40 km) away. I waved at William as I passed him on the highway then rode ahead.

A few miles before the gas station, I caught up to, and passed, some road cyclists; I was going a good 25% faster than they were. I held them off until just before the gas station where I slowed down to 'cool down' my legs in preparation for the break. They passed me just before I stopped and maintained some of their pride. William rode up a while later and we picked another meeting spot before continuing separately.

Just as I arrived at the next gas station that we'd agreed to meet at, it began to rain torrentially; I refilled my water then waited for William. We turned off into some side roads afterwards and followed them the rest of the way to our host's house. Our way turned to dirt after several miles and the roads were slick with mud. William slid out while going down a hill and tumbled through the mud while his panniers rolled off down the hill in different directions. I made sure he was okay before I started laughing at him then rode up and held his bike while he reattached the bags.

While we were checking our maps at an intersection, someone in a nearby house saw us and invited us in for a beer. We happened to be ahead of schedule to arrive at the time that we said we would arrive at our host's house and accepted the offer. Our temporary host was an older man who'd traveled South America on a motor scooter and told us that people had been very kind to him. The conversation was in Portuguese and I translated everything I understood for William though he was picking up on a good bit of it by now. We were invited to stay for lunch and probably would've had a place to sleep too if we'd been so inclined, but we had to get going to make it to the barbecue. We thanked our host and continued on our way.

The roads were dirt for the last few miles and rolled steeply. It was raining again and we counted down the dwindling miles to our goal as we checked our maps at every intersection. The rain made the roads slick and less than half a mile (1 km) away from our host's farm I heard William shout while I was riding ahead down a steep descent. His front tire had slipped out from under him in the slick mud causing him to crash and go rolling down the road for several yards and get covered in even more mud in the process. I helped him with his bike again and we found Jose's parents' house after a bit more navigating.

Unfortunately, there had been a misunderstanding when we'd been texting back and forth using a translate app and something had gotten lost in the process. The barbecue had been on Saturday after all but the good news was that we had arrived a few hours early to Sunday dinner. A couple of the guests spoke some English and were able to fill us in on the Portuguese we couldn't quite understand. We had an enjoyable evening just the same and we were glad for the experience and grateful for the generosity of our new friends.

CHAPTER 41

Day 402, March 9, 2017

Curitiba, Brazil

One of the things we accomplished over our couple of days in Curitiba was rinsing the heaviest of the mud off of our bikes. My back tire had leaked itself flat again and both of William's tires were flat. The Brazilian Barbecue Brevet had been ill fated from the start: huge distances, busy roads, and an insane amount of cumulative climbing from all the rollers. To top it all off, we'd been plagued by flats the entire way. The most common culprit was pieces of wire that littered the road; they were placed there by the damaged tires of heavily laden semi-trucks. Our flat count for the stretch was 16 flats total, split exactly in half at 8 each. We'd persevered, nonetheless, putting in 10 hours or more of riding per day for the first few days and completing the distance in just 4.5 days. It was worth the effort just the same, even though we hadn't made it to the barbecue. Jose's parents were great hosts; they only knew a few words in English but, they were patient with the language barrier and my Portuguese had progressed at the fastest rate yet. They stuffed us to bursting with excellent homemade meals and we helped around the farm where we could. One of their dogs had recently had puppies too and we got to play with them.

When we were getting our bikes ready to go, William noticed that his front hub was grinding, the exact same problem that had happened to his rear hub a couple of days before we got to Curitiba. We tried taking it apart and the bearings were destroyed. Jose's dad went by a hardware store with the remaining bearings and came back with as close as a match that they had but they didn't work either. While he was gone, I checked my wheels. My rear hub felt weird; I couldn't quite place the problem so I tried taking it apart. Some of the bearings had broken apart too and were disintegrating inside the hub. I hated to ask Jose's dad to go back by the hardware store but I had no other option. He went with one of the few intact bearings and came back with some replacements; they weren't an exact fit but the wheel would roll. Neither of our bikes were in good working order and at that point; we'd both need new hubs but they were good enough to ride on for at least a few miles and hopefully they could get us to a bike shop.

We rode into Curitiba; the one day we couldn't ride a full day was the one day it wasn't raining. We found the bike shop Jose's dad had recommended and showed them our problems. They had hubs in stock and would be able to have them switched out in a few hours. My rear rim was cracking in the same manner as the rims on the recumbent had and I opted for getting a new rear wheel built. William's rims were fine and he just had his hub replaced. The process took five hours and there was an hour of daylight left when we got going with both our bikes back in working condition. We'd booked a hostel for the night and raced across the city to try to get there before dark. We found the hostel at sunset and called it a day.

We'd planned to take a circuitous and more adventurous route to our next destination but, the hub problems had cost us an entire day. We were both on a schedule to get to Santos for our respective transportations to the next section of our adventures and we couldn't risk being late. As such, we'd have to ride highways much of the way to Santos. It took a couple of hours to ride out of the city; Curitiba's landscape much resembles that of the rest of Brazil, steep rolling hills. Some of the hills were steep enough that William had to push his bike going up. Up again then down again for endless miles and we were jockeying with traffic the entire way.

Eventually, we found ourselves on quiet dirt roads and the traffic dropped as low as one vehicle per hour. Still steep rolling hills, but quiet enough roads that it made for good cycling. William and I would ride together going up most of the hills and the few flat sections. I'd ride ahead on the descents for fun and wait for William at the bottom. On one particularly steep and rocky descent, my rear wheel hit a jagged rock and it blew out my rear tire. I heard and felt the bump but didn't recognize the tire had blown until William had caught up. At first, I thought it was just a pinch flat, but soon realized it was much worse. The rim that I'd replaced not 25 miles (40 km) earlier in Curitiba was bent and I was suddenly very excited to get to Europe where, according to William, the roads were not littered with giant rocks

My options were limited; I tried smashing it back into shape with a rock, but that only served to scratch the rim and it didn't budge in the slightest. William reached into one of his panniers and magically produced a pedal wrench that he'd carried across nearly four continents but had only used a couple of times to disassemble his bike for the flights between the continents. Despite my lack of understanding as to why he would carry such a heavy tool with such a limited use for so many miles, I was able to use it to bend the rim back into place and, of course, was grateful that he had it.

The moment of truth was next, re-installing and filling the tire. Tensions were high as I slowly pumped up the tire; both of us expected it to blow off the rim at any second. The rim held and I got the tire all the way up to operating pressure without issue. Next was riding; I got on my bike gingerly while expecting the wheel to collapse or spontaneously combust in some freak accident but hold it did. I took it slow at first before I gained confidence that it wouldn't fail suddenly and, eventually, went back to riding ahead on the smoother descents, but, I was more careful to avoid any large rocks.

Rain was threatening on the horizon so we cut our dirt detour short to avoid riding in the mud, then stayed on highways the rest of the day. The precipitation never got past a sprinkle but, lightning was flashing in the distance. On a few occasions, we witnessed lightning striking repeatedly five times or more in the same spot in the span of a single second.

The lightning was enough to put us off of wild camping and William wanted to watch a rugby match that evening. We set our sights on a hotel and sprinted out the last couple of miles when William felt his rear tire going flat. We arrived just in time; shortly after we got our bikes inside, it began pouring rain. The hotel was reasonably priced and, lo and behold, they had a buffet livre downstairs that was impossible to turn down and we had a beer each too. My time in countries that were cheap enough that I could afford to treat myself on occasion was soon coming to a temporary end and I decided I'd enjoy it while I still could.

It was raining when we left the hotel in the morning. We had all highways to the next town that we planned to stop in and chose to do a leapfrog progression again. We picked a place to meet up then I'd ride ahead and wait for William and so on. William got some chicken wings at one of the gas stations and the chickens that lived at the gas station kept trying to eat William's gas station chicken wings. The BR-116 was a divided highway; it had a good shoulder most of the time but it would disappear whenever the highway went from two to three lanes while going up or down a steep hill; this, combined with the high traffic, made for a few sketchy sections because of the aggressive drivers, but we didn't have any serious incidents. Per usual for Brazil, the terrain was rolling hills. In this case, they trended upward most of the day and we were rewarded with a couple thousand foot descent in the last miles before our goal.

We planned to stop in Cajati; the town looked big enough to have a fire station, but, once we asked where it was, we found that the nearest station was 30 miles (48 km) away. We tried asking at a police station but they weren't able to help us. The weather was threatening rain again, it'd drizzled for a good part of the day, and it looked like we were in for another storm tonight. There was a hotel within sight of the police station and we asked the price, but, didn't realize that we'd mistranslated the price until they were ringing it up on William's card; what we thought we'd heard had sounded a little too good to be true for the room they showed us. The actual price was the equivalent of about $19 US each per night when we thought they'd said something close to $12. It did have air conditioning though, the first time I'd had that luxury for about a month and a half, and they had wifi. It was too late to change anything so, we made the best of it by turning on the A/C, full blast, and leaving only to get food at the nearby store.

By some miracle, I slept until after 9:00 the next morning; air conditioning is awesome! William woke me up once he realized that we were in danger of missing the included breakfast at the hotel. Breakfast was nothing remarkable and we finally got on the road around 10:30. We took gravel roads to avoid the highway as much as possible; all the traffic the previous day had made riding a chore. The dirt roads wound past houses and through the jungle and had almost no motor vehicle traffic. After the dirt roads, we took a quiet secondary highway to the town of Pariquera-Açu. We went to a store there and William had his signature snack, an energy drink and bar of chocolate, which he indulged in quite frequently while I had chocolate milk and some cookies. After we refilled our water, I felt my back tire going soft; one of the many patches on the tube had failed in the humidity and was leaking air. We pulled into the shade of a gas station to escape the worst of the sun and I re-patched my tube.

The vehicle traffic increased significantly after Pariquera-Açu and we took the next dirt turnoff to avoid the worst of the traffic. The dirt road we took changed slowly from a two lane road to a one lane road with barely enough room for a single car to fit through the dense undergrowth and minor flooding in the road from the recent rain was common. The road opened up again after passing through a tiny village. We cycled past flood plains and some water buffalo farms with steep hills in the distance; the scenery reminded William of his cycle through Southeast Asia.

We'd messaged a Warmshowers host on a whim the previous evening and we'd had a reply from them that morning before we left the hotel. Our host's place was in Ilha Comprida and we got there just before dark where we were welcomed in by Mauro. He and a friend ran a fledgling casa de ciclistas in Ilha Comprida, just a few miles away from the small town of Iguape. Within an hour of our arrival at Mauro's casa de ciclistas, a storm blew in; all the wind and rain made us glad that we had shelter for the night. Mauro bought a pizza for us and we conversed for a couple of hours in the blend of Spanish and Portuguese that William and I had refined during our time in Curitiba before Mauro went home for the night.

Mauro brought us breakfast in the morning too! After breakfast and some pictures, Mauro rode with us to the edge of the next town where we said our farewells and gave our thanks once more. We still had rolling hills all day but, they'd backed off in size and frequency significantly. A light rain started a couple of hours into our day. My back tire went flat; another patch had failed from all the moisture, though it was a different one than the day before. We sheltered at a bus stop and I was able to re-patch it again. We took another dirt turn-off in lieu of several miles on the busy BR-116. The overnight storm had turned several sections into mud but I was able to ride all of them. The heavy mud and soupy roads slowed our progress, but we pressed on.

Our offline maps showed a gap of 100 yards (90 meters) or so in the particular road that we took but we confirmed with Mauro that said gap was passable. The break in the road turned out to be a river. A bridge was under construction at one time but the project had been abandoned years ago and the skeleton of the partially completed bridge gave an eerie atmosphere to the place. I was able to ride most of the way across the river until my progress was impeded by a small truck that was stuck in the river. After getting our bikes across, we helped get the truck out of the river before continuing. Away from the river, we went straight into a 1,200 foot (360 meter) climb. The climb was inconsistent most of the way up but, the last mile or so kicked up to a grade beyond 20%. I rode the entire way with no small effort and waited for William at the top; he rode up several minutes later and we began descending the other side soon after. The delays caused by the mud had taken up a huge amount of time and we were in danger of running out of daylight.

We passed a small hamlet but couldn't see anywhere that we may have been able to stay; we rode on and, eventually, the road turned back into pavement. It was dark when we rode into the town of Pedro De Toledo and began looking for somewhere to stay. With all the paid accommodation we'd had recently, I wanted to find somewhere free to stay. We asked at the military police station about somewhere to camp. It took a bit of waiting but, eventually, we were escorted to a community building and told we could camp outside. They had showers in the building that we both made use of and there were some trees that I could hang my hammock on. While I was cooking dinner, some people came by to say, "Hello"; I didn't think anything of it, but they made William nervous. The more people who knew we were there, the more likely it was to be an issue.

The night had passed uneventfully and it didn't rain. We left our camp at the community center around 8:00 and coasted into town to get some groceries. That day was my last full riding day in South America so I got chocolate milk and some pastries for breakfast as an early celebration. It was overcast and relatively cool all day. In stark contrast to our entire time riding together, we had almost completely flat roads the entire way north so, we rode together most of the day. The only mildly interesting event was William getting a flat from the notorious pieces of wire that had plagued our time in Brazil. This brought our combined flat count to 22 flats since Foz do Iguaçu, split evenly at 11 apiece. William, doing his best to make light of our difficulties and ever in search of a good pun, was quoted as saying, "You could say our contest for the most flats was down to the wire."

We made decent time and, around midday, we saw an American fast food restaurant just off the highway; both of us had a craving for something that resembled a taste of home and we hauled our bikes over the concrete barrier separating us from our goal. We feasted on burgers, fries, and ice cream but by the time we finished we were feeling more like an afternoon nap than cycling the last 30 miles (48 km) to our goal for the day. Both of us had a schedule to keep so, we pressed on. It began pouring rain an hour after lunch; the temperatures were warm enough we didn't bother with putting our rain jackets on. We pedaled along completely soaked, but not at all cold.

Our obstacle of the day was a rough neighborhood with such a reputation for being dangerous that we'd been warned about it a few days prior by a local we'd talked to about our route. The borough was known as 'Q-town', short for the mouthful of 'Queventenádo'. It was most definitely a rough area; trash and the remains of burned tires littered the streets. Unlike my travels so far, William had had a few seriously negative experiences with people on his travels and was riding faster as a result. While traveling for several years, the odds of encountering a few people with malicious intent are fairly high; but, that's just a part of the risk of this kind of adventure. It was still pouring rain and, apart from a few dirty looks and stares from the locals, we rode through without incident.

Once we were a few miles past Q-town, I tried checking a couple of bike shops to see if I could get my wheel trued. It was a bit bent still from the rock incident that happened the day after I replaced it. The mechanics I spoke to were puzzled by my request, their logic was, "Why would I bother trying to get my wheel straightened if it wasn't close to rubbing the frame?"

We'd arranged to stay with the casa de ciclistas in São Vincente, just a few miles away from where my transatlantic cruise/ferry would leave in Santos. They'd asked for our arrival time earlier in the day; I'd accidentally replied to the wrong person and our hosts were clueless as to our arrival time. Unfortunately, we hadn't discovered that was a problem until after we'd stood outside the casa in the rain for a good 20 minutes and then cycled in said rain through town to find wifi; however, once we'd found a connection, we heard back from them in minutes. Their reply was that the São Vincente casa de ciclistas doesn't have any permanent residents and we'd have to cycle the few miles into Santos to get the keys to the casa. William, at that point, would have been fine with getting a hotel. I almost was, but, we checked online for a price quote and saw it'd run close to $20 US each, per night, for a hotel. I offered to ride across the city while William waited. I preferred to sleep somewhere for free and spend the money on a good dinner instead. William didn't object and I sprinted the 4 miles (6.4 km) across the city to get the keys before riding the same distance back. I was back within 45 minutes, with the keys, and we got into the casa without any trouble.

After getting out of our wet clothes, we showered off. William went first and warned me about Carlisle, the cockroach he'd named while taking a shower. Carlisle was a bit of a creep; he hung out in the corner and watched while I was taking a shower. There weren't any restaurants nearby so we had to save our celebratory dinner for the following evening.

CHAPTER 42

Day 408, March 15, 2017

São Vincente, Brazil

The sun was out in the morning and the residents surrounding the casa de ciclistas had marked the occasion by burning some of the numerous piles of trash in the streets outside the casa. South America was supposedly 'discovered' where São Vincente was now and the cobbled streets we'd ridden on weren't much younger than that. In just a few miles, we went from one of the rougher areas in the city to one of the nicest. We'd followed a cycle path along the beach into Santos during which William completed the standard for his west-east round the world ride by reaching the Atlantic Ocean and ceremonially dipping his wheels in the water having been on the Pacific side and done the same ceremony a few months earlier and having successfully cycled every inch since his arrival in Colombia.

Of all the people who I'd reached out to, to take the transatlantic cruise with me, my grandma was the one person willing to step up to the plate and join me on my latest adventure as she had both the time and money to split the "double occupancy only" cost of my cruise to Europe. She'd arranged for a hotel a day earlier than she would arrive in Santos and had offered to let William and I use the extra night she'd paid for. It was an offer we couldn't refuse and we arrived at the hotel shortly after the 2:00 pm check-in time. The contrast to last night's accommodation was huge. The lobby of the hotel was intimidating. We rolled up on our bedraggled bikes, wearing our riding clothes that still smelled musty from not having dried properly after the previous day's rain. We carried our bikes up the extravagant entryway stairs and a confused bellhop held the door open for us after a moment's hesitation of deciding whether we belonged at the hotel or not. William made sure our somewhat dirty bikes weren't forcibly removed from the marble clad lobby of the hotel while I did my best to act like I belonged in the hotel, despite my ragged appearance, and I checked us into the hotel without incident once the receptionist saw that we had a reservation. Now that we had our room key, we confidently wheeled our bikes through the marble lobby, past marble statues and gold lined mirrors, to the elevators and finagled them into separate elevators before heading to our room. That hotel was easily the nicest place I'd stayed in the entire trip so far.

We spent the majority of the afternoon enjoying the luxury of large beds, fast wifi, and air conditioning. We found an all you can eat rodizio steakhouse while we were resting and walked over for an incredible celebratory dinner (at which I consumed several pounds of meat) to mark our completion of cycling South America. It was, once again, an anticlimactic event for me; there had been some hard days along the way but, overall, it wasn't too difficult and was actually quite enjoyable for the most part. Part of me had thought I wouldn't make it that far and I was happy with the result. I can even say the incident of losing half a finger from mountain climbing was a good thing as it's served as a strong and consistent reminder of my own mortality. Hopefully, that would keep me grounded well enough to use good judgment in future situations. I had a feeling that the anticlimactic aspect would be a similar feeling to when I finished my world tour even if I accomplished all my goals.

My grandma arrived at the São Paulo airport the day after we got to the hotel and she'd arranged a pickup van through the hotel. William had completed his coast to coast goal for

South America and, shortly after demolishing the extravagant breakfast buffet at the hotel, we packed his bike into the airport shuttle so he could avoid a long, dangerous, and probably illegal cycle up the mountainous highway to São Paulo for his flight to South Africa. William and I met my Grandma at the airport with the shuttle driver. The airport shuttle was on a schedule and couldn't take William to find a box for his bike, then give him a ride to the other airport for his flight, so we dumped him off at the parking garage of the airport. He made it to South Africa, I checked. William was off to cycle Africa and I was going to catch my cruise to Europe.

My grandma had some jet lag from the flight and we didn't do very much for the rest of the day but, all the gear that I'd ordered and had sent to her house had made it there in her luggage: a new lightweight tent, tires, a couple of pairs of socks, a new pair of off bike shoes, and an e-reader to replace that one that had failed on me a couple of months ago. The remaining couple of days before the cruise were pretty relaxed. Our e-tickets, that we'd spent a couple of weeks worrying about the necessity of, for the cruise arrived two days before we were scheduled to depart and I got a box to put my bike in.

We'd packed most of our bags the night before and had an earlier than planned departure for the cruise terminal after the last night at the hotel. Once I'd made sure my grandma and her bags were safely in a taxi and that the taxi was going to the correct location, I rode my bike to the terminal. The new high quality tires were incredible, buttery smooth and fast. I arrived a few minutes after my grandma and we went to check in. The people checking the bags said it wouldn't be necessary to pack my bike into the box and I could pick it up after we'd finished the paperwork check in. After waiting in line, the receptionist checked over our papers and we were good to go through security. The security check was more of a formality than an actual check. All my electronics and my pocketknife were in my backpack along with the metal lid to my pot and my tire pump; I expected to have my backpack hand checked and it concerned me when it passed through the X-ray machine without anyone inspecting it further. I got my bike back from the baggage check, unscathed. They hadn't found or didn't care about large metal objects that were my stove and fuel bottle but apparently they'd found my tent stakes interesting enough to warrant further inspection, but they hadn't confiscated them.

I wheeled my bike onto the ship without issue; people seemed more intrigued than bothered by the idea of bringing a bicycle on board and I eventually moved it into our cabin. I'd been endlessly concerned about getting everything in order for the cruise and the boarding process; I was concerned that something would go wrong whether it was a paper missing or a problem with getting my bike on board but everything fell into place and it worked out just fine.

After an evening safety brief, a couple of hours later, we were underway.

CHAPTER 43

Day 420, March 27, 2017

On a Transatlantic Cruise

Almost the entirety of the following week was spent aboard the cruise/ferry to Europe and my grandma and I spent the majority of our time aboard the ship, alternating between the "20 hour per day" buffets and finding somewhere to sit and read, occasionally with the accompaniment of live music. We went to two ports the first week; Illheus, Brazil on the second full day of the cruise and Salvador Bahia, also in Brazil, on the following day.

The following four days were spent out to sea, journeying across the Atlantic. Highlights include my being entered into a ping pong contest and promptly losing by a large margin to a woman who was probably triple my age and me somehow convincing myself to go to the gym more days than not; I got on the stationary bike once for about 20 minutes, the fit was awful and it was terribly dull. I tried running one day and found that I could run a six minute mile for a couple of miles but it hurt to walk for several days afterwards; I didn't do any more running. I turned my focus to picking things up and putting them down again with some prehab/rehab exercises thrown in. I'd developed some minor back and joint pain while riding over the last week or so in Brazil and hoped that some strengthening would curb it.

There was live entertainment every evening that we went to at the onboard theater. The performances were always of a musical slant, ranging from a Batman themed ballet, to opera, to Grease the musical. During those days at sea, we crossed the equator; the captain announced the crossing over the loudspeaker and most everyone rushed outside to take a look. Several people seemed disappointed that there wasn't a physical line marking the equator. The following day, there was a celebration coined 'Neptune's Baptism.' The adventurous passengers who chose to participate were paraded around the pool then anointed with iced sea water before taking seats along the edge of the pool. This was not yet pleasing to Neptune and said passengers were crowned with various foodstuffs, such as flour, milk, and chocolate powder, while Neptune's toga clad intermediary asked if he was happy yet after each round. There were 5 rounds of that nonsense before everyone jumped into the pool. Neptune soon followed with a belly flop into the murky depths of the pool that had turned brown from the chocolate powder.

We were already in port in Cabo Verde when we woke up one morning. Cabo Verde is an island nation about 400 miles (640 km) away from the coast of Africa and is part of the continent of Africa. My grandma had booked a tour for herself and I was going for a bike ride. Since I'd been allowed to wheel my bike directly into the room, getting it off the boat was as easy as wheeling it through the ship and down some stairs to the dock of my 19th country.

One of my shifter cables was frayed and had broken while I was checking my bike over the previous evening. My first priority of the day was finding a new cable. They speak Portuguese in Cabo Verde and I asked a taxi driver just outside the port where I could find a bike shop. I was directed to a group of men and I showed them the cable that had broken near the shifter and asked about a shop. One of them had a bike and offered to ride with me show me where it was. We rode less than a mile into the town of Mindelo and directly to a bicycle shop. The bike shop had the cable and I installed it myself. I didn't have any of the local currency to pay for the cable and they wouldn't accept US dollars. The man who'd shown me where it was said there was an ATM nearby and that I could pay him back for it. We rode over to the ATM and thankfully my card worked so I was able to get the money to pay for the cable. I rode out of the town, alone, afterwards; I'd downloaded maps ahead of time and had already planned out a route around the island.

I rode a loop around the island, at least 2/3 of my distance was on cobbles and my new tires were working wonders. The ride wasn't quite smooth on cobbles but it was pretty close. I probably could have lowered my tire pressure a little more but the tires were doing an excellent job as it was. Just before reaching the other coast, the road turned to pavement for a few miles. Cabo Verde is an archipelago and we were on the island of São Vincente. The island wasn't all that big and many of the people on the cruise were out on various tours. I saw a couple of people that I recognized and many people were waving and shouting as they passed me in tour vans.

Not too far away from the biggest settlement of the island, Mindelo, was the tallest point on the island, Monte Verde. There was a road going up that I wanted to ride. The road was entirely cobbles and it climbed steeply up the mountain, with sections of the road carved into the cliff side. I didn't bother with watching how long it took but I got to the top eventually. There was a radio array on top and an armed guard at the entrance. There were a few tour vans at the top and I was confident it was relatively safe because of that. The top of the mountain was around 2,500 feet (760 meters) above sea level and enshrouded in passing clouds that blocked the best views. I snapped a few pictures before beginning the descent. Even with good tires, going over 30 mph (48 km/h) on cobblestones is a rough ride and my joints began to protest as I neared the base of the mountain. Back in Mindelo, I went to a small restaurant with wifi and sampled a local beer. Once I'd taken care of everything that I wanted to do online, I rode back to the ship.

CHAPTER 44

Day 424, March 31, 2017

Funchal, Portugal

After a few more days at sea, and a port in the Canary Islands, we arrived in Madeira, Funchal, an island in the Atlantic a couple of hundred miles north of the Canary Islands and part of Portugal. I went for a bike ride there too while my grandma walked around town with an Australian couple we'd met onboard. We were docked again and I had no trouble getting my bike off the ship. Right away I noticed how much better the drivers treated cyclists, one of them cut me off and almost made me crash; there are terrible drivers everywhere.

While I was checking my maps at a stop light, a policeman started blowing a whistle and yelling at me in Portuguese. I couldn't understand a word he was saying and told him as much. Portugal has a law against texting and driving; he had assumed that was what I was doing and cyclists are apparently not exempt from that law. He spoke English and I explained to him that I had no idea where I was going and that I was checking my map; he asked where I was going and gave me directions afterwards that were good enough that I didn't get lost again.

The route I chose climbed through the city of Madeira, narrow streets and steep grades the entire way up, but, most of the drivers were patient enough that it wasn't dangerous. I wasn't feeling that great; our dolphin spotting day cruise in the Canary Islands, the day before, had had an open bar and, after two weeks without any consistent riding, I was feeling weak and out of shape. Going to the gym onboard had stopped after the first week. My appetite, though slightly diminished from its previous levels, was still as large as ever and my pants were getting tighter every day.

I was at the top of Pico Alto in about two hours; I'd climbed from sea level up to about 3,700 feet (1,120 meters) in elevation then I rode down the same way I'd ridden up on what was probably the best paved descent I'd done since switching from my recumbent. Soon, I was in the city traffic again and had to slow down; I passed a few vehicles going downhill but eventually the streets became too crowded to pass. I went by a bike shop in town and bought some self-healing tubes; changing flats turns a great day into a difficult day in a hurry and I thought I'd give them a try. I switched the tubes out at the shop and used the wifi for a while before riding back to the ship.

CHAPTER 45

Day 431, April 7, 2017

Messina, Italy

Excessive amounts of reading and eating were quite common for the stretch following my day ride in Funchal. So was a distinct lack of any form of exercise. After Funchal, we did a two day transit to Lisbon. My energy level varied widely throughout the day as I finally began to recover from almost a year on the road without a significant break. I'd go from extreme fatigue, barely able to stay awake, to hypertension and being unable to sit still. I was experiencing multiple cycles of this throughout each day. Supposedly, these are similar symptoms to Zika, but, I never got checked so I don't know if I had it.

The day after we visited Lisbon, Portugal, we went through the Strait of Gibraltar and entered the Mediterranean Sea. The sight of the landmasses of Europe to the north and Africa to the south served to increase my eagerness to get back on the road. The ship made two more ports in the Spanish cities of Valencia and Palma de Majorca; all good fun, though I didn't ride my bike at either of those stops. I chose to get off my 'ferry' in Messina, Italy so I could ride the entire length of the country as opposed to looping down and back from Venice. I was on a schedule; I needed to be in Lausanne, Switzerland on April 17th for a side trip. This would require me to average in excess of 100 miles (160 km) per day to get there on time. This would be by far the most strenuous schedule I'd ever attempted. Let Jacob's 'Giro d'Italia' begin!*

*Tour of Italy- after the famous bicycle race of the same name

The ship docked in Sicily, just after sunrise, and I was at the ship's reception soon after waiting with my grandma to pick up my passport. It was not as easy as showing up and getting it; the clerk said I'd have to wait for the immigration officer to return it. After almost three hours of screaming internally, my passport was ready and I was off in a flash. I made it less than 2 miles (3 km) before I had to catch another ferry to the mainland, Messina is on Sicily.

After the 20 minute crossing I arrived in mainland Europe. My energy and excitement to get going had been accumulating over the last week and I had the same nervous excitement that I felt when I was first getting started on my tour in Idaho.

I rolled off the ferry and started turning the pedals. Suddenly everything went smooth just like it had on the day I started more than 15 months earlier. I was on the brink of the cumulative landmass of three continents, with a fourth not too far away. Several years' worth of riding could be linked with no more than a few short ferry rides in between and I could hardly wait to get going.

End of Book One

BUDGET REPORT FOR FEBRUARY 1, 2016-JANUARY 31, 2017

I maintained a log of everything I spent for my first year on the road; I'm sharing it in an effort to show people that cycle touring is not all that expensive. At that budget, I was not comfortable every single night, a few times it was cold but more often too hot. My tent protected me from the rain when I had it and I was able to find some kind of shelter almost every time I needed it after I got rid of it. I never went hungry due to a lack of money, but I didn't always eat well. I cooked the vast majority of my dinners myself, and I eat a lot. Seriously, it's beyond most people's comprehension how much I eat. I had a water filter and therefore avoided paying for water as much as possible, if I remember correctly I spent less than $20 buying water this year. It takes a little effort to filter water but it more than paid for itself.

Totals are rounded to the nearest dollar, and then rounded up more often than not; it reflected the approximate change in my bank balance too. If anything, it's slightly higher than the dollar value cost. This list also includes: my San Blas cruise, the extraordinary cost of the gear I replaced and sent home, and buying a new bike in Santiago. It was above my goal of $20 per day by a little more than the cost of my new bike; it was an unexpected cost, but I'm content with it. This does not include the transatlantic cruise that I booked in August 2016. I hadn't taken it by the end of my first year so, it will go in next year's budget.

Categories:

Food: all consumables, going out to eat, groceries, and everything I drank including alcohol. $3055

Bike, parts, and gear: buying a new bike, parts and paid labor for bike maintenance, all the gear I replaced and the cost of shipping for what I sent home. $3372

Accommodation: hostels, hotels, camping, and anytime I paid for somewhere to stay including that old woman in Peru who charged Jesse and I to stay at her house after she invited us in. $766

Visas: costs for entering and exiting every country I've been to. $389

Other: the San Blas cruise, ferries, park and museum entrances, other, that kind of thing. $927

Frostbite medical care and amputation. $0

Total expenses for one year of traveling by bicycle: $8,554 USD

AFTERWARDS

As of this writing in the autumn of 2019, I'm still touring! If you'd like to follow the continuing journey I'm maintaining a blog at:

www.crazyguyonabike.com/doc/niktia

On Instagram @worldbybike_niktia

And on Facebook: NIKTIA, a Bicycle World Tour

Flicker gallery to go with the book:

https://www.flickr.com/photos/155467799@N08/albums/72157711087308616

Also, to help raise some money to fund my travels I'm selling postcards each month made from my best pictures. You can join the postcard club or help me out with a dollar or a few at:

www.patreon.com/Worldbybikeniktia

Hope you enjoyed the book! I look forward to writing more in the future. Thank you for your support!

Jacob Ashton

Made in the USA
San Bernardino, CA
02 December 2019